Psychology & Kabbalah

By the same author

Psychology
&
Kabbalah

Z'ev ben Shimon Halevi

Gateway Books, Bath

First Published in 1986

This edition published 1991
by GATEWAY BOOKS
The Hollies, Wellow
Bath, BA2 8QJ

Printed and bound in the United States of America

British Library Cataloguing in Publication Data

Halevi, Z'ev ben Shimon, 1933-
  Psychology & Kabbalah. – Rev. ed.
  I. Title
  135.4

ISBN 0946551863

for Rebekah

Contents

Illustrations

Preface

When Adam and Eve came down from Eden there began a process of incarnation and comprehension into why they had been brought into being. This situation recurs each time we are born as we learn about physicality and how it differs from that other reality whence we came. Most soon forget this prenatal memory, but some seek to return to that state of soul by looking within. Psychology is the study of this archetypal world that hovers between Earth and Heaven; and Kabbalah is a spiritual tradition that places the psyche's inner and outer counterparts in the context of the greatest reality. Combined, these bodies of ancient and modern knowledge can bring into focus the nature and purpose of our descent into matter as the Self of each individual passes through level after level to become one with the Divine SELF who gazes through our eyes upon its own reflection.

London, Summer 5745

Introduction

Psychology is the science of the mind. The root Greek word 'psyche' means soul or that which is not of the body, but is the invisible component of a person. In prehistoric times, death was recognised as the moment of division between the body and what animated it. All over the world people acknowledge this phenomenon and indeed take enormous pains to placate or honour the departed intelligence. Anyone who has seen the corpse of someone well known to them experiences the same sense of total absence, not only of life, but of that peculiar essence which made the person unique. This recognition of an unseen, yet palpable dimension of a human being, must have generated the first enquiries into what it was that came into being at birth, possessed a certain character during life and disappeared at death. Here began psychology.

In the earliest stages of humanity's life on Earth, the main preoccupation was to learn to survive. People had to adapt to the interplay of the four elements, to use plants and relate to animals. Now while these first human beings may have been primitive, their consciousness was of a quite different order from anything they might have encountered in the wilderness. Not only did they observe the ways of nature as the seasons turned, but they recorded and collated experience in a manner that no other species could. Animals might respond to a drought by migrating or sleep through the winter to avoid its difficulties, but this was an inbred instinct completely unconscious at the individual level. Human beings saw the rhythms of the Earth as recurring patterns, then as principles from which they built up a picture of the Universe they lived in. The most intelligent and sensitive of these early shamans formulated their conclusions into myths that explained the processes in the world about them. These speculations included the origin of the human race, whence it came and whither it was going. It is known that not a few had an experience of revelation in which they were shown the situation of mankind from a higher dimension. One such person was Enoch (Genesis V). He, according to Kabbalistic legend, is said to be the source of various esoteric traditions that pass on these mystical illuminations.

By the time the first civilisation arose in Egypt and Mesopotamia complete cosmologies had come into being about the World that lay behind the mundane events of daily life. The periodic upheavals of war, earthquake or famine were accepted as moods of the gods and goddesses who inhabited the invisible realm from which people came at birth and returned at death. Great priests and kings by sacrifice and deed might influence events, but ultimately, the upper worlds ruled the lower, because no one, except perhaps the mystics and magicians, understood the laws of those unseen levels.

Now while birth and death were the dramatic entry and exit points of the unknown region and therefore of great interest to everyone, there were some who were particularly interested in what went on between. Most people, it was noted, just existed, oblivious of any purpose but to survive; others were more outgoing and dominating, while still others, retired or sought to live an interior life, either in madness or deliberate contact with the invisible realms. These observations led to speculation about types of people, temperaments and fate, which is the distinct pattern of a life as a person's particular nature interacts with the conditions into which they were born.

The Jews and Greeks were the first in the Western world to consider these questions methodically. Although influenced by Persian and Indian views of the universe, the Jewish approach was basically prophetic in mode while the Greek applied intellectual analysis. Both pondered the place of mankind in the universe and examined the performance of the individual. The stories of the Bible and the Greek legends are about people relating to the supernatural worlds. In each tradition, certain characters embody a human vice or virtue under trial, thus Jacob and heroes such as Ulysses undergo their development, while others around them move unconsciously through the drama of existence. The theme of inner evolution occurs in all mythologies, as individuals struggle to emerge from a tribal group to become people who do not just live on the mundane level, but who consciously participate in the cosmic process of Divine manifestation. Moses, Jesus and Mahomet were examples of highly developed human beings who could not only talk with ordinary folk but converse with beings of the upper worlds and God.

Between the poles of simple physical consciousness and total realisation is a great spectrum of human experience. This is divided by all esoteric tradition into the realms of the body, soul, spirit and Divine. Psychology is concerned primarily with the world of the mind, which has access to body, contains the soul, is penetrated by spirit and touched by the Divine.

This book is an attempt to set the study of psychology within the scheme of Kabbalah, which takes into account the origin of all human beings and their Divine, spiritual and physical composition. We shall give particular attention to the psyche and the great journey of destiny that each one of us makes as we descend into incarnation and then return whence we came. However, in order to understand and fuse the disciplines of psychology and Kabbalah, we must examine the history of our present situation at every level. This means extracting the most important elements of each subject and interweaving their relevance so as to make a synthesis which can give new insights into both. Various schools of thought will be drawn upon, not only to give a broad view, but to cover all the stages and levels of unfoldment. Naturally, there will be omissions of some areas, owing to the limit of space and my own experience. However, if this work brings the Kabbalist and psychologist into contact, then it will have served its purpose.

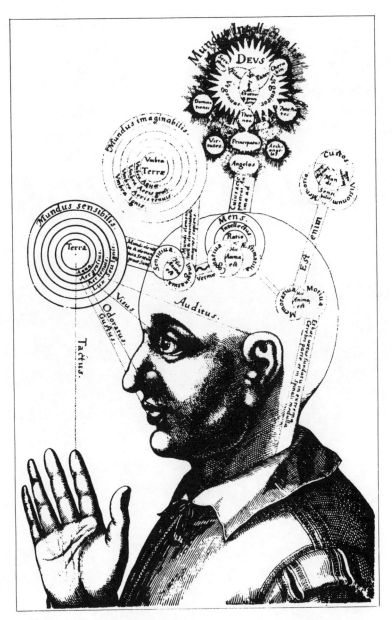

1. MIND AND THE WORLDS

In this seventeenth-century engraving Robert Fludd, who was familiar with Kabbalah, shows the various levels of consciousness. The mundane senses relate to nature, while the world of Form is perceived by imagination. The intellectual level, that corresponds to the Spirit, is based upon the Sefirotic Tree which is the model for the Macrocosm of the Universe and the Microcosm of Man.

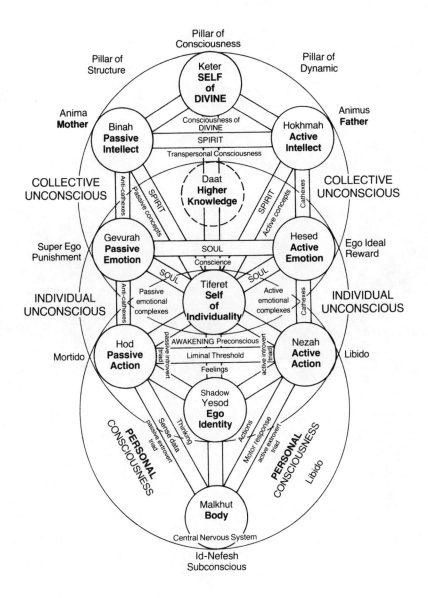

2. GENERAL SCHEME

Here the psyche is set out upon the Tree which is the key diagram of Kabbalah. The notations place various aspects of the psyche at different levels and within their functions. The interactions and penetrations of these factors generate the structure and dynamics and the degrees of consciousness and unconsciousness.

Psychology & Kabbalah

1. Observation

Prior to the ancient Greeks, a systematic study of the psyche in the Western world did not exist. The presence of the soul was recognised, but what was known was either confined to the esoteric schools, such as the one at Eleusis, or embedded within folklore. Such information might be in the observation of apparitions of the dead, the meaning of dreams and stories about adventures among the gods. Fragments of knowledge have come down to us, but they are usually cast in the form of allegory which needs interpretation into the language of our time. At that point in history, Western man was still at the superstitious phase of development in which unusual phenomena were noted but not understood, so that the natural and supernatural were confused. An example of this was the belief in the gods of the Underworld, and that the soul went downwards, after burial, into their domain.

When the Greeks came into contact with the older and much more advanced civilisations of the East in their campaigns of conquest and trade, there occurred a cultural alchemy in which the rational intelligence of the Greeks was fired and fused with the religious and philosophical experience of the oriental mind. Besides the contacts with the Persian and Indian civilisations and the connection with the Egyptians, there was also the meeting between the Hellenic and Judaic cultures that produced the groundbed of Christendom and Islam. The impact of this interaction stimulated not only an intellectual approach to cosmology, but psychology, as the Greeks began to examine their own myths and extract a rationale to the structure and dynamic of the macrocosm and microcosm of the Universe and mankind.

Around the sixth century before the common era B.C., Greek science had concluded that there was a distinct difference between sense and reason, inasmuch as the mind synthesises what the body perceives. Likewise the notion of different temperaments was observed and related to the four elements in an 'as above so below' formula, so beloved by the mystical philosophers. Around the fifth century B.C., the Pythagorean school differentiated between the

1

psyche and the body, which they saw as a prison for the soul while the person was incarnated. They believed life was a process of learning as the soul slowly worked towards inner freedom, purification and immortality, in its transcendence of the cycle of natural birth growth, decay and death.

The schools not so concerned with the developmental aspect focused upon more pragmatic questions; and here we get the great division between the Platonic and Aristotelian approaches, which have split the study of psychology right down to our day. Plato followed the mystical line, in that he saw the universe emerge from an invisible realm into a manifestation, while Aristotle, the scientist, observed that these subtler realms were inherent in the material world. He saw the psyche as the sum or essence of a living body, while Plato perceived it as a non-physical organism which could be reborn again and again after death.

At a more detailed level of observation of the incarnate psyche, the Greeks began to differentiate distinct functions of activity such as the nutritive, sensitive and rational, which corresponded to the plant, animal and human levels of a person. They also became preoccupied with the morality of the psyche and the various drives of the body as they came into conflict. The process of primitive impulses slowly being organised into conscious complex actions was also recognised, as was the principle of wish and fulfilment in dreams, when the higher faculties were asleep and the baser appetite could be released without social condemnation. Many of these early conclusions were incorporated into the various systems that arose in the Hellenic view of the psyche. The Stoics, for example, saw a sense impression as an awareness in the consciousness of the psyche, and they differentiated between imagination and hallucination, and a subjective conviction from an objective reality. They also concluded that the innate reason in animals that caused them to behave in certain ways should be defined as 'instinct' which is quite different from a human being's capacity of conscience, based upon an inner knowledge of the Laws of the Universe.

The effect of Hellenism upon the Jewish, and later the Christian and Islamic view of the psyche was enormous. Philo, a Jew who lived in Alexandria about the same time as Jesus of Nazareth was born, sought to amalgamate the revelation of the Bible with Greek thought. He rationalised many of the themes contained in the scriptures as allegories of reality, relating various Biblical characters to certain qualities and levels of development. This process was taken up by the more radical Jewish thinkers, but it was not incorporated into the orthodox outlook until it had passed through the NeoPlatonic versions of Christianity and Islam, by which time the psyche had been examined and defined in great detail. The open acceptance came when Kabbalah moved out of its traditional seclusion to oppose the philosophical logic that was attracting and threatening the unquestioning faith, not only the intelligentsia of Judaism, but of Islam and Christendom in the early Middle Ages.

In this crisis between reason and revelation, the nature of the psyche was brought into deep focus, as various mystics spoke openly about the many components, functions, problems and resolutions related to the inner life. Discussion about the soul in the rabbinical study house, the monastic cell and Sufi school explored every aspect and level, until the creative impulse was spent and the universities became mere places of repetition and information based upon what the ancient and medieval masters had said. It was not until the Renaissance that psychology started to move again as enquiring people began to look at the field afresh. Work by the anatomist Vesalius in the sixteenth century removed many ideas about the psyche being dependent upon the body as some ancients had said, and social observers such as Machiavelli, who wrote a practical textbook for princes, swept away the academic ideal that people were inherently noble. It was only too clear in that time of political expediency that the primitive side of a human being could predominate. This led to a reformulation of psychology and its implications with studies of the effects of society upon the individual.

Conversely, scholars like Thomas Hobbes moved in another direction and developed a mechanistic approach, seeing dreams, for example, as caused solely by external factors. This mode was in line with the influence of Galileo, who had destroyed the ancient picture of the world and all its mystery with celestial mechanics. The Age of Reason that was born out of these standpoints was opposed by the Platonists of the time, such as the Cambridge school of Henry Moore, but they were out of fashion. Even Newton, a mystic of the first order, had to hide the fact that most of his notes were about religious issues. Outwardly little real psychological study was carried out during the seventeenth and eighteenth centuries, although much work was done on the mechanistic and theoretical approach, which led to many conclusions based upon the empirical method.

The extreme rationalism of this period produced its reaction from the most pedantic edifices of theory to a blind fascination with the irrational, such as the magnetic process of Mesmerism. In an age obsessed with exquisite style and the perfecting of machinery, madness was not understood and was treated in the most barbaric way. It was not until the emergence of social consciousness that people thought to examine the psyche of the individual. By the late nineteenth century there were numerous schools of psychology; some studied from a physiological standpoint, while others considered the sociological, functional, and behavioural aspects. Schools like the Gestalt explored the effects of the environment on the psyche, in contrast to the analytical procedures then being developed to probe the structure of the mind.

Out of this melee of scientific investigation came Freud, who opened up the World of the Unconscious with its powerful forces that permeate consciousness to influence people without their knowledge, causing neurosis, psychosis and occasional irrational behaviour in the so-called normal. Freud's contribution to Western psychology was enormous. He not only rediscovered what the esoteric schools had talked about for centuries, but began to systematise the mind in a scientific way, although he did meet a lot of resistance from his own profession. Jung, his younger colleague who had been developing his own views of the psyche, took up the Platonic stance to Freud's Aristotelean approach. He saw that while the psyche had its primitive drives, it was also subject to a deeper influence coming from the higher levels of the unconscious. Thus the ego of the lower psyche was separated out from the Self which supervised the process of development described in spiritual texts and myths.

Today there is a great interest in the West in the esoteric. This has brought many people to recognise that psychology is a prerequisite before moving on into the study of the Spirit and Divine. Here is where psychology and the esoteric can meet, mutually adapt and start an alchemy for our age. But before this can begin we must consider the idea of revelation as a source of knowledge.

2. Revelation

In one sense the history of Kabbalah is unimportant because its essential teaching has always been the same through the ages. Only the form of it has changed over time. The content of the Torah, as it is traditionally called, is about the origin, nature and purpose of the Universe and mankind's place in a Divine process by which God beholds God in the reflection of Existence. This theme runs through the Bible and every esoteric system that emerged out of that circle of human beings who can perceive the transpersonal dimension of reality. A culture may clothe and sometimes obscure the teaching, but its presence is sensed in rituals, devotions and metaphysics by all who seek a meaning to life, and even by those who have only a superstitious appreciation of that which lies behind the surface of the physical world.

The original Gnostics or 'those who know' were the people who had direct access to higher knowledge. This may have come about through performing correct actions, devout prayer or deep contemplation. It could also be revealed by the instruction of one who knew from personal mystical experience, what lay beyond the ordinary mind, and perceived its upper levels and their workings. Unfortunately, as has been noted by mystics, there is always the problem of describing the indescribable. Many, therefore, have had to reduce their perceptions into earthly terms in order to convey something of these finer and subtler dimensions. The following legendary events give a flavour of this order of reality.

According to Jewish tradition, Enoch ('the initiated'), who lived in the earliest period of Mankind's sojourn on earth, was an individual quite unlike the other people of his time. He had not forgotten his origin in Paradise and become immersed in the flesh. He lived in seclusion pondering the reason why human beings had been incarnated. Others before him had read the Book of Raziel (the Secrets of God), which had been given to Adam that explained the reasons of Existence, but Enoch wished to know for himself, so he lived a life of intense inner work, the result of which was his ascension. He was taken up in a vision to view the higher regions of Existence and see how they operated. Here he was shown the past, the future and the souls of the yet unborn, as well as those of the dead. He also saw the angelic realm of Paradise with its multiplicity of forms that are the archetypes of the material world below, and the Heavenly realm of the archangels who watch over and supervise the creative processes of the Universe, before being brought into the Presence of the Holy One in the Primordial World of pure light. Tradition says that the archangel Gabriel then said to him, "Enoch, be not afraid. Come with me and stand before the Face of the Lord". But Enoch fell down before the Holy One and worshipped even though the Voice of the Divine said, "Be not afraid. Rise up and stand before my Face forever". Then Great Michael, the Captain of the Hosts of God, lifted Enoch up and took his earthly robe from him (his physicality), and annointed him with Holy Oil and clothed him in celestial raiment — he had become equal to the angelic creatures around him. He was then instructed in the Torah. For thirty days and nights Enoch remained in this exalted state of consciousness recording all that he heard and saw. Afterwards he was told by the Holy One of the secrets that even the archangels do not know — the reason for Lucifer's fall and why sin occurred in Eden. He was also informed about the origin of Adam, the manifestation of the Worlds, and shown the great curtain that hangs before the Throne of Heaven, whose threads represent all the generations of mankind. After this revelation he was instructed to descend to the reality of Earth and teach about these matters until he was called up to take his place permanently in the higher worlds.

After he had transmitted what he could to his household (his school), he told them to pass on this knowledge, concealing nothing from those who truly wished to know. He was then, tradition tells us, hidden by a darkness so that he was lost to earthly eyes. At this moment, in the same month, day and hour of his birth he was taken up to the highest Heaven. When the darkness lifted the people saw that he 'was not' as the Bible puts it, that is he had discarnated without having to go through the natural procedure of dying and leaving a corpse.

While his children built him a memorial at the earthly location of his departure, Enoch was going through the various stages of ascension, called in Kabbalah the lower and upper halls. Here he encountered the angelic and archangelic hosts of the Worlds of *Yezirah* and *Beriah*, or Formation and Creation, who were not initially friendly toward this terrestrial intruder, for we must understand no human being up to that time had reached full potential. Enoch was the first, and if it had not been for Divine protection, then some angelics might have harmed him, for they were not a little jealous of mankind's special place in the scheme of Existence. This problem had caused the downfall of Lucifer, the highest of the Archangels, when he refused to acknowledge the superiority of Adam who was the most perfect image of the Holy One.

Enoch was now to fill Lucifer's vacant place in the Seventh Heaven, which is the closest point to the Face of Divinity. Thus, when Enoch arrived at this level, he was transfigured by the Fire of the World of *Azilut* or Emanation into the human-angelic status of Metatron who has the title 'he who bears the Name of God'. As such, Enoch became the Master Teacher of all mankind, the source of every esoteric tradition. He was recognised in Egypt as Thoth, in Greece as Hermes Trismegistus and in the Bible as Melchizedek. As such he initiated Abraham into the secrets of Existence. Later, he appeared as Elijah, who was also without earthly parents. In Kabbalistic tradition he turns up at crucial points to instruct or help people in difficult situations when the laws of the earthly level need overriding for some higher purpose. This is called the miraculous and is witnessed in the preservation of individuals in dangerous circumstances who have certain spiritual jobs to do.

The story of Enoch belongs to a different kind of reality. At the level of Nature only the senses perceive but this is confined to the ever-present moment so that only the obvious is provable. However, the psyche that inhabits the body can go further, recognise other levels, and link together various phenomena to make some sense of the continually changing situation, detecting rhythms and patterns not only in the exterior world, but within the body and psychological processes of emotion and thought, and memories that have their origins in the near or remote past. This is the realm of the psyche that acts as the medium between the outer and inner dimensions of a human being and that other reality hinted at in the legend of Enoch.

Enoch represents the complete development of every level in an individual, from the physical to the psychological and spiritual organisms of consciousness, to the Divine present in everyone. This leads to the premise which must be at least provisionally accepted, that within the deeper parts of the psyche are unconscious areas that hold not only memories of this life, but of all humanity, even as the body possesses an inherent knowledge gained over millions of years of physical evolution. Kabbalah takes the notion even further in saying that a human being is a miniature version of the primordial Adam, who is the model of all that exists. Thus, each individual like a hologram, is a microcosm of the whole Universe. Here, we take the Platonic line and begin by setting out the grand design of Existence according to Kabbalah, so that we may fit some Aristotelian-type conclusions into a general scheme, making a balanced blend of the empirical and the mystical.

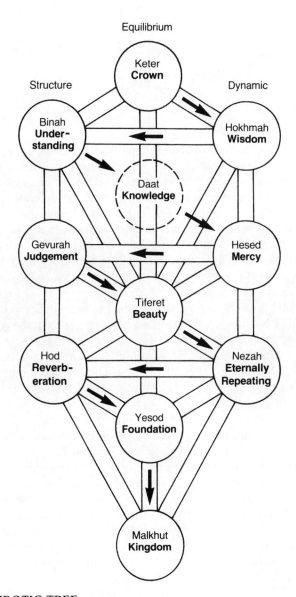

3. SEFIROTIC TREE

This shows the sequence of the Sefirot as they unfold in the Lightning Flash to form the two outer pillars of active and passive function with the central column of consciousness. The twenty-two paths describe the relationship between specific Sefirot and the triads show their combined interaction. The Hebrew names and their root meaning are approximate translations.

3. Origins

How does one describe that which has no substance or form? How can we speak of the origin of all things? All that can be done, mystics of every tradition conclude, is to convey an approximation of what was, is and shall be. Kabbalists have applied many devices to express how Existence came into being. Some used the symbol of a nut, with its kernel and shell, others told fables of how the Holy One wished to become known, and yet others constructed metaphysical models which they said gave only the faintest hint of the Reality. In this book, we will use a composite of several views held by Kabbalists down the ages to make a coherent picture for our frame of reference.

According to some rabbis, God wished to behold God and so out of the *En*, or Nothingness, emerged a point from which the Absolute withdrew, thus allowing a place of non-Existence to come into being. Then that which is *En Sof*, or Absolute All, surrounded this space with what has been called the *En Sof-Or*, Endless Light, which penetrated from the periphery of the place of non-Existence to its centre in a series of ten radiances. Those *Sefirot*, as they were called, unfolded in an instantaneous sequence to set out a configuration that was to be the paradigm for everything that would be called, created, formed and made in Existence. Composed of pure consciousness this realm of light was the reflection of the Holy One. As such, it both revealed and concealed the Absolute in an image of Divinity.

Called *Olam Ha Azulit*, the World of that which is 'next to' this realm of Emanation was continually in process of becoming, as it emanated from the first *Sefirah* of manifestation called *Keter*, the Crown. This highest *Keter*, the Crown of Crowns, is associated with the Divine Name of EHYEH ASHER EHYEH or I AM THAT I AM, which carries the intent of the Absolute to behold Itself in the reflection of Existence. The following sequence of *Sefirot* are the different aspects of Manifestation as they unfold and compose an eternal Unity of the Divine Attributes. Thus, the Crown is the point of Origin, while the two that follow form the active and passive counterbalance of Divine Intellect. These are called *Hokhmah* and *Binah* or Wisdom

10

and Understanding, and together with *Keter*, the Crown, they form the Supernal Triad which occurs in all esoteric teachings. Here are the principles of equilibrium, expansion and contraction as the Divine flow is sent forth and held between consciousness, dynamic and structure. In ancient China, this was known as the Tao, Yang and Yin and in India, the Principles of Sattva, Rajas and Tamas.

Below this Supernal Triad is what is called the non-*Sefirah* of *Daat* that separates the lower *Sefirot* of Construction as they are called, from the three Supernals. In medieval times, it was called the veil or abyss before the Face of God, but the modern notion of a 'Black Hole' like those found between universes, might give a sense of its mystery and function. It is said that when the Holy One willed it, the impulse radiating out of the Supernals then crossed the dark place of *Daat*, which means Knowledge, to continue the process of expansion, contraction and equilibrium at the next level of Divine Emotion. Here, the *Sefirot* of *Hesed*, *Gevurah* and *Tiferet* act as the Merciful, Judgmental and Principle of Beauty, as the expansive, controlling and unifying aspects of the Heart of the Image of God. The next pair of *Hod* and *Nezah* continue the sequence as the practical *Sefirot* of Action, and indeed the Hosts of God are seen to emanate from these two, whose names originate from the Hebrew words, to 'reverberate' and 'eternally repeat'. These *Sefirot* of Glory and Eternity, as they are sometimes called, are concerned with the routine matters of vibrations and cycles which govern the three lower worlds which are to emerge from the Primordial World of *Azilut*.

The final pair of *Sefirot* are vertical and central, and act as the foundation and resolution of the Divine process. Indeed, their names are *Yesod*, which means 'Foundation', and *Malkhut* or 'Kingdom', which contains all that has been brought down in the Lightning Flash flow from the Crown. *Yesod* may be seen as the place where the image can see its own image, like the ego of the psyche can picture itself. *Malkhut* as the receptacle of all has sometimes been called the Body of the Divine. The complexity and subtlety of the *Sefirot* is further increased by what are called the twenty-two paths between the Divine Attributes. These are specific relationships that bind the three pillars of what is called by some 'The Tree of Life' into a symmetry that contains all the Laws of Existence. The seven-branched candlestick or *Menorah* in the Tabernacle and Temple is an early version of the Tree with its two sides, central column, six arms and their four junctions plus the twenty-two decorations. This was the basis of the Tree of Life diagram, that was used by the rabbinical circles of medieval Spain.

Early Kabbalists not only saw this first world in the form of a Tree or candelabra, but also as the image of a human being which is the most complete reflection of the Divine. This image of Adam Kadmon or Primordial Man was the synthesis of the *Sefirot* as it expressed their unity, function and radius of operation in the limbs, body and head as well as the various levels of Divine thought, emotion and action. Most important of all, this human image was seen to possess a consciousness that could reflect upon itself; thus fulfilling God's will to behold God in Adam's realisation of Who gazed upon Who. This was the purpose of Existence. However, at this point in manifestation Adam was only aware of the unity of the Primordial World; there was no differentiation or experience of existing. Here was complete innocence. Such a state meant there was no knowledge, no knowing and being known. All was just potential. If this situation had remained, then the Divine image would never become conscious that it was a reflection and there could be no realisation Who was Who. The lower worlds were created, formed and made for Adam Kadmon to go forth and then return in consciousness of what was, is and shall be. In this experiential process through all the various levels of reality, I AM THAT I AM beholds ITSELF) in Adam's reflections. The Kabbalistic diagram of Jacob's Ladder describes the four interpenetrating worlds that make up the full extension of Existence. This is the Holy Firm, or the groundbed of our scheme.

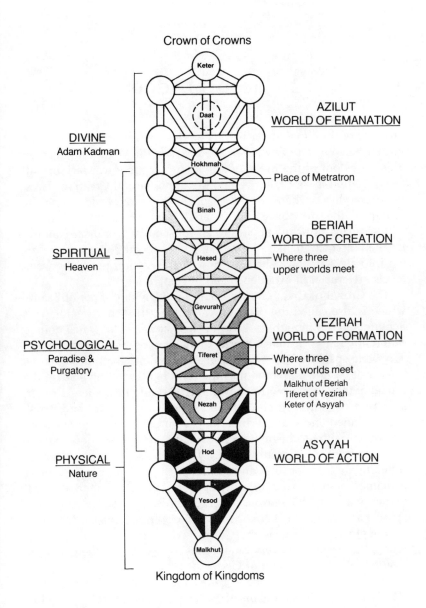

Crown of Crowns

DIVINE
Adam Kadman

SPIRITUAL
Heaven

PSYCHOLOGICAL
Paradise &
Purgatory

PHYSICAL
Nature

Keter

Daat

Hokhmah

Binah

Hesed

Gevurah

Tiferet

Nezah

Hod

Yesod

Malkhut

AZILUT
WORLD OF EMANATION

Place of Metratron

BERIAH
WORLD OF CREATION

Where three
upper worlds meet

YEZIRAH
WORLD OF FORMATION

Where three
lower worlds meet

Malkhut of Beriah
Tiferet of Yezirah
Keter of Asyyah

ASYYAH
WORLD OF ACTION

Kingdom of Kingdoms

4. JACOB'S LADDER

Here the four worlds are set out as interpenetrating Trees that form one great Tree
that stretches from the first Emanation to the last manifestation. Each world is a
complete Tree in itself with crucial points where the different realities can meet. This
is the Macrocosmic setting of Existence.

13

4. Jacob's Ladder

The first of the three lower worlds to emerge from the realm of the Primordial World of Divine is called *Beriah*, the World of Creation. This arises out of the midst of *Azilut* so that the lower face or half of Emanation is concealed behind the upper face of Creation. Thus, there are places where the *Sefirot* of the superior world match the *Sefirot* of the inferior world in an interpenetration of different realities. This principle applies to all subsequent worlds and allows for their interaction, like air dissolving in water, and water evaporating into air. Later, we shall see how such junction points between levels are crucial in experience and development.

The Crown of Creation arises out of the Divine *Sefirah* of Beauty which is also called the place of YAHVEH ELOHIM the Creator. This *Beriatic Keter*, although an echo of the *Keter* of *Azulit*, has quite a different quality, in that it marks the beginning of time and space. The Bible speaks of the seven days of Creation which describe the phases of cosmic unfoldment as the *Sefirot* create a universe on the model of the Divine World above. Such a World is of a lesser order, a more dense and complex nature as the laws of *Azilut* and *Beriah* are combined and interact. In a dimension that is one remove from its origin, 'things' begin to appear and move, for now having emerged from the Eternal World of Unity, potentiality can begin to differentiate into location and duration, thus the upper and lower firmaments are separated; land appears and plants and celestial bodies marking the seasons emerge. Birds, fish and animals are created and finally the *Beriatic* Adam, the spiritual image of Divinity is brought forth. Here is the Cosmic World of Ideas — the place where the essence of everything that is to be arises in the Universe, like thoughts in the mind of God.

Out of what is traditionally called the Throne of Heaven upon which sits the Divine Adam of *Azilut* emerges the third world of *Yezirah* or Formation. This arises out of the midst of *Beriah* so that its *Keter* corresponds to the *Tiferet* of Creation and the *Malkhut* of *Azilut*. Here is where the three upper realms meet. The quality of *Yezirah* is like that of water; if *Beriah* is likened to air and *Azilut* to fire. This symbolism gives some idea of the character of the four worlds. Fire radiates, air moves and water takes up different forms, while earth, represents the tangible quality of the lowest and most solid world. The fluidic zone of *Yezirah* holds the position of being the intermediary between the physical and the spiritual and Divine. It is also said to be the emotional level of Existence, with *Beriah* as the intellectual and *Azilut* as the level of pure consciousness. The quality of *Yezirah* is caught in the various descriptions of Paradise with all the various shapes and sizes, colours, sounds and sights to be experienced there. Here, the creative ideas of *Beriah* and Will of the *Azilut* manifest in form as the laws of the superior levels combine and interact with *Yezirah*. This world is of particular interest in our study as it is the habitat of the psyche and all the archetypes, or gods, demons and angels, as the ancients called them.

The lowest world in Jacob's Ladder is called *Assyah* or the World of Action and the elements. Here, the combined influx of all that happens in the worlds above manifests in the transient moment by moment reality of the concrete; the states of solids, liquids, gases and radiations being the result of all that has happened in the upper worlds. An example of this is the effect of the Sun upon the atmosphere whose winds stir up the ocean and then precipitate rain over the Earth. *Beriatic* ideas and *Yeziratic* forms produce the forces that make the minerals, plants and animals arise in the elemental world of *Assyah*. Modern science sees materiality as the wave-particle ground bed of physical existence but not its origins. Everything we observe with the senses is made up of a vast and subtle combination of all four worlds concentrated into the material spectrum.

Kabbalah sees the interaction of the Worlds as the twin processes of descent and ascent, or Creation and Evolution. The Will of the Absolute is implemented in the downward impulse of consciousness through the Worlds, to reach its maximum range in the denseness of materiality. Here, it turns and begins to reflect back in increasing stages of consciousness, in metals, minerals, primitive and advanced plants and lower and higher animals. These in turn add to the wider consciousness of Nature as it refines and adds more intelligent levels to its species, that in turn enhance the capability of the Earth and subsequently the solar system. The notion that planets and suns are living beings is an ancient one, and as scientists observe the characteristics of celestial bodies, so their likeness to living organisms has been noted. For example, the Sun's 11-22 year electromagnetic rhythm has been seen as the pulse-beat of the Solar System, which is like a cell within the body of the Milky Way that in turn has the qualities of a creature on the cosmic shore of a higher ocean of reality.

The esoteric concept of 'as above so below' is seen in the micro-cosm of the body and the macrocosm of the Earth. Both have enormous populations of creatures, each performing their task in an ecological chain, whether as the intestines or rivers, or the lungs and the forests that breathe for the body and Earth. If this law is valid, then it is not unreasonable to speculate, if one has not had direct experience, that there are also creatures who inhabit the higher worlds. Sensual logic will deny such a possibility, but then this same faculty of (so-called) reason thought the earth to be flat for millennia; nor did it believe in bacteria until they were seen under the micro-scope. Up to the eighteenth century, the reality of non-physical entities was accepted in the West, but with the Age of Reason their presence was denied, suppressed or rationalised into subjective phenomena. Some modern psychologists, however, have begun to recognise that not everything they encounter is a product of the unconscious. A few even acknowledge intrusion and interference from the invisible realms. This opens a door that has been bolted for centuries in the study of psychology.

According to Kabbalistic tradition there are many levels of beings. Some, for example, are responsible for vast operations such as galactic development. These are the great spirits or archangels. Others, of a lesser order, act as intermediaries, carrying out specific tasks like watching over planets or species of plants and animals. Yet others are involved with more routine matters such as cycles of weather or the maintenance of particular areas such as lakes or mountains. These were seen as the old nature gods or devas in the Indian tradition.

In Kabbalah the angelic and demonic beings are often defined in terms of the *Sefirotic* Tree. Some, like those responsible for diseases or migrations, for example, work on opposite pillars, one to stimulate the process of expansion, while its partner holds the function of containing on the other pillar, so that a balance is kept. Yet other beings might operate in the vertical mode, with one above and one below, carrying out a reciprocal flow operation, such as the annual process of springtime manifestation and autumn's dissolution, as the seasons switch hemispheres. These creatures, like those in the terrestrial seas and jungles, are part of a celestial ecology that maintains a field of consciousness at their level, like a flock of gulls expresses the mind of the Great Gull that resides in the World of Creation. These angelic and demonic beings are the archetypes of dynamic, structure and maintenance. Within the worlds of *Beriah* and *Yezirah*, they exist in their own right and should be regarded in the same way as the flora and fauna of the physical world, because within their realms they are quite real and powerful.

The existence of a whole hierarchy of beings who live in the upper worlds is accepted by most spiritual traditions although they may see them in different cultural forms. In Kabbalah, these hosts are seen in terms of Jacob's Ladder with each order limited to a specific level in the same way as the whale and the worm are confined to their habitats. The human race, however, is regarded as quite unique in that, because it has its origin in *Azilut*, it is not limited to any particular world.

5. Human Beings

Human beings are not like any other creatures in existence, because they come from the World of Emanation and not Creation. While it is said in the Bible that Adam was created on the sixth day, it will be remembered, according to Kabbalah, that Adam Kadmon pre-existed Creation. The appearance of a spiritual Adam in *Beriah* is another way of presenting the idea of the Divine image at the next and lower level. As such the *Beriatic* Adam represents, by being the last to be created, the image of spiritual perfection. Lucifer, the highest Archangel, could not accept this and fell. His place, as said, was later filled by Enoch, the first man to return from the descent into matter, and transfigure his experience of all the worlds into self-realisation to become Metatron. Enoch-Metatron marks the beginning of a vast process in which Adam Kadmon is transformed by humanity from a state of innocence into that of experience. Tradition says when the last human being has been born and begins his or her cycle of illumination, then the Messiah, the most perfect of incarnate Mankind, will manifest upon the Earth to everyone, because Adam Kadmon will be close to full consciousness. These final days at the End of Time are still some way off, we are told. Meanwhile, humanity must continue the process of individual and collective development as it works its way through fate and destiny.

According to some rabbis all human beings begin existence as *Nizozot* or sparks within the radiant image of Adam Kadmon. Others go further and say how different people originate from specific parts of Adam's anatomy, some coming from the arms or legs, others from the head or organs such as the liver or eye. This is a symbolic way of defining the particular quality and task in the destiny of that human atom of the Divine. Thus, there are those who are concerned with action, while others operate primarily through emotion or intellect. Each one of us has our root in a particular cell of Adam's body and carries out the role of that unit in relation to a particular system within the organisation of the *Sefirotic* Tree. Some rabbis add that there are righteous, unrighteous, and common sparks. This is to say, those strongly inclined to progression or regression within the context of the Tree, with the more ordinary being concerned with the routine processes of Existence. Here one must discriminate carefully. For example, the symbolism of coming from the Line of Cain as against Abel (the two sons of Adam), means that one expresses the just rather than merciful mode in one's chain of lives. The ancient Greeks had the notion of uncommon men and common men, that is those with a special purpose, and those who carried out general duties. The Indian caste system originally had the same idea in the privileges and obligations of each level; the highest and most advanced carrying the greatest responsibility. The division of High Priests, Priests, Levites and Israelites has the same connotation in the Bible.

Kabbalistic tradition goes on to describe how these sparks or atoms from the World of Light are sent down into Creation to participate in a vast cycle of self-realisation. A vignette of this process is the image of a human being coming out of *Azilut* and entering the Seventh Heaven with the cry "I AM" as it comes in the spiritual Universe. Here, energy is added to consciousness, and the first differentiation occurs as the photon of Divinity becomes aware of moving in space and time. The contrast between this cosmic dimension and Eternity must be enormous and many seek to return to the Radiance whence they came. However, the velocity and density of Creation, plus the impulse that sent them forth carries them downward through all the Seven Levels of Spirituality to a place called the Treasure House of Souls that is situated beneath the Throne of Heaven. This is an allegorical way of saying they have come out of *Beriah* and are now enclothed in a form in the realm of *Yezirah*.

Here, Kabbalists say, they wait until they are born, as there appears to be a definite sequence of arrival and departure between the upper and lowest world of physicality. No one is moved without reason, for that would be contrary to the whole scheme of Existence which is founded upon laws that control an ordered progression. Like the construction of a building or the gestation of a child, each phase must proceed according to a plan that allows both the general and the particular to emerge at the right moment and place. Thus, while individual sparks experience the descent into spirit, psyche and body as a very personal event, it is in fact carefully co-ordinated with other sparks. These might come from the same root, to act in support or be fated to oppose or facilitate the development of that specific human entity. The *Pargod* or great curtain that Enoch saw hanging before the throne of Heaven holds the grand design of human destiny. As the pattern of threads intertwine throughout the fabric, so a human spirit weaves its cosmic destiny through many fates. Some of these configurations are complex and produce numerous encounters while others may experience only few, but deep connections, that help individual's to relate their potential and play a vital role in Existence.

According to some, at the beginning of the present Great Cycle or *Shemitah*, only a few human beings were incarnated upon the face of the Earth. These propagated and died, that is they returned to the upper worlds before being born again as the children or grandchildren of their children. In this manner, the human population of the planet has increased in numbers and experience until there are possibly more people living in the body than there are in *Yezirah* or *Beriah*. Tradition says there is a set number (II Esdras 4.36). The population explosion is expected to level off. As people come and go, so the ebb and flow of the living and dead set up a tidal rhythm of generations that influences history according to personal and collective karma. Thus, the infamous holocaust of the Second World War, for example, served its cosmic and individual purpose in bringing about the state of Israel. Many who died in the gas chambers, it has been said, have been reborn into that country with the deep conviction of 'never again', as the unconscious personal and collective memory of a former life turns the current generation of Israelis into a nation under arms.

Over the millennia, a field of fatal patterns, based upon karmic relationships and stages of development, has been built up to affect not only the individual, but their soul groups and spiritual associations as well as their social and cultural settings. These personal and collective connections are part of the organism of mankind and have a great bearing upon where individuals are born, who they meet and mate with. Thus, the law of reward and punishment determines the conditions people find themselves in and what lesson they need to learn before they pass again through death back into the upper worlds for recapitulation and rest prior to rebirth. This process is known as the *Gilgulim* or Wheels in Kabbalah and will be dealt with in detail later, for it has a direct relevance to the study of psychology. However, before this we must examine the Kabbalistic theory of the four worlds and see how they correspond to the levels within a human being.

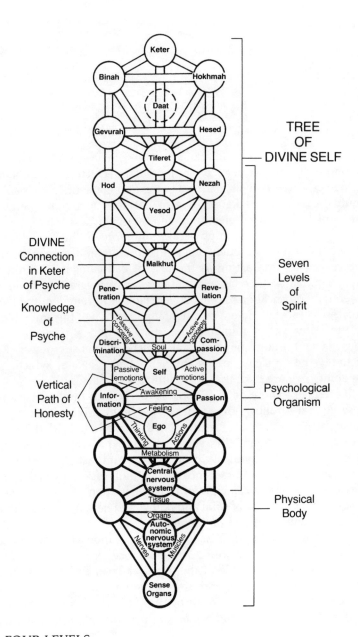

5. FOUR LEVELS

Each living individual has four levels of reality within them. The physical body forms the natural base to negotiate the outside world, while the psyche is the intermediary organism for the spiritual vehicle with its Divine dimension. The whole constitutes a complete human being capable of attaining consciousness in all the worlds.

21

6. Four Levels

Approaching the composition of a human being from the Aristotelian or empirical view, we begin by setting out the structure and dynamics of the body. The body is made up of the four elements, that is solids, liquids, gases and radiance. It also has four levels of operation: mechanical, chemical, electronic and consciousness. Here, we see the four worlds echoed in physicality. In terms of the Tree, there is the interaction of the outer pillars in structure and dynamics, with the central column acting as the axis of consciousness within the organism. Thus, there is a mineral level of awareness in all the essentially physical operations, a vegetative awareness in the living processes, a social and environmental perception at the animal level of the body and a human dimension, in that a person can be conscious of things beyond that which the senses detect. This includes the capacity to be aware of being aware, which is a capability, we are told, that only humanity possesses.

If we take a more detailed look at the Tree of the body, we will observe that it follows the model of the highest Tree of the *Sefirot*, but at the physical level of reality. Thus, the body's *Malkhut* contains the four elements and the sense organs which look outward to perceive solids and liquids, through touch and taste, gases through smell and hearing, and radiance through all, especially sight. Here we also observe the principle of interpenetration of levels as taste, for example is a blend of solid and liquid, and hearing a combination of gaseous vibration and radiation.

The triad surrounding *Yesod*, or the foundation of the autonomic nervous system that governs routine procedures, is made up of muscle, on the active side of the physical Tree, and nerves on the passive or receptive side, with the horizontal triad of organs above processing what comes in through *Malkhut*. Beyond the path stretched between *Hod* and *Nezah*, or the voluntary and involuntary principles exampled by selective listening and heart rhythm, lies the triad of tissue. This is where the ingested elements pass out of the mechanical and into the chemical level, represented by those processes concerned with building structure or releasing energy.

This resolving and dissolving is monitored by the *Gevurah-Tiferet-Hesed* triad of the Metabolism which is governed by the central nervous system at the pivot of the body Tree.

The upper zone of the body Tree is composed of the side triads that control the positive and negative electrical process that, for example, accelerate or decelerate various functions, such as muscular action and brain waves. The central great triad of *Binah-Tiferet-Hokhmah* contains the electromagnetic field of the body, which includes those finer frequencies that no machine can detect, but can be perceived by individuals with a sensitivity to the aura of the body. This phenomenon is not as mysterious as it seems, as most people respond to someone with a disturbed auric field by sensing it as a peculiar atmosphere about a person. In this scheme, *Binah* and *Hokhmah* represent the body's organisational form, and the life principle that activates it.

The *Keter* of the body Tree in our scheme corresponds simultaneously to the *Tiferet* of the psyche and the *Malkhut* of the Spirit. Here, we see how the three lower worlds can be perceived by a human being. By this is meant that a person cannot only cognise through the senses but be aware of the psychological and spiritual dimensions of reality. As the body reacts to the physical world so the psychological organism experiences the World of Formation and the Spiritual Vehicle, the World of Creation. However, although their interaction enables the person to be aware of all three realities, most people are only conscious of the physical dimension. The higher levels are usually confined to the unconscious, until a shock like death or a developmental crisis occurs to raise the question of what life might be about. More of this later.

To be precise, most people live in the area between the lower physical functions and the higher psychological faculties. In Tree terms, they are oblivious of the autonomic processes of the body below the central nervous system of *Tiferet* and unconscious of events beyond the *Tiferet* of the psyche. This leaves the upper face of the body and lower face of the psyche which operate at the same level but in different realities. At the centre of this interaction of perception of different worlds is the place of *Daat* or knowledge of the body, and *Yesod* of foundation of psyche. Here the exchange of physical and psychological data is rendered into an intelligible image by the ego which can become aware of a pain in the body or a mood in the psyche. The ego in most people is the chief mode of consciousness. It perceives through the senses, and can recognise

and differentiate thoughts from feelings. It can initiate action, recall
past events, deal with routine matters like driving cars, and select
what the body and psyche can relate to. This is possible because of
many factors that we shall discuss. At this point, however, we shall
keep to the outline, the general framework in Tree terms, so as to
build up a key vocabulary.

The triads around the ego of the psychological Tree are composed
of thinking, on the passive side, and action on the active, with
feeling in the triad that corresponds to the organs on the lower
physical Tree. This is not without reason, as there is an 'as above,
so below' relationship between the triads of one Tree and another.
Thus, feelings are associated with such organs as the stomach and
heart, while thinking is related to the systems of nerves, and action
with the triad of muscle. These correspondences are relevant to the
interaction of body and psyche, either through feeling precipitating
thought and then action or some other combination. Here is the
mechanism of psychosomatic disorders as psyche and body resonate
in the two Trees.

Above the threshold line stretched between the *Hod* and *Nezah*
of the psyche, which represent the voluntary and involuntary processes of the mind, lies the triad of Awakening, where the data
collected by *Hod* and the power of *Nezah* come into contact with the
Self of the psychological *Tiferet*. Here consciousness is elevated and
one becomes aware of being aware. Everything is clear and a lucidity
is present to perceive the lower part of the psyche, especially the
ego, quite objectively. Such an event can occur during a dramatic
moment, or while particularly at peace. It has the quality of seeing
the body and the physical world from another place, and indeed
that is precisely what is happening as one's centre of conscious
gravity is shifted out of the sensually orientated ego into the realm
of *Yezirah* when seen from the *Tiferet* of the Self. From here the
unconscious can come into consciousness, for suddenly memories,
drives and restraints normally unrecognised come into view, as the
side triads of emotional and conceptual complexes may reveal their
contents. These, it will be seen in the diagram, are divided into
active and passive, that is, the emotional and intellectual experiences
that form the structure and dynamic aspects of the psyche. An
example of a passive complex may be seen in certain disciplines one
learned as a child, such as not expressing one's emotions or holding
firm to certain values. An active complex may take the form of a
zest for music or a political ideal.

The soul triad of the psyche defines the zone of free will. While all the other triads perform important tasks they are nevertheless under definite laws. The body must concur with these or die, and the main part of the psyche is unconscious and therefore not accessible to choice. Only when a person is centred in the Self, if only for a moment, can he or she alter the patterns of their life. This is because the soul triad, it will be noted, is not part of the lower world of Nature or the upper realm of the Spirit. It is quite independent of either, although it has the *Tiferet* connection with the *Keter* of the body and the *Malkhut* of the Spirit. The Self is the place where the three lower worlds meet in the psyche.

The *Binah-Hokhmah-Tiferet* triad of the psyche is a blend of the upper part of *Yezirah* and the lower part of *Beriah*. Here the individual relates to the spiritual dimension. Thus deep within the unconscious is a connection to the transpersonal World of Creation. This cosmic aspect reveals the relationship of the individual to the universal. Here, the Divine spark that is impelled through space and time is held by the Spirit that animates the psyche which lives within a physical body. Thus when and where we are born is not accidental; nor is the form of our fate, which is, under psychological laws as exacting as those which govern the body that give it distinct characteristics and limits. This is so because, according to Kabbalistic tradition, Divinity watches over each of us through the Divine connection at the *Keter* of the psyche where the three upper worlds meet in the *Tiferet* of *Beriah* and the *Malkhut* of *Azilut*. As the Sufis say, "God is closer to us than we are to ourselves." This completes the general scheme of the psychological Tree. Detailing will come later.

Each of us is the image of Adam Kadmon. Within every human being are, in miniature, all the levels of Emanation, Creation, Formation and Action. We have been called forth from the Absolute for a distinct purpose and have been given four vehicles that allow us to operate in all the worlds. Having outlined our frame of reference let us now examine the subject of reincarnation which has a profound bearing upon the psychology of an individual.

7. Transmigration

The notion of reincarnation is common to many cultures and has been held since antiquity. The fact that it was unofficially declared a heresy by the Second Christian Council of Constantinople in 553 A.D. and that it has no place in Islamic doctrine does not invalidate it, as many examples bear witness to its reality. It was accepted widely in the Orient, and among Celtic Druids in the West. Plato acknowledged it and so did the Gnostics and the Essenes. The early Christian scholar Origen observed that it was the only explanation to certain scriptures, and many other thinkers concluded that it was the reason why some people have fortunate or unfortunate lives, irrespective of their good or evil deeds. The rationale behind this is that reincarnation was seen as the redressing of personal and universal balance carried over in a continuous sequence of lives that adjusted each fate according to merit. Out of this process emerged the lessons to be learned about the laws of Existence and the purpose of that particular person's destiny.

There is abundant evidence of people recalling past lives. Some are in the form of vague feelings about a certain place or period; others are distinct and precise in their recollections. A certain American general, for example, had his driver take him off the beaten track during a North African campaign to view an ancient battlefield. When asked how he knew so much about it, he replied that he was there at the time. He went on to say that he had been a soldier through all his lives over the centuries. In another case, a child in India declared that he was from another village far to the north, and that he had been murdered by his wife and her lover, and buried in a particular place. Subsequent research revealed that the name of the village and man were real and he had indeed been murdered in the way described. It has been argued that stories and facts can be relayed by gossip or can be unconsciously absorbed material, but while this does occur, the volume of facts that could not be known by the person remembering a past life is weighty. One example was a woman who recalled an old crypt in a certain church which was later discovered during repairs to the building.

More recently, researchers have been collating recollections of past lives in a methodical way, using the technique of hypnotic regression. In this method, the person is taken back before birth into a zone of memory that holds images of extraordinary clarity in some cases. For many, the moment of death is still very real. One person, for example, vividly recalled falling off a tentpole in her forties at a market in ancient Iraq. Another remembered dying of an intestinal growth in eleventh century England and another in sixteenth century Normandy of old age, after a rough life as a soldier. Some people recall earlier lives without being hypnotised. One individual recognised the streets of a certain old city the moment he arrived, and another had a dim recollection of lying under the rubble of a house as the Cossacks set fire to it. As might be expected, the humdrum aspects of a life are forgotten, or rather blend into a general feeling, while the more dramatic moments are deeply etched upon the memory. This suggests that the psyche, or at least some part of it survives physical death and continues to retain the experience through the post-mortem period and into the next life.

One researcher using the regression method, explored a sequence of fourteen lives of the same person. First, the man was moved into a state of consciousness that detached him from his physical body. When this occurs, the workings of the psyche are freed from practical constraints, as in dreams. Then the attention was focussed by the hypnotist in a series of probing questions that explore time and place. The result was a picture of a series of historic periods lived through, ranging from 2000 B.C. up to the twentieth century. The detail of the conditions of some periods is quite striking, such as clothing and customs. Sometimes the person held rank and sometimes a humble position. In one life he was preoccupied with a dying young wife. In another, he married into a wealthy family; and in another lived in Lebanon and enjoyed being a merchant while studying with the local sage. Later, he found himself in Greece in a homosexual relationship with a Roman, and at another time in a village in Central America around 1300 A.D.. During these and subsequent lives, he was sometimes a man and sometimes a woman [it was noted by the researcher that there was a predominant tendency to be male or female in a person's pattern]. The subject of this experiment lived in Portugal as a woman and in Italy as a man where he did not get on with his aristocratic neighbours. Later, he was a Welsh girl who died in childbirth after a relationship with a Spanish sailor. He could still feel the guilt and shame of this incident.

These memories, like his attachment to a particular wooden spoon while living a French peasant's life, left deep marks, as did his feelings about the American colonies hurting his business when he was an English wool merchant in the eighteenth century. Such details as these, and many others, indicate a complete bank of unconscious memories stored somewhere deep in the psyche.

From a Kabbalistic viewpoint all this is theoretically quite feasible. The *Yeziratic* vehicle of the psyche is in principle exactly like the body but in a different reality — that is, as the physical organism can store the experience of a single life and evolution in its skills and instincts, so the psyche can hold ancient memories as well as recall the events of the present life. The psyche is just as subtle and complex as the body and indeed processes thoughts, feelings and actions in the same way as the body does the four elements. Dreams, for example, are part of the psyche's digestion system. The deeper memories, however, like fat or alcohol, are buried in the unconscious recesses of the psyche, only to emerge in special situations, which release what is embedded there. Such events occur during analysis and certain Kabbalistic exercises. In most analyses the analysand only goes back to the moment of birth, although some go beyond into the prenatal situation. The implication is that what one is born with is a great deal more than a genetic typology.

Kabbalah takes this longer view into account. According to tradition, the process of *Gilgulim* is a 'turning' of lives. It is also called *Ha'atakah* or 'transference'. Generally termed 'transmigration', the concept first appeared only in the twelfth century among the Kabbalists of southern France, after being opposed by the more conventional schools of Iraq. This is not unusual as the academics can never accept what they cannot prove. The argument of the *deja vu* or 'already seen' as a perception warp is the most commonly used to refute 'double take' memories but the volume of previous life memories far outweighs this sense-based conclusion.

According to Kabbalah all human beings originate from different parts of Adam Kadmon. This gives each of us a particular quality and tendency so that we may be sympathetically inclined to this or that *Sefirah*, triad or Pillar. Moreover, tradition says that individuals descend in groups of a similar kind which remain connected at the higher levels as they pass down through the lower worlds to incarnate from time to time and perform their individual tasks. Books have been written about these groups, their relations and collective destinies and identity over a sequence of lives. The most obvious have been identified by certain Kabbalists in different historic roles. For example, the patriarch Jacob is seen to return as Mordecai in the Book of Esther, while the sixteenth century Rabbi Isaac Luria was considered to be a reincarnation of the great mystic rabbi Simeon ben Yohai of the Roman epoch.

Transmigration is seen in some cases as a corrective punishment for discrepancies in a former life, and in others, as a continuing process of perfection. Among some Kabbalists, it was considered a privilege to be incarnated in order to aid the Holy One bring Adam Kadmon into full realisation through their experience. Here we see the appreciation of levels, for various stages of human development have different needs and situations in order to evolve. Some people require easy conditions after a hard time, and others the reverse. Certain individuals have to suffer because of misdemeanours in a previous life, and others go through it with them in order to help. Many good individuals support quite evil people so as to get them out of a karmic cesspit. This process is sometimes called 'Ibbur' in Hebrew, and can apply to incarnate or discarnate individuals who perform such tasks.

All these possibilities suggest a complex situation. Each human life has its Divine root, spiritual level and psychological karma which are the hidden part of the iceberg of the current life. The reason, we are told, that so few people recall any previous existences is that today is where we live and have our being. Our past lives, like yesterday and yesteryear are background to the present; for as one great Kabbalist remarked, "Sufficient unto the day is the evil thereof". In reality, the moment 'now' is the only time and place we can act upon. Incarnation is necessary because out of the flesh we have not the power to affect all the worlds and make our contribution to Adam Kadmon's education through a series of fates that compose the chain of our destiny. Transmigrations are part of a great design, but they are carefully planned to give the individual the maximum possibility of development. Here is the prenatal factor in any esoteric psychology.

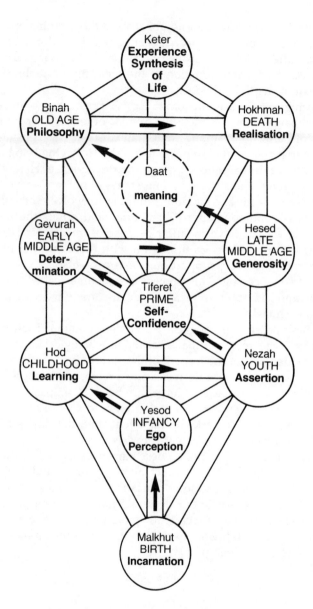

6. AGES AND PHASES OF DEVELOPMENT

Here the progression from birth to death and beyond follows the Sefirotic sequence, with each Sefirah indicating a stage of physical and psychological growth. The qualities of the various positions show how the body and psyche mature according to Divine Law and Cosmic principle as the individual ascends the Tree.

8. Fate and Destiny

The moment a person is born, that is, takes the first breath and is separated from the mother, he is subject to the Laws of Nature. This is because the physical body on birth finally manifests into the *Malkhut* of *Assyah*, the lowest of the four worlds, after passing through the descending sequence of gestation. Having produced the physical vehicle, which enables the entity inhabiting it to exist in the natural world, the process then reverses and begins the return back from the materiality of the body through the various stages of growth, maturity and ageing towards death. The first phase, after investing the *Assyatic Malkhut* is *Yesod* or the stage of infancy, the next *Hod* or childhood, and then *Nezah* which relates to youth. *Tiferet* marks the point when a person reaches their physical prime, while the *Gevurah* and *Hesed* stages correspond to early and late middle age. *Daat* brings the phase when one thinks about death as the symptoms of mortality are experienced. The *Binah* period is of early old age, and *Hokmah*, the epoch of late old age arrives before the individual comes to *Keter* and dies, leaving the body Tree to dissolve back into its *Assyatic* elements.

The *Sefirotic* stages of life echo the planetary ages of the ancient art of Astrology which many Kabbalists see as the study of the influence of the *Yeziratic* world upon the psyche. Because there are clearly a set of universal principles at work in both the body and the psyche, so the horoscope drawn up for the moment of birth was considered to hold the key to each fate, as their relationship was fixed at the first breath. This leads on to the idea that fate is the resultant pattern of a life as a particular individual with a certain karma and in a specific environment, passes through the various phases of physical and psychological development. Seen this way, fate is a highly complex combination of factors operating at many levels. That is why there are so many different views of it. For example, some see fate just as what happens to the body; others view it as the history of the psyche; yet others perceive it as a combination of the two, but only at the level of ego and conditioning, while others take just the inner life into account and detach it from physical reality. Fate contains all these factors, that is the physical situation, its psychological aspects and its spiritual and Divine dimensions. Few see them as a unity that produces exactly the right conditions for the realisation of each individual at their particular stage of evolution.

In order to get a general sense of the developmental sequence, let us outline some examples of the planetary and *Sefirotic* stages that can pervade one incarnation and their qualities. A person who has not progressed beyond the Earth or *Malkhut* phase of incarnation, for instance, would not outgrow and master the elements, and so would be preoccupied with physical security, while the individual at a Lunar or *Yesodic* phase of development might be childlike and egocentric in all their dealings with the world. Those at the Mercurial stage of *Hod* are often eternal students always looking for novelty and information, even as those at the *Nezahian* or Venusian phase frequently carrying on as they did in their youth throughout their pleasure-orientated life. Those who are in the Solar or prime stage at *Tiferet* often assume a great self-confidence, unless their pride has been broken or modifed by the tests of fate, while people who are at the Martial or *Gevurah* stage, usually spend their lives in an endless compulsion until they learn to control themselves and serve a higher purpose. Those stuck at *Hesed* or the Jupiterian phase can be the excessively generous givers who seek to buy love or respect, and not a few who have reached *Daat* or the Pluto phase live preoccupied with death and the beyond; while others at the Saturnian or *Binah* phase become old before their time in deep understanding or the lack of it. Those at the Uranian stage of *Hokhmah* frequently live their lives according to visions which may be profound illuminations or madness; and those whose fates have the quality of *Keter* or Neptune often have a deep religious dimension to their fate, which can be genuine in some and a delusion in others.

As will be seen each one of these stages has different possibilities. This is determined by two critical factors. The first is the element of free will on the part of the person, in response to their situation and the second is the purpose of that individual's fate in relation to the lesson they have to learn about their place in the Universe. The old rabbis said, "Not a sparrow falls that is not noted in Heaven". And also, "Are not the hairs of your head numbered?" That is to say everything occurs according to the grand design, and everything is taken into account. This concept was symbolised by the great curtain hung before Heaven, in which each thread, representing the destiny of an individual, is made up of segments that follow the *Sefirotic* sequence from the top to the bottom and back again. In some cases one stage may take many lives to complete; in others the process may move quickly over one lifetime, such as in the example of the Buddha. This overall plan is, of course, too vast for most people to recognise in a fleeting three score years and ten, but many individuals have felt or seen, at crucial moments of their lives, some sense of purpose to their existence. Not a few have actually perceived what their destiny is and followed it. These people are quite distinct from the rest of humanity, which for the most part is oblivious of its personal and cosmic objectives and seeks only to survive and propagate. However, there are millions who have developed *Hod*- and *Nezah*-type fates and appear as great discoverers and entrepreneurs or creators and innovators while advanced *Tiferet*-centred people act as leaders at every level. Likewise, those at the *Gevurah* stage manifest in various disciplines such as professional soldiers or lawyers, while people who are cultivating *Hesed* are often seen in religious communities or doing charitable work. Individuals operating a powerful *Daat* may be the seers of their generation. Well developed *Binah* people are frequently found running large organisations while talented *Hokhmah* types can turn up as ideas people in the laboratory or political party. The *Keter* initiates are sometimes seen in monasteries and asylums, although they are rarely observed in ordinary life, even though they are undoubtedly there to give it the Divine dimension. All these are well individuated types, who, it must be said, may be good or evil.

Every human being possesses free will, but few care to use it fully. Most people prefer to choose, and it is their choice, to come under the power of one of the functions. This means they are ruled by their bodies or by their egos, or that they are dominated by one of the other *Sefirot*. Many people have not got beyond the *Yesodic* stage and so they are governed by what society imposes on them, as they conform like grown-up children. This may seem a harsh judgement, but if one considers human history and how the majority allow their lives to be ruled by others, it is easy to conclude that real and mature individuality is indeed quite rare.

The purpose of each Fate is to create the conditions for such individuality to emerge. This notion is based upon the recognition that nothing occurs in Existence without a reason and that no event is without significance. If the organisation of the human embryo can occur in perfect sequence with each stage of development phasing in just at the right point to create, form and make billions of cells arrange themselves into such a complex organism, then it is not unreasonable to think that the plan of an individual's Fate follow the same laws.

It is no accident that the Earth is just in the right place in relation to the Sun, Moon and planets to be able to support life; and that the most delicate web of Nature is maintained by an integrated network of flora and fauna. Nor is it strange from the viewpoint of universal principles, to see how each life and death is part of a whole in which each generation is but a season in the general evolution of the planet. In humanity's case, the development of individuality arises out of the collective groups of families, tribes, peoples and civilisations as they emerge over the cycle of many incarnations to psychological and spiritual maturity. This process, however, has to be monitored, because free will and resultant karma lead to many twists of fate before people get in touch with their original spiritual group, or meet their soul mate with whom they can carry out their particular destiny or cosmic task.

Sadly, many who are trained to observe the psyche are oblivious of these larger dimensions which require an awareness of things beyond the normal view of the world. Such a sensitivity is often concealed for professional reasons or lost beneath clinical observation. However, in this exercise of relating psychology to Kabbalah we can explore such ideas and dimensions freely. Therefore, in our next chapter we shall leave the sense and logic-based perception of reality and examine the moment of death, and what follows, in order to see what goes on prior to a new life. In this way, we may glimpse the situation of the psyche before it is affected by the conditioning of its next incarnation.

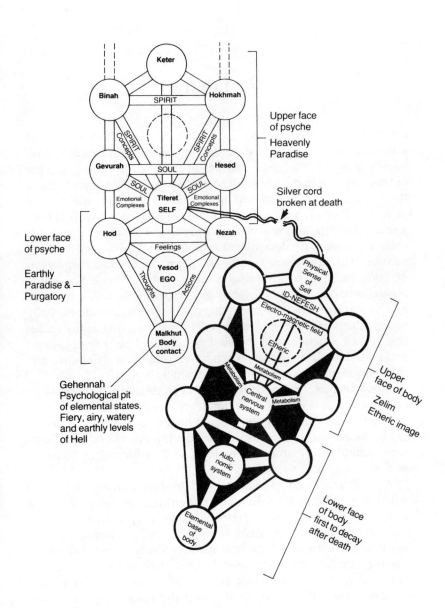

7. DEATH

On dying the psyche and physical body separate permanently. During sleep, anathae-sia or shock a complete parting is prevented by the traditionally called Silver Cord, which is broken at death. When this occurs the devitalised body begins to disintegrate, and the psyche enters the post mortem phase of recapitulation of that life.

35

9. Death

Out-of-the-body experiences are not uncommon. They have been known to occur during medical operations and while people have been gravely ill. The characteristics of the phenomenon is a sense of separation from the physical, so that a person finds himself above the operating table or sick-bed looking down on what appears to be an inanimate body which they recognise as their own. Much as been written about the subject and the theory is, in Kabbalistic terms, that there is a temporary detachment between the *Assyatic* and *Yeziratic* vehicles. This disalignment of the two normally coincident organisms of body and psyche can also occur in traumatic events such as accidents or during acute psychological crisis. Generally, it resolves, and the detached consciousness that observes from outside the body usually drifts or is sucked back into its cohesive union as the senses regain their function, and the vital principle reasserts the powerful gravity of Life. Death occurs when the separation is maintained and the connection between body and psyche is broken.

Many near-death experiences have been collected in recent years by qualified researchers who found to their surprise, that such incidents were quite common when it became acceptable for people to talk about such moments. Many, like the out of body incidents were stimulated by unusual situations such as drowning, being hit in battle or having accidents.

After several hundred such observations had been collated, it was noted that all exhibited a distinct set of phases, depending upon the length and depth of the experience. Some people only perceived their consciousness set apart from their bodies, but others, on reaching the extreme of physical pain, suddenly found themselves passing through what appeared to be a dark tunnel or veil. Yet others went beyond this stage and actually heard themselves pronounced dead, for they could still hear the voices of the so-called living. Those who passed through this phase recorded that they became aware of people, whom they knew to be dead, approaching them and many were conscious of a powerful presence or bright light that spoke about their lives. This in many cases rapidly flashed, in reversed sequence, before their consciousness, as if in a review of their performance. All who reached this point said this was the frontier between life and death, and that for various reasons, they were drawn back into the body, often with great regret, because they experienced a wonderful ecstasy in being discarnate.

These records of partial discarnation find an echo in accounts of the first stages of death in such volumes as the Tibetan *Book of the Dead*. The cultural form may be different but the essence of the experiences is the same. So too are the many descriptions found all over the world of the post-mortem conditions in which those who have lost permanent connection with their physical bodies find themselves. Much superstition and distortion through ignorance has blurred what has been recorded, but nevertheless the general principles of what happens between death and rebirth has been known by various esoteric traditions. The Platonic myth of Er who was believed to have been killed in battle, but awoke at his funeral to tell the tale of the process, is a classic example of allegory being used to describe events in the Upper Worlds.

In Kabbalah, there is the advantage of the metaphysical system of Jacob's Ladder, so that one can see precisely what myth and experience reveal. Taking the moment of death, and there are 903 forms of death according to the rabbis, the way a person dies is considered as an indication of how he or she will fare in the *Olam ha Bah* or the World to Come, which means, in fact, the next world or *Yezirah*. For example, a righteous man or woman will die gently, like a hair being removed from a bowl of milk, but the evil person will suffer great pain as the psyche is pulled out of the body; for resistance against facing their deeds in the action replay of their lives is very strong; or they may simply be too immersed in materiality and be frightened by the separation. It is also said that when a person dies their cry reverberates throughout all the Worlds, even as a newly born babe's does. This is a symbol of the cosmic effect of passing from one world to another. The rarest transformation is called 'the Kiss of Death by the Holy One', who takes a highly evolved person gently across the divide between the living and the dead.

According to tradition, the *Shekinah* or Presence of God comes to the good and true person, giving them the opportunity to go straight up the central axis of the Ladder in a moment of pure consciousness into union with the Divine. The Tibetan *Book of the Dead* describes the same phenomenon and urges the dying person not to be distracted from the light and so be reborn. This is a very Buddhist understanding. Kabbalah sees much work to be done in the lower worlds before such an illumination, and so it regards rebirth as part of an ongoing process. Every tradition has its view.

Seen in greater detail, the process of dying begins with the separation of the two lowest bodies. Anyone who has witnessed someone dying slowly will recognise that sense of withdrawal which makes them stand out in a hospital ward from those still strongly incarnate. The moment of death is when the physical and psychological become so separated that the vital soul, called the *Nefesh* in Kabbalah, cannot keep their systems synchronised. In Tree terms, the *Daat* or Knowledge of the body is parted from the *Yesodic* ego of the psyche as the upper face of the physical Tree becomes detached from the lower face of the psyche. At such a moment, we are told, the body actually loses a fraction of its weight. The processes described in the near-death situation are then passed through, but this may take up to three days to complete, as the vital forces still hold the two bodies in a kind of orbit until they are exhausted and the *Nefesh* collapses. During this time, it is not unknown for relatives and friends to hear or see the newly deceased person. Such apparitions are based on the fact that there is still what is called, the *Zelim* or shadow image that is held until the vital energies are spent. This is a period of taking leave of the material level for most newly dead people who accept they have finished that life and withdraw, having taken their farewell of those whom they love. It is also why we are told not to hold them back by excessive grief, but to help them on their way with prayer and a ceremonial of saying goodbye at a funeral. This is common to all cultures.

There are those, however, who wish to stay for various reasons, such as the person who clings to their material possessions because they believe in nothing else, or those who for some reason are excessively attached to a certain place or event in their lives and wish to relive it over and over again. These account for the phenomenon of ghosts which eventually disappear, sometimes only after centuries, unless someone with spiritual knowledge or psychic gifts can release them from what, in some sense, is a form of discarnate insanity. A more common form or apparition is found, for example, at the scene of recent accidents where the deceased are seen wandering about in shock for a time, before they realise that they are dead. A more unusual case is recorded in the Talmudic commentaries of how the great rabbi Judah Ha-Nasi used to visit his home after his death on the eve of the Sabbath, to be present at a rabbinical seminar. He eventually, we are informed, ceased to attend, out of respect for the other scholars. His work was done and he had to leave them to do things their way.

The initial process of dying is complete when the connection between body and psyche has finally been broken. This takes place around the third day. At such a point, it is said, the *Nefesh* loses contact with the psyche and hovers about the corpse as it begins to decompose back into its original elements. This accounts for the quite different atmospheres found in new and old cemeteries. According to Jewish tradition, the *Nefesh* hangs around for about a year in a state called the condition of *Sheol*, or the Nether World, that is, here below, where they can still observe the living. This is why the final stone setting takes place on the anniversary of death. It is also because a year was seen as about the length of time generally required for the recapitulation and purification of the soul of the deceased. Here, it must be said that a different order of time was envisaged, in that a turn of the seasons on Earth symbolically corresponded to the cycle of a life at the *Yeziratic* level. During this period, the detached psyche underwent several phases of process. The first was an expansion of perception as the psyche was released from the constraints of the flesh. Thus everything became more intense, so that during the period of reflection over the just-passed life, both pleasure and pain were experienced to an extreme. This gave rise to the symbolic states of Paradise and Purgatory, which can be seen in terms of Jacob's Ladder as the upper and lower faces of *Yezirah*. Traditionally, they are sometimes called the Heavenly and Earthly Edens; the lower obviously related to the level that is closest to the upper face of *Assyah*, and the superior to the lower face of *Beriah*. Some Kabbalists see the left and right pillars of the psyche as the Severity of Purgatory and the Mercy of Paradise. Either way, the experience of the life lived is distilled into an essence that is stored in the psyche and remains after the old body has been discarded.

Tradition adds that according to a person's quality of life and consciousness, so they rise or sink to an optimum level. *Gehennah*, the Jewish equivalent of Hell, is the state of being of those who insist on breaking universal laws. This harsh place of retribution can be with or without a body, because being at the base of the *Yeziratic* world the forces and laws concentrated there (often symbolised by the extremes of the four elements, such as ice or boiling mud) operate upon anyone who holds to a completely egocentric or material view of Existence. Such people are held in these extremes until they realise why they are there and experience guilt and then remorse. The act of repentance automatically releases them and they rise up out of the 'Pit' as it is sometimes called because it occupies the lowest region of *Yezirah*. Most people, we are instructed, abide in the middle zone of *Yezirah* until they have completed their time of rest, contemplation and instruction. Those at an advanced stage of development reside beyond what are called by some, 'the summerlands', into the great Silence of *Beriah*, the World of Pure Spirits. Here they undergo further training to perfect what they have learned during life. These are the true Gnostics, those who know the secrets of life and death and the reason for their existence. Here they bide their time, for unlike those below, they can choose when to incarnate, so as to carry out some task. Most of humanity, tradition states, goes forth and returns within the orbit of the *Gilgulim*, or the wheels of life and death. This cyclic motion carries within it both collective and individual factors that determine the time and place for each new fate as it moves through its stages of destiny. But before this can happen much preparation has to occur prior to conception and birth.

10. Intermission

As mud, water and oil each find their level in a glass jar, so the *Nefesh*, psyche and Spirit go to their respective places in the three lower worlds. The *Nefesh*, or vital soul disperses into its elemental aspects in a relatively short time, its matter returning to dust and its energy rejoining the general pool of vitality in Nature. The psyche is of a more subtle composition and greater duration; even this, over a certain period, dissolves like the *Nefesh*, back into the fabric and force of *Yezirah*, as it too is only a vehicle for holding the dynamic of the Spirit and the spark of Divine Consciousness. However, many lives on Earth have to be passed through before this occurs permanently. Likewise, the spiritual vehicle also eventually dissolves back into its World of Creation, when the photon of consciousness within an individual, having reached its full potential reunites with the being of Adam Kadmon and goes beyond, into the Nothing and All of the Absolute. Until then, each human being goes to his or her appropriate level; the most evolved, according to tradition, to the higher reaches of Jacob's Ladder, where they await recall or enter the inner councils of mankind that watch over the human race. Here, they may remain for many centuries, working from above, until it may be necessary for someone to descend and operate directly at the lower levels. Such people as the great saints and sages are of this order, selecting their moment to incarnate according to the general situation in which cosmic trends are taken into account. The influence of masters like Confucius and the Baal Shem, who turned up at a crucial point in Chinese and Jewish history are examples of careful timing at the transpersonal level.

Most souls do not reach the lofty chambers of the *Beriatic* world where Providence organises and adjusts the grand design for our planet, but remain below in the realm of *Yezirah* where they complete and assimilate the lessons of their previous life. During this time, many old connections are reviewed with the already-dead, and the long-term effects of even earlier lives are seen in the light of the last, as patterns are recognised as repeating, or progress has been

41

made to break or develop certain tendencies. Meanwhile, those of their own generation, with whom they have karmic or group relationships come and go in the merry-go-round of birth and death. Some people, we are informed, remain only for a short time, either because they cannot do much work at the *Yeziratic* level or because it is better for them to learn while incarnated. Not a few return to a body very quickly, because they are drawn back by their still primitive nature, or have to complete a task within a certain time and must follow it through. Many people have this feeling in relation to situations or certain individuals.

The notion of soul groups gathering and dispersing in the Upper Worlds and then re-meeting below upon the Earth is not without evidence. Thousands of men and women recognise each other, though from where they cannot recall. Some call it *Kismet*, others *Nemesis* as they work something out together. Occasionally individuals actually perceive the reason why they have been brought together. Some become spouses, lovers or friends, and some just companions on the way of the Spirit who have met and worked together before over the centuries and in different countries. It is not uncommon, for example, to find these people operating within the same religious or esoteric order, or others who form a multi-racial group that always meets at the centres of civilisation, like medieval Toledo or seventeenth century Amsterdam where the conditions allow cross-connections and pollination between traditions, as happened in tenth-century Baghdad or in present-day London.

It will be appreciated that much organisation is involved in bringing about these situations. This is carried out by the laws of cause and effect and conscious management. Thus, while the angelics take care of the cosmic cycles of Nature, discarnate human beings with experience and insight watch over and determine the right moment for individual reentry into the flesh. For the bulk of mankind, the rhythm is fairly regular. In the same way, many people live their lives on Earth as a routine, unless disturbed by larger events, like war or economic recession. Most individuals come and go between the worlds in the ebb and flow of families that leap-frog each other over the centuries as they pass through the roles of children, parents and grandparents, sometimes exchanging positions in relationship and sex. Tradition says there is a tendency towards one sex, and that any reversals are to teach the other sex's viewpoint. According to legend, psyches are paired and seek each other out. If they work with integrity, they will meet and mate, but too often people are side-tracked by preferring security, social standing or a dozen other diversions that make them miss that fatal meeting with their other psychological half. It has been said that the *anima* for a man and the *animus* for a woman, which are the feminine and masculine counterparts in the psyche are in fact, the *Yeziratic* images of their partner in that World. This is one of the reasons why the *anima* and *animus* projections are so powerful and have little to do with the physical reality of the partner.

According to esoteric teaching, when the moment for descent comes a new process begins. Having synthesised the previous life's lessons, now deeply etched into the *Yeziratic* body, the experience is then blended into all the knowledge acquired by that human being since it was first incarnated. This sometimes manifests as vague memories of past epochs that form a backdrop to the psyche. However, if a last life had been traumatic, for example, then it will leave a particularly strong residue that may affect a person's new life from deep in the unconscious. A violent marriage, for instance, will influence any relationship in the next life. Here we begin to see how an individual comes into a fresh incarnation with a distinct set of tendencies, based upon perhaps a series of disastrous or harmonious lives. The Buddhist notion of all that we are is the result of what we have thought not only includes the experiences of this life, but of others. An example was the young man born after the Second World War who felt constantly guilty because he had betrayed friends in the French Resistance. Being executed had not expiated him in this life and he subsequently committed suicide.

Whatever was done in the previous life must have an effect on the next; for it is inevitable that certain fixed attitudes will generate corresponding situations. The quick-tempered man must invariably attract conflicts, and the highly emotional woman, love or hate deeply. This is where the supervisors, as they are sometimes called, come in, for they might arrange for such a woman to marry such a man, in order to learn how to solve their problems. Clearly, the arranging and timing of those matchings is a complex business. According to some, people belong to karmic groups. These have senior and junior supervisors who relate the individuals in them to the bigger scheme so that karmic connections form an integral part of family and society at large. Most people, we are told, are assembled for their descent without too much trouble, and are born in a general sequence so as to live what, for many, is a relatively simple life in urban or rural communities all over the globe. These are for the most part the as yet unawakened level of humanity and form the ground-bed of mankind. Kabbalah defines them as mineral and vegetable levels of humanity who seek physical security and basic sustenance. Usually they live quite regular lives and come for the most part under the collective psyche of tribes, peoples and nations. The village in Mexico, the market town in England and the industrial city in Russia contain many such people. Individuality is as yet undeveloped as people conform in dress, customs and attitudes to the image of a true Bedouin Arab, Yorkshire miner, Chinese farmer, English civil servant or Spanish aristocrat. This level has nothing to do with class.

The animal level of mankind is composed of those with compulsive drives. These people have ambition and exhibit all the qualities that make a person want to get to the top of a profession, a political party or a street gang. Such people do not live like their less aggressive contemporaries. They incur, in their struggle for superiority and domination, much karma. By their nature, they will generate both strong friends and foes who are fatally involved with them over many incarnations. The ruling families that murdered each other for power in the beautiful chambers of the Alhambra Palace in Moorish Spain did not just leave an atmosphere of their violence that still can be felt, but took with them the karmic effect which may still be working itself out in modern dynastic struggles of business, crime or politics. These are the things that have to be taken into account when a group of souls is being organised for its next incarnation.

Those who have reached a certain level of development and are defined as being the 'human' level of mankind, are under a different set of laws. Here is where the misunderstanding about people being reincarnated as stones, plants and animals comes from. All humans are born as people. It could not be otherwise, but they may live at any one of these levels which are a state of being, not an entity, like becoming a dog. Some animal people, for example, behave like pigs or lions, and some vegetable people are like oaks or daisies. They exist at that level and as such can be good or bad at being what they are, like an exquisite rose or a mad dog. The 'human' human beings are often individuals who have lived many lives and have reached a point when they are not just seeking security, nourishment or dominance, but realise that life and the Universe have an aim. Some are awakened souls and others conscious spirits. There are several levels. Such people are not so easy to place in the usual timetable of births and deaths. They require more exact postings and may have to wait until the right combination of conditions and companions can be found on Earth so as to able to live their fates consciously and carry out their destiny.

Long-term plans, made at the level of *Beriatic* Providence, are referred to since 'human' humans are rare and have to be strategically placed. Thus, one person may be born in Argentina in order to give him a specific training; while his future wife is raised in England where the conditions for her karma are perfect, so that when they meet, in New York, at the right moment, they are ready for each other and the work they are to do together. Kabbalah states that each soul is shown, before they are born, the general outline of their life to come, the places they will be and the main people they will encounter. This memory, like those of previous lives is more or less forgotten in the business of being a baby, although some people do retain a dim recollection. However, before we discuss this phenomenon we must examine the situation prior to the conception of a new body in the future mother's womb.

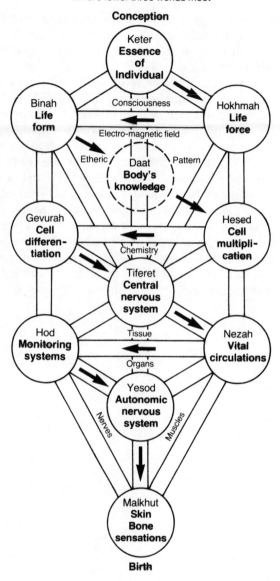

Where lower three worlds meet

Conception

Keter
Essence of Individual

Binah
Life form

Consciousness

Hokhmah
Life force

Electro-magnetic field

Etheric

Daat
Body's knowledge

Pattern

Gevurah
Cell differen-tiation

Hesed
Cell multipli-cation

Chemistry

Tiferet
Central nervous system

Hod
Monitoring systems

Tissue

Nezah
Vital circulations

Organs

Yesod
Autonomic nervous system

Nerves

Muscles

Malkhut
Skin Bone sensations

Birth

8. GESTATION

Conception starts at the Crown of the physical Tree and the impulse works its way down from the finest to the coarsest levels of the body in the Lightning Flash sequence. Thus the body emerges out of the lowest point of Creation, through the bottom half of Formation to fill out and manifest in a solid physical vehicle that has access to three worlds.

11. Gestation

The great Kabbalistic classic the *Zohar*, compiled in medieval Spain, says, "At the moment when the union of the soul and the body is being affected, the Holy One sends on Earth an image engraved with the Divine Seal. This image presides over the union of man and wife; a clearsighted eye may see it standing at their heads. It bears a human face; and this face will be borne by the man about to appear. It is this image which receives us on entering the world, which grows as we grow and which quits the Earth when we quit it."

The phenomenon of a presence and even an image is not uncommon at the moment of conception. Some people have described it like someone else in the room. Others have actually seen a figure standing near by and still others sensed something special occur while making love, which they recall with great clarity, when it is established that the woman is pregnant. In rare cases, a name is presented and even the character of the person about to be incarnated.

In order for this momentous moment to occur, many things have to be in the right place. Not only do the prospective parents have to be brought together in sexual union below, but the conditions for conception must be set up above in the higher worlds. It is well known that sexual intercourse at the right time of the menstrual cycle does not always produce a child, nor does contraception always prevent the male sperm from meeting the female egg. Moreover, a prolonged attempt to produce conception over many planned months is not a guarantee that it will eventually occur, although a single sexual encounter with a complete stranger has been known to get an unexpected result. This is because the timing is crucial in conception and subsequent birth.

Providence, which oversees the grand design, organises events according to the needs of the Universe and the individual. Thus, there is a juxtaposition of considerations that takes into account the general planetary situation, the state of human society on Earth, the condition of a particular nation, the phase of a certain community, the circumstances of a specific family and the karma of an individual. Most of these factors are part of a general pattern that is unfolding, but the closer we come to the particular, the more exacting is the timing. For example, a national revolution usually takes years to generate a sparking point; like the first shot on Lexington Green in the fight between the British and the Americans. And the person to lead the struggle, like Washington, has to be ready and at the right age. This required considerable precision in organising his fate. Thus a person is born at a certain time in order to deal with a certain situation, connect with specific people, relate to peers or marry a particular individual. A twelve-year-old boy cannot wed a ninety-year-old woman, even if they are soul mates, and produce a child. The sequence has to be synchronised to produce the most profitable conditions.

This synchronicity is not confined to events below in the World of Action and Elements. It must also occur above, in that the levels of spirit and psyche must be ready for the descent. Tradition says that first, as indicated by the 'Divine Seal', the process is started from the World of Emanation which brings the essence of the person's spirit and the essence of the person's psyche together. These 'atoms' or 'seeds', as some traditions call them, are the residual experience of all previous lives which regenerate the *Beriatic* and *Yeziratic* organisms in the same way that the physical body is manifested. At first, we are told, the structure and dynamics of the spiritual and psychic vehicles are brought into contact and united. They are then held ready for the gestation period while the person is prepared and briefed. More developed individuals are usually aware of what is involved, and can actually recall this pre-natal state, after being incarnated as they remember being 'somewhere' before being born, and having conversations about the nature of their future life. Most people remember nothing, but experiments in hypnotic regression have brought back to many people quite startling recollections. For example, some remembered what it was like to be in the womb, and what relationship to various members of their present family they had had in former lives. Some recalled looking forward to being born, and others that they were quite reluctant to come. There were some who saw they had a particular job to do in their next life, while others that they did not want to live again at all. The laws of karma, however, govern the moment of conception and incarnate they must be under the impulse of cosmic and developmental necessity.

The process of conception, seen Kabbalistically, is the bringing together of all the worlds, and their fusion in the manifestation of a physical body for the incarnating entity. Thus, while the couple make love so there is union between male and female *Yesods* of their body Trees, resulting in a rising up of consciousness into the *Yeziratic* triad of Awakening or Ecstasy, as there is a descent of the spiritual and psychological vehicles of the individual to be incarnated. Conception occurs, when it is willed from *Azilut*, in the place of the Self where the three lower worlds meet, so that, as the *Daat* of the body and the *Yesod* of the psyche, and the *Daat* of the psyche and the *Yesod* of the Spirit come into creative contact so that fusion on all the levels takes place and the way is open for the sperm to unite with the ovum. Such an event is not a random selection of seeding, but a precise orientation of conditions. Thus while the parents who perhaps come from totally different backgrounds, might appear to meet quite casually at a party, it is in fact a fatal coming together that could affect many lives. Such events are the result of tremendous preparation to get them together at the right moment, to court, marry and conceive a particular person.

Once the ovum has been fertilised, the *Assyatic* process of building a physical body is begun. Following the descending lightning flash sequence, the essence of a person is held at the *Keter* of *Assyah*, which is simultaneously at the *Tiferet* of the psyche and *Malkhut* of the Spirit, that is the place of the Self. Thus, the individual's core qualities will be fused in with the physical characteristics of the parents. The process moves on down to the *Hokhmah* of the body that gives life, and then across to *Binah* that determines the structure. If the process of gestation passes the critical point of *Daat*, the abyss of the Body Tree and the momentum of incarnation is not withdrawn, as sometimes happens for various reasons, then the genetic procedures continue in the expansion of *Hesed* in the multiplication of cells and their differentiation in *Gevurah*. The essence of the body and the base of the psyche are established in the *Tiferet* of the body, that later becomes the central nervous system which serves physical consciousness. The process is then continued as the various *Nezahian* cyclic systems are built in and tuned in the data procedures of *Hod*. Examples of this are blood circulation and the adjustment of the sugar balance according to needs. The three triads around the autonomic system of the body's *Yesod* manifest the organs, nerves and muscles. The creative impulse finally resolves in the *Malkhutian* level of the bones that support the body and the skin with its sense organs that give access to the external world of physicality.

The process of gestation is complex as the four elements of fire, air, water and earth are blended into the levels of mind, electronics, chemistry and mechanics. These mirror the four worlds in the body. So, too is the interaction of the pillars of structure and dynamic and the vertical axis of consciousness. The various stages of gestation moreover, repeat the pattern of manifestation, but in miniature, as the atom of Eternity emerges out of the energy of Creation to take on a form and then substance. All the experience of Existence goes into the gestation of the body, as every creature that has been brought forth is present in the embryo. This is seen in the way it passes through the various stages of evolution. first it looks like a primitive plant, then a simple animal; later it takes on the forms of a fish, reptile and mammal before finally developing into a human embryo.

During the period of gestation, as the various higher vehicles of psyche and spirit are gradually brought into alignment with the body, the consciousness of the person about to be incarnated hovers about the embryo. At first the relationship is quite flexible, which is one reason why miscarriages can occur almost without noticing. Later, as the psyche begins to fuse into the physical organism, the bond grows stronger. Some people dimly recall this period and many, under hypnosis, remember quite clearly floating around in their mother, fully aware of their own and her feelings about the coming birth. Most people are pleased to make the association; but others, it has been noted, would rather not and retreat. This can lead to spontaneous abortions or Down's syndrome children, who, in wishing to remain discarnate, retard the normal process of gestation at the genetic level. The same may also be said of autistic children, who almost complete the process, but have not quite come into full incarnation. As will be realised, gestation is a highly critical period, when the new body is at its most vulnerable and therefore, susceptible to influences coming from both the incarnating individual and the mother. Thus what she thinks, feels and does physically and psychologically can affect the embryo. This is why many pregnant women go into a deeply cocooned state and lose all interest in anything but their baby. It is a natural and psychological protection designed to shield the growing foetus from unhelpful influences before its birth.

The timing of birth is as crucial as conception. Many doctors see the process of pregnancy in terms of a standard model, but the moment of birth is not like that. To be born too early or too late is a clinical abstraction. A person is born at the most propitious time for that individual to enter the physical world, and Providence is not above using the medical profession as an instrument to get an individual in on the dot. There is no such thing as a premature or late birth when seen as the first intimation of Fate. The way an individual emerges into the World is of great significance.

12. Birth

During the process of gestation the mineral, vegetable and animal levels of the embryo, are built by a field of force and form present in the womb. This is a combination of the mother's vital energy and the *Zelem*, or image of the individual to be incarnated. Slowly, the necessary elemental base of the foetus fills out the already-existent *Yeziratic* plan as the vegetative principle takes in nourishment from the mother and builds up the structure. Around four months, the body is sufficiently developed to move about, like an animal restless within its confines. During this time, the psyche, while relating to the growing foetus is relatively unbound. According to research under the hypno-regression technique thirty-three per cent of tested subjects observed that they did not fuse with the foetus until just before or during birth. Moreover, some did not fully incarnate until afterwards. Many people gave remarkably clear descriptions of their own state and that of their mother's, and others described crucial periods during pregnancy. All this indicates a lucid awareness of what was going on.

In one case, for example, the person observed that they were frightened by the rapid growth of the foetus and the on-coming birth, while another, one of twins, recalled the conflict over which foetus was theirs. This echoes the Biblical story of Jacob and Esau who fought in the womb of Rebecca, indicating a high degree of consciousness prior to being born. In many cases, detailed observations of the mother's physical states were recalled, so too was her attitude and that of the father, because the psyche was not, like the foetus confined to the womb. In some cases, the person could recall coming and going, as if hovering between two worlds, and in one instance the individual was aware of checking the foetal state of development from time to time, while spending the rest of the period elsewhere. The degree of involvement with the foetus during pregnancy seems to be variable. For example, only twelve per cent of those regressed reported being attached to the foetus at six months after conception.

The connection between body and psyche, at this stage of their relationship, is not strong. This means that in some cases the privilege of free will can be applied to abort the process or to go on, like the person who saw that the foetus had webbed fingers, but chose to continue the pregnancy because the mother was so happy. Others are not so steadfast and withdraw, precipitating a miscarriage. This might be caused by a negative attitude on the part of the mother or external events that are more than the incarnating person can endure, generating natural or accidental stillbirth which may be an unconscious form of abortion. In the case of deliberate abortion, the issue is different. It is a matter of choice and from this flow certain consequences of karma — good or bad. Rabbinical law discusses the problem and concludes that under certain conditions the mother's life comes first, providing the child's head or greater part of the body has not emerged during birth. Abortion prior to this state was not considered. Seen from an esoteric viewpoint, there may be a moment of choice, for many reasons, to terminate a pregnancy, but the effect on the parents and incarnating individual has to be considered very deeply before any action should be contemplated. Many who have decided to abort, have preserved their lifestyle, but experienced a profound loss of more than a child. For the soul who was returned to the Upper Worlds, it is perhaps less of a shock. They can at least come in via another couple, or if right, and the original parents have learned a vital lesson, return again as a second child, who is often given as a second name, the one intended for the first foetus, because the parents sense it is the same soul, but in another body.

As we have described, the time and place of a birth is taken into account by those responsible for organising the incarnation. The cosmic rhythms and patterns ebb and flow each year, and it is a question of inserting an individual into the physical world at the best moment for their development. Traditionally, there are twelve human types, held in the place of the Self, at the *Tiferet* of the psyche and the *Malkhut* of the Spirit. Each one of these dynamic forms has a distinct character which contributes to a general spiritual-psychological experience. Tradition suggests that we incarnate as one of these types in order to learn and perform certain cosmic tasks and psychological roles, moreover that we slowly move round the Zodiac from type to type as we proceed from life to life. Seen Kabbalistically these forms are the various modes by which each Divine atom of Adam Kadmon experiences all the levels of Existence. Astrology is the study of these principles, and so the moment of birth, when the fluid quality of the psyche is crystallised in the solidity of the body is of great interest.

Anyone who has been present at a birth, and is aware of more than just the physical action, is struck by the presence of something very powerful and other-worldly in the room. Indeed, for anyone who has witnessed death, the same sense of the Upper Worlds is present as the soul departs. At birth, the process is reversed, with considerable effort needed to bring the person down, because besides the problems of getting the psyche into the very small glove of the body, there are dangers as the individual shifts their centre of gravity from one world to another. This can be intrusion by lost discarnates who still seek a body or entities that simply like to interfere with the transference process. Such an idea may sound medieval, because it is no longer fashionable in our age of science, but many highly intelligent and sensitive people discreetly acknowledge that this is possible and that the notion of possession by an alien psychology is not just a myth. In earlier times, people accepted the reality of other worlds and their inhabitants and took precautions with prayer and amulet. Now, while we depend mainly upon physically con-ducive conditions in the labour ward, it is noticeable that more care is being taken of the psychological conditions that the child comes into. The new technique of birth taking place in warm water is an echoing of an esoteric idea of bringing the individual slowly out of the *Yeziratic* World of Water into the Earth of *Assyah*. There are, however, other spiritual procedures. As there are traditional watchers in the room of death, so there can be those at birth.

Besides the preparations of those below to create the best con-ditions for birth, those above also attend an incarnation. It was observed for example by one, who was given the task to act as watcher at the labour of a woman under the discipline of Kabbalah, that as the moment of birth approached, so there appeared a ring of light that encircled the room. This was augmented by four columns of cold blue fire which passed through the floor and roof of the chamber. As the labour increased, so too did the intensity of psychic activity. The doctors and midwives did all they could to encourage the birth, but it became very apparent, to the Kabbalists present that nothing would happen until certain conditions were in alignment. At a specific moment, the final contractions began, and while everyone else was involved in the delivery, the watcher saw several figures, high over the bed, helping someone down. The image was blurred but they were unmistakably quite human. These attendants worked above with the psyche as those below laboured with the body. When the child emerged the figures above the bed faded, but the circle of light and the pillars of blue flame remained for some time after the birth.

Perceived from the babe's view, many who underwent the hypno-regression procedure vividly recall entering the birth channel. Descriptions of darkness, pressures, texture and light at the end of the birth canal remind one of many near-death experiences which tell of going through a tunnel towards a brightness. Kabbalistically, this is the passage through *Daat*, the black hole of Knowledge that bridges the Worlds, to bring about fission or fusion between the physical and psychological realms. Many people regarded this transition as a traumatic event as they were squeezed through the canal. Some could actually recall the midwife's hand or a surgical instrument grabbing at them. Most were shocked by the coldness of the air, the blaze of light and the noise in the room. Nearly all experienced a profound sense of loss on being incarnated. This was probably not just for the security of the womb, but the dramatically reduced contact with the higher worlds they had just emerged from. Many, it was noted were acutely aware of those about them and their state. For example, the relief of the mother, the indifference of a doctor, and in several cases the disappointment of the father over the sex of the child. Some actually recalled what people said, like, "Oh, what a fat boy!" This indicates that the psyche is not infantile at birth, but is a perfectly cognisant intelligence. The state that a child enters this world with, likewise, is more than just a physical reflex. One person remembered being intensely angry, while another, remained calm. It has been said that the way a person reacts at birth is crucial to their life. Indeed many mothers have observed that this response is often retained as a major quality of character. Examples of this are the quiet watchful babe who became a philosopher and the furious infant who has been angry ever since.

It has been noted by many people that new-born babes are very like old individuals. It is not just the wrinkled face that gives the impression but the eyes that radiate a mature intelligence, and the general feeling that here is an adult mind locked inside the small and delicate body. This reality is alas, soon forgotten in the projection of most parents, relatives and friends who only see the body of a baby. It is interesting to note that many of the hypno-regressed subjects recall thinking and feeling like adults and how they drifted in and out of the babe's body, for the connection between the psyche and body is quite fragile. One person described how the body diminished their scope in that they could not relate to so small a vehicle. In Kabbalah this stage of infantile-adult consciousness is called the 'Days of Wisdom'. In some it soon passes as the body begins to make its demands, and the incumbent psyche slowly becomes immersed in learning how to relate to heat and cold, hunger and bowel movement. In time, the adult element of the psyche shifts into the unconscious although it is partially regained when the body is asleep, as the connection between the body and the psyche is loosened. The incarnation has now taken place and slowly but surely the memories of former existences are overlaid as the individual starts to live a new life. The possibilities of this incarnation, however, are revealed in the horoscope or macrocosmic time picture made for the moment of birth.

13. Paradigm

Astrology is the study of the effects of cosmic influences upon mankind. It is one of the oldest sciences and certainly the most ancient form of psychology. This complex body of knowledge about celestial effects has been built up over several thousand years by empirical observation. The Babylonians formulated the general scheme of interacting levels and the Greeks refined the detailing. The Arabs added the more precise dimension of the Mundane House system and western astrologers have deepened and widened the subject with the aid of the modern scientific method. Today, astrology is a subtle synthesis of mythology, psychology and technology. Seen Kabbalistically, it is a discipline that relates events in the World of *Yezirah* to what is happening in the World of *Assyah*. Looking at it in a more contemporary way, astrology is the study of a system of cosmic dynamics and structures and how it affects the sub-system of the psyche according to the tensions, eases, blocks, and releases occurring at a given moment. Its rationale is that the solar system with its ever-changing set of planetary relationships affects, by resonance, the delicate infrastructure of the Earth and particularly human beings who are especially susceptible to events in the greater worlds. This is because each is a miniature version of the universe and resonates in sympathy with cosmic rhythms and patterns. A natal horoscope is simply a picture of the celestial situation at the moment of birth when the incarnating psyche gells into the body.

The reason why such a chart can be useful is because there is a analogic relationship between the nature of the *Sefirot*, the planets, and the psyche. Thus, for example, *Malkhut* and the Earth correspond to the body while the Sun and Moon relate to the Self and *Tiferet* and the ego and *Yesod*. The planets correspond to the various functions and levels of the psychological Tree that is based upon the image of Adam Kadmon. The model becomes individuated at the moment of birth as each of the heavenly principles leaves the mark of a particular sign of the Zodiac upon the first breath. Here, it must be said to astronomers, that the picture is not of the stellar constellations or actual celestial bodies, but twelve earth-orientated divisions of the sky when the luminaries and planets are related to a particular place and moment. It is like the difference between a perceptive, but impressionistic painting of a person and a highly resolved image of a photograph. The former is concerned with depth and emphasis, the latter with a surface accuracy that is, in fact, often a misleading picture. A horoscope reveals, to a good astrologer, what in a character is likely to predominate tendencies which could be checked and what needs to be worked upon. A highly skilled practitioner can make certain predictions about a life, like a good diagnostician can prognosticate the course of a disease, but this must be based on great experience and a profound understanding of human nature, which many astrologers and indeed doctors do not have, because most people assess by the obvious or go by the rule of established opinion, which is subject to intellectual fashion.

The position of the Sun, Moon and planets give each chart and Tree a unique loading, for only rarely are two people born within four minutes of each other at the same place. The manner in which this configuration is spread out or cluttered can indicate the way a person may be a good or bad all-rounder or an obsessional type, such as is found when Sun, Moon and Mars are conjuncted in a particular Sign or Mundane House. Without being too technical, for astrology is not the focus of our study[1] a House is that department of life in which a planet manifests itself. For example, Saturn in what is called the tenth House, which relates to achievement in the World, would tend the person towards a powerful ambition. Both Napoleon and Hitler had this in their charts. Here, it must be said, to quote Sir Thomas Browne, the seventeenth century physician:

> Burden not the back of Aries, Leo or Taurus with thy faults; nor make Saturn, Mars or Venus guilty of thy follies. Think not to fasten thy imperfections on the stars, and so despairingly conceive thyself under a fatality of being evil. Calculate thyself within. Seek not thyself in the Moon, but in thine own orb or microscosmical circumference.

This is to say that while the horoscope indicates trends, they are no more than tendencies that can be utilised or checked, because the factor of free will is always available. Alas, the choice is usually

---

[1]See author's *Anatomy of Fate, Kabbalistic Astrology*. Gateway Books, Bath, 1986, and Samuel Weiser, Inc., York Beach, Maine, 1986.

to be unconscious of one's inclinations, especially the bad ones, so a chart has great relevance to most of us. Therefore, let us take an example and see the *Sefirotic* and celestial principles involved and their effect upon the psyche that has been incarnated.

A horoscope is usually drawn up for the moment of the first independent breath when the psychological and physical bodies fuse to a greater or lesser degree. If they do not lock then the child dies and the psyche retires to *Yeziratic* world again as happens in a still birth. This fusion of body and psyche produces a patterning of forces and structure not unlike snowflakes that take on certain forms according to the conditions. In the case of people, the psyche is crystallised into a kind of personal hologram of the cosmos as it unfolds the grand design. This sets in motion what we call fate. The process can be likened to an arrow shot from a bow under particular conditions of angle, tension, wind, humidity and aim. Once the arrow has been loosened it will follow a specific trajectory. In Hebrew, the word *Het* or 'sin' means 'to miss the mark' and this is related to a person who does not use the fate given to develop, for unlike an inanimate arrow, we can make in-flight adjustment, even though the general passage from birth to death may be fixed in this or that way, according to the karma that set up the aim.

If, for example, our subject was born just after dawn, with the Sun, in say, the sign of Cancer, then empirical evidence would indicate that they might be essentially retiring and preoccupied with domestic matters; whereas someone born fifteen minutes earlier would still be interested in family and security but this would be expressed very outwardly in a drive for better and new homes in society, or the founding of communities in pioneer conditions. A Moon, in say, Leo might add a charismatic or a megalomaniac ego according to the Moon's relation to the other planets and its position in the House system; whereas a Moon in Virgo, which is favourably related to the Sun could, if well handled bring a practical ego-*Yesod* to aid the Self-*Tiferet* symbolised by the Sun. If badly utilised, despite its good aspect, such a person might become excessively petty or possessive in their pursuit of security and turn a potentially excellent family situation into one of tyranny. This illustrates that so-called good and bad horoscopes are not as clear-cut as they might appear. Many a person with an apparently difficult chart has mastered its problems and grown out of being what Shakespeare called an 'underling' of their stars.

If the Ascendant, Moon and Sun are considered as the bodily

form, the ego and the Self, then the planets represent, on the Tree, the various functions of the psyche. Thus, a Mercury at *Hod* in the Sign of Gemini in the third House of communication would indicate a high degree of intelligence and inquisitiveness, while a Venus in the same Sign and House would suggest a sensual curiosity that might lead to promiscuity. Likewise, any of the planets when analysed according to their position and mutual relationship will indicate the propensity for a particular *Sefirah* in their psyche. An afflicted Mars or *Gevurah*, for example suggests bad Judgment or conversely, if worked upon, real discrimination. A well-aspected and placed Jupiter, or *Hesed*, however, could create laxity in limits so that the person is continually in debt or loves people who always hurt him. This, of course, could be his fate, that is either to learn not to, or to clear some karmic backlog. Likewise, a Saturn in Aries in the House of partners could lead to an impetuous and contentious marriage to someone much older, in which some past life problem is worked out in a parent-child relationship, until one or both become adults. The position of Uranus or *Hokhmah* factors could be quite critical in a person's life, if it is found in the House of possessions. This indicates sudden gains and losses in practical things, if it is in an earth sign, or perhaps emotional matters, if in a water sign. The planets Neptune and Pluto, according to Kabbalah, are associated with the central column of consciousness and would indicate the kind of contact with the Divine and Knowledge of the Spirit the person might have. Neptune in Pisces, for example, might mean a mystic approach as against Neptune in Taurus which would produce a more material and practical connection.

All the foregoing can only give a faint impression of what can be got from a birth chart. With a trained eye, much can be gleaned by scanning and focussing, analysing and synthesising all the factors. Like an X-ray plate, the paradigm of a horoscope contains many minute details of the situation as well as the general picture. It can indicate talents and lessons of character, the inclination to lead this or that kind of existence, and when astrology is intelligently applied, detect the crucial periods of growth and crisis. For, as the body has to grow into an already existing image, so the psyche has a pattern which follows a particular path as the person moves through the various ages and stages of development.

Seen objectively, the birth chart sets out the potential of a person. People do alter the pattern of their lives, but this is quite rare, as few know themselves well enough to modify or develop their traits.

Astrology is useful because it is a detailed map that contains the kind of information which normally takes years to acquire. Having seen the emergence of the psyche into the material world of the body, let us now look at the parallels as we begin to see the relation and resonance of the psychological and physical organisms.

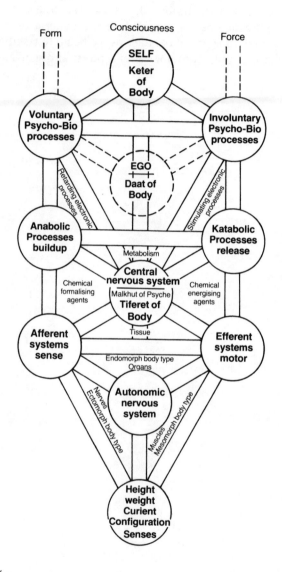

Form   Consciousness   Force

SELF

Keter of Body

Voluntary Psycho-Bio processes

Involuntary Psycho-Bio processes

EGO

Daat of Body

Retarding electronic processes

Stimulating electronic processes

Anabolic Processes buildup

Katabolic Processes release

Metabolism

Central nervous system

Chemical formalising agents

Malkhut of Psyche

Tiferet of Body

Chemical energising agents

Afferent systems sense

Tissue

Efferent systems motor

Endomorph body type
Organs

Autonomic nervous system

Nerves Ectomorph body type

Muscles Mesomorph body type

Height weight Curient Configuration Senses

9. BODY

Here the mechanical, chemical, electrical and conscious levels of the physical organism are shown in their active and passive roles with the lower and denser parts acting as instruments of the higher and more subtle alchemies of the etheric field and direction of the lower face of the psyche.

14. Incarnation

Seen Kabbalistically, the body begins as a single fertilised cell which in the process of multiplication and differentiation slowly fills out an already existing form. This picture of the body is held in the lower face of *Yezirah* at *Yesod*, which is the *Sefirah* concerned with holding images. It is also the place of *Daat*, in this case, the Knowledge of the body. The scientist sees the template of the whole within each cell, but these are only the building blocks. The design of the organism is of a higher order of law and the cells merely conform to a pattern that is repeated in millions of human bodies. This process of filling out the form does not stop at birth, but goes on through the various *Sefirotic* phases until the body reaches its prime around twenty years. During this growth period many phases have to be passed through and they are seen as distinct stages in the development of the psyche as well as the body. The basis of the psyche, according to those who only see the material dimension is the genetic structure of each cell that determine sex, body type, skin, hair and eye colour and many other characteristics of physical make-up. They also connect the instinctive memories of all mankind to that particular individual's race, nation and family as well as the character of the person's body, which is made up of the combination of the parents' chromosomes. This unique mix of physical elements greatly affects the lower face of the psyche which is now embedded in the upper face of the body Tree.

An example of the above are the three major racial divisions of mankind, symbolised by the three sons of Noah who populated the world after the flood. As a wide generalisation the white, yellow and black races represent the thinking, feeling and action aspects of humanity; and the civilisations they have generated, exhibit these distinct qualities in Western science, Eastern religions and African dancing. Of course, there are many blends of the three found in the sub-ethnic groupings, where intermarriage has taken place, and racial sub-divisions, because within each strain there are thinkers, feelers and doers. However, although clear-cut divisions have been blurred, there is nevertheless still a strong collective trend in most people who recognise their roots and conform to the group mind of their race, nation and community. The conflict in the Republic of South Africa between the white and black tribes is an example of quite different attitudes which not only consider a person's colour of skin but the psyche and its general outlook. This occurs all over the world, even in so called advanced countries like Britain where the Scots still regard the English as the 'auld enemy' at international soccer matches where the tribal level erupts.

The three types are also observed in individuals who are defined by some scientists, as ectomorphic or the thin nervous thinkers, mesomorphic or the strong, muscular active people and the endomorphic or slightly plump, sensitive and moody feelers. These originate, according to biologists, in the predominance of the nerves, muscles or gut processes during gestation. The Kabbalist would argue that such differentiations arise because of the type of the psyche being incarnated, in that a person needs this or that kind of body in order to correct or develop that or this quality.

The classification of body types fits on to the basal triad of the physical Tree where the muscles, nerves and organs are seen to be clustered around the autonomic system at *Yesod* with *Malkhut* at the elemental level of skin, bones and external sense organs. This relating of the body to the Tree is seen in the example of the peripheral nervous system with its sub-division of sympathetic and parasympathetic which correspond to the outer pillars. The sympathetic, (right column) dilates the pupil of the eye while the parasympathetic (left column) constricts it; and the sympathetic stimulates the heart, while the parasympathetic does the reverse. Here, we see the principles of structure and dynamics that operate throughout the Worlds at work in the body. To continue, the relationship between the central and the autonomic nervous systems matches the *Tiferet* and *Yesod* of the physical Tree. This is because the autonomic acts as the flywheel foundation which takes care of routine processes of the body, while the central nervous system, being of a higher order connects the *Malkhut* of the psyche with the operations of the brain, as the *Yesodic* ego of the psyche, overlays the *Daat* of the body. These fuse into a working relationship at birth as the lower part of the psyche interlocks with the upper part of the body Tree.

When a babe emerges from the womb and is detached from the mother it is still far from being independent, for although the umbilicus has been cut, the psychological cord between mother and infant is still present and has to be maintained. This is called the 'bonding' process. In simple societies, mother and infant are rarely separated. In recent years, however, in the Western world, the two are sometimes parted for various technical reasons during the immediate post-natal period, which, it has been observed, appears to have a detrimental effect on both, particularly the baby. In more enlightened birth situations, the infant is now immediately given to the mother to hold and nurse. This is not just the becoming externally acquainted, after the long inner relationship of pregnancy; but the vital setting up of a connection that is very subtle and deep between humans as the *Malkhut* and *Yesod* of the child's psyche seeks to establish contact with the physical world, represented initially by the mother.

The failure to facilitate such a bonding, it has been noted, generates an inability for the incarnating psyche to relate to physical reality. Experiments on monkeys stopped from establishing such a *Yesodic* foundation with a mother have resulted in extremely disturbed animals, which, if not corrected, become permanently unstable and withdrawn from their society. The same is true of human babies which, if prevented from forming a solid *Yesod* connection with their mothers, can become psychotic or neurotic in later life. Such a situation occurs when a mother is sick herself, indifferent to the child or has another situation that needs, in her view, more attention. From a Kabbalistic viewpoint such events are no accident, but the first fatal effect of a cause rooted in karma. This does not mean that all the individuals concerned should not take responsibility for their actions as parents, for here one must take into account free-will and the notion that the person who has just been born is also quite cognisant of what is going on for the first few days and sometimes weeks after birth. The actions and reactions of both parties is crucial and forms the ground-bed of physical and psychological security as the *Malkhut* and *Yesod* of the babe's psyche are impressed with their primary experience of the new life. Here is where a fundamental trust or mistrust of the world outside originates.

When the body and psyche start to knit together with increasing momentum so the ability to maintain the prenatal consciousness will be buried beneath an ever-deepening accretion of sensual experience. Gradually, the infant body and its needs will overcome the clarity and freedom of the psyche. Most people soon forget it, although as we have been shown, many, through hypno-regression, can recall what happened with great precision, which suggests a remarkably mature appreciation of the circumstance in some cases. The loss of this psychological perception, seen Kabbalistically, is the shift of the centre of gravity of consciousness down into *Malkhut* as the *Yesod-Daat* relationship of ego draws the attention away from the psyche and into the body with the development of the most direct sense of touch. This and the other *Malkhutian* organs[1] of perceiving physical reality will be examined in the next chapter.

[1] For a more detailed account of the body, see the author's *Adam and the Kabbalistic Tree*. Published by Gateway Books, Bath, 1985, and Samuel Weiser, Inc., York Beach, Maine, 1985.

15. Perception

Most people believe that they see the outside world as a reality. In fact, what they perceive is a very subjective image of the physical universe. The reason is that everything that we touch, taste, smell, hear and see comes into our consciousness via one of the senses. This means that what we perceive is basically an impression that has been filtered through a particular organ that is only sensitive to a specific set of frequencies, which may be influenced by physical disability then passed through mechanical, chemical and electronic processes before it is screened by an individually, psychologically and culturally biassed mind in a particular state of consciousness.

As will be seen, there is no such thing as an objective view. Even the most fastidious scientific procedure can be distorted by the desire for a certain result, because the scientist's personal view will always influence the result, unless he or she is a person who is conscious at every kind of reality. This is why there are so many contradictory theories about the Universe. It depends which level is being viewed. For most people, the only world that is real is the physical, and therefore they assume that the senses are quite objective in their perception of it. This, science is just beginning to see, is not so. For example, one of the more recent discoveries is that the two hemispheres of the brain work in quite a different way from one another. The left side, it is observed, is more precise in its perception and talents. It has skill in mathematics, language, logic and literature, whereas the right hemisphere is inclined to the irrational skills of music, dance and creative fantasy that underlie all the arts. This discovery, based upon research into normal and damaged brains, is of particular interest to the Kabbalist because it concurs with the notion of the pillars of the Tree where the right of *Nezah, Hesed* and *Hokhmah* are related to the more creative processes and the left of *Hod, Gevurah* and *Binah* to the more analytical approach. It is of equal interest to note that there is a criss-cross of impulses that occurs in the brain, so that each hemisphere influences the opposite side of the body, to balance any tendency to be lopsided or split. Thus the right, generally active side of the body is checked by the logical half of the brain and the more passive half is stimulated by the creative hemisphere. There are, of course, left-handed people who use that side in a more active way, but this indicates some double counter-balancing process well illustrated by Leonardo Da Vinci who was not only left-handed but wrote mirror-wise. The reason for being this way probably lies in the psyche rather than the body and here we have the relationship between the *Daat* of the body and the *Yesod* of the psyche as the critical factor in the way we view and respond to the outer world.

At birth the *Daat* or Knowledge of the body is united to the *Yesod* or ego of the psyche. This means that impressions coming in from the outside world, through the senses, come into the ego and start to build up a picture of external reality. The way this occurs is important because as said, the infant is laying down the basal foundation of the ego. At first, tactility is the most important sense in that it can touch and receive a direct impression of the physical. This earth-sense is served by thousands of cells near the surface of the body that pick up heat, wet, pressure and a dozen other bits of information about what is impinging upon the skin. Some areas of the body have concentrations of tactile cells such as the hands and face, so that these parts of the body can react quickly to circumstances and learn to respond to the dangers or delights of the physical world. Inner sensors, for instance, are found in the mouth and these react to whatever is placed there by the instinct to feed the organism. Thus, the first image an infant builds up in its *Yesodic* ego is related to pleasure and pain and nourishment. These instinctive drives to seek comfort, avoid discomfort, and be satisfied are quickly absorbed by the psyche's *Yesod* as the *Daat* of the body translates the sense impressions rising up from the psyche's *Malkhut* as it receives data from the nervous systems and sense organs of the *Tiferet*, *Yesod* and *Malkhut* of the body.

Taste and smell, the intermediary senses of earth-water and water-air expand the image being focussed in the *Yesod* of the infant. The taste of mother's milk and skin, together with the aroma slowly build up an ego-centred picture for the newly incarnated psyche. Gradually, memories of the pre-natal world are swamped by a preoccupation with learning how to suck the breast, get more warmth and absorb as much support as it can from the mother because it cannot sustain itself in what appears to be a hostile environment where, for example, either hunger is contracting its stomach or its bowels are over extended. Warmth and love counter-balance cold and fear as strange sounds and unfamiliar sights impinge upon the little world slowly being formed on *Yesod's* screen of ego consciousness. The outer world and its ever changing state must be very threatening to the infant whose only refuge initially is sleep. For while the mother may alleviate bodily tensions and act as a substitute ego for the babe's *Yesod* is not sufficiently developed to tell the difference between inner and outer events.

Ego is the sense of 'me and mine'. This is quite different from 'I' which is more objective and will be reserved for the term 'Self' which we will encounter later on. Ego arises out of experience of the World and its synthesis within the lower psyche. This begins with the senses inasmuch as the body and the environment starts to form an image of external reality within the physical *Daat* and psychological *Yesod* of ego. Let us look at an example of this process.

A baby sticks its fingers into a hot cup of coffee, while seated on someone's lap and finds that it hurts. This is because the afferent nerves inform the autonomic nervous system that the skin is being scalded and a paired loop of efferent nerves makes the hand jerk back. This experience of hot coffee will be passed on by the body's *Yesod* of the autonomic system up to the physical *Tiferet* of the central nervous system which will then inform the body's *Daat* that in turn communicates to the psyche's *Yesod* that fingers in hot coffee hurt. All this will occur while the lowest physical triads of nerves and muscles deal with the practical situation. The *Yesod* of ego will meanwhile file the experience for future reference in the memory. At a more complex and subtle level, visual shapes, like the human face will slowly be differentiated by the same process into mother and non-mother, and then eventually father and other people as physical and then psychological experience focusses and fuses ego consciousness, if only for a split second at a time. Such moments of cognition leave an imprint upon the memory that can then be recalled and used to recognise what has been known.

Memory is seen Kabbalistically as occurring both in the body and the psyche. First, there are all the recollections of previous lives deeply embedded in the psyche, making a general matrix; then there are those acquired in this life that come from the interaction of a person and the world. These are composed of countless sense impressions and the psychological outlook formed by a particular view of the environment and the individual's relation to it. The image is held partly in the millions of cells of the body, particularly those of the brain, where every cell has at least sixty thousand connections that act as a memory bank, and partly in the psyche that stores every moment of consciousness in its vast library of emotional complexes and system of concepts. The argument that the physical brain retains all memory is invalidated by the phenomenon that some people with severely damaged brains can still function, although certain motor activities and memories may be impaired or lost. The brain of a man, who is only aware of the physical world, may sense that it is the location of his mind, but consciousness, as we shall see, does not reside there.

The process of learning to use the senses and co-ordinate their findings not only goes on from moment to moment, but deepens the general perception of the psyche, of the outside world. This, however, is greatly influenced by two factors, namely the particular balance of the psyche and the specific conditions a person finds him or herself in. The former is the result of many lives and the individual set of the temperament that occurred at birth, and the latter by the type of family and the kind of culture that the individual lives within. These factors, together with the genes of the body and their inclination towards this or that physical tendency creates a conditioning that must affect how experience is interpreted. An example of this is the differing views of the Red Indians and the White settlers towards the Black Hills of Dakota in the last century. To the former, the hills were a sacred and commonly shared area devoted to the Great Spirit. To the latter, they were a wilderness, inhabited by savages and full of gold. Such opposing perceptions of the same place are based upon impressions and attitudes built up since infancy that have slowly filled out a *Yesodic* image of how things are. Most of us are oblivious of our subjectivity. To counterbalance this, the psyche has to learn what is objective, in order to be able to live in the physical world. Here, we begin to differentiate between practical skills and the psychological patterns that are learned as the baby slowly extends its radius of action.

16. Orientation

If the *Daat* of bodily knowledge and the *Yesod* of the psyche generate the ego and its World view by their interaction, so the *Binah* and *Hokhmah* of the physical organism correlate with the *Hod* and *Nezah* of psyche in the sensory and motor functions, while the *Malkhut* of the psyche overlays the physical *Tiferet* of the central nervous system. Thus, experience is processed by the co-operation of two systems. Take, for example, the eating of an apple. The teeth and tongue of the sensory organs test the consistency and taste of the fruit, after it has been seen and often smelled to check if it is ripe. This procedure is quite unconscious and automatic, in that having passed through the *Malkhut* of the sense organs, it is then worked upon by the body's interior mechanisms to reduce it to a pulp that can be absorbed. These are the instinctive or subconscious operations of the *Nefesh* or vital intelligence that takes care of the body. But supposing a worm is discovered by the tongue, then quite a reaction is precipitated. Suddenly an image arises in the mind and all the associations with worms comes into the ego's awareness. A shift in level from the autonomic to the central nervous system occurs, and that portion of the apple with its inhabitant are ejected in a blend of body reaction and ego consciousness. In an infant, such an event would not occur, because a child has no association with worms. Certainly, the psyche's *Hod* as data gatherer would register the difference between apple and worm, but the *Yesodic* image is not yet present, so that the *Nezah* principle would not respond. This is why very young children can swallow stones, coins and many other objects that would revolt adults. Discrimination has to be learned.

Learning is a process of receiving sensory information by the psyche's *Hod*, seeing its significance, that is, in relation to the world picture held by the psyche's *Yesod*, and responding to it in an appropriate way, through the psyche's *Nezah*, or motor reaction. To set up this situation requires many phases of physical growth and psychological development. Let us look at a particular sequence that has been detected. According to one researcher's findings there are six distinct stages of sensory-motor intelligence. It is said that an eye can pick up the stimulus of one photon, which is the equivalent to seeing a candle at thirty miles, that the ear can detect the tick of a watch at twenty feet in a quiet room, and that the taste buds can identify a few molecules, or the equivalent of a teaspoon of sugar dissolved in two gallons of distilled water. It has been reckoned that the nose can also detect a few molecules or the density of a drop of perfume spread throughout a three-roomed house and that the tactile sense can notice the weight of a bee's wing falling from 39 inches onto the cheek. With this highly sensitive equipment an infant perceives, but as yet cannot comprehend the environment in which it finds itself.

The first phase that has been defined is called 'activating reflexes'. In this, the infant's sensory-motor intelligence or *Hod* and *Nezah* principles operate simply as functions, such as sucking and moving arms and legs. Objects have no meaning or separate existence, nor is there any sense of space or time other than what is present. There is no idea of cause and effect. The second phase, called 'primary circular reactions' is when the infant starts to co-ordinate random actions, as for example, when hungry it will, at first by accident, find its fingers in its mouth and then attempt to gain sustenance by sucking them. Objects now begin to have significance, although they as yet have no meaningful setting. The third stage, called 'secondary circular reactions' occurs at about six months when the infant begins to be interested in specific objects and starts to make purposeful movements such as touching a toy. Here an appreciation of space comes into play and a sense of power when it realises that if it moves in a certain way, the object will be given to it. The recognition of time arises at this point as memorable incidents, such as feeding, come and go. The fourth stage called 'coordination of secondary circular reactions' which appears towards the end of the first year, takes various perception and response circles and begins to combine them in specific operations in order to obtain a desired effect. New combinations are developed and events can be perceived in relation to each other, such as extracting an object hidden under a cushion. Memory at this point begins to extend, although time and space are still not understood. In the fifth stage, called 'tertiary circular reactions' the sensory-motor intelligence is sophisticated enough to take what skills the infant has to evolve elaborate operations, such as using one toy as a tool to move another closer. At about this time, interest in the nature of objects deepens with handling and closer examination. Spatial consciousness increases as the relationship between objects is appreciated and time slowly begins to fill out in relation to the external world and the infant's actions. Let us look at this Kabbalistically.

Up to this point, the sensory *Hod* and the motor *Nezah* combination in conjunction with the central nervous system and the psyche's *Malkhut* have been building up a working system as the ego, at *Yesod* slowly focusses everything experienced into a co-ordinated picture of the infant's world. This can occur because the triads of psychological action, thought and feeling are also being activated by experience so that an inner dimension is added to the mechanical proficiency that has been acquired. At about eighteen months, the infant enters the sixth phase, called 'devising new schemes in combination with mental activity'. This means a profound shift, from a purely *Assyatic* or physical trial and error technique, to internal or *Yeziratic* manoevring. Because the *Yesodic* ego has developed sufficiently to work with just images it can now manipulate forms in the abstract. This gives the capability of insights the senses cannot have, such as deducing that a certain object must be hidden under another even though it was never seen to be put there. Here is quite a different order of awareness. The capability of thinking things through in *Yezirah* is to appreciate what may not be physically visible, and this requires the skill to identify cause and effect and the ability to recall past events and relate them to the future. Here is where the human being begins to go beyond the sensory-motor intelligence level that all the higher animals have, although the more mechanistic developmental psychologists would not agree with this, because they only perceive the World of *Assyah*.

Some researchers, for example, hold the view that a child learns by conditioning, that is, it responds to a stimulus, and if this is repeated often enough, then a pattern is established. It is, they argue, a question of conditioning natural reflexes. This is taken further in that as the child grows up in its surroundings so its temperament, created by its genetic make-up, is conditioned to become this or that type of person. In opposition to this behaviourist view, is what is called 'nativism' which says that infants have all the knowledge they need inherently, and that this only has to be activated by experience. Such inborn knowledge is observed in children everywhere. The reality of the matter lies between these two viewpoints and many child psychologists combine elements from both in what is sometimes called 'a cognitive structure'.

For the Kabbalist the view is much wider for one must consider what most psychologists are oblivious of, and that is all that went before the infant was born. First, the psyche that has been incarnated has a great deal of experience already, although this may be quickly overlaid by having to contend with learning how to live in an infant's world. This, however, does not obliterate the innate level of development. Such can be seen in certain children who advance with great rapidity and are way ahead of the average in that they learn to speak quite early and are remarkably perceptive. In exceptional cases, like Jean Cardiac, an eighteenth century prodigy, the alphabet was known by his third month and he could talk his native French at one year. By the age of six, he could speak English, Latin, Greek and Hebrew, before dying at seven. This suggests more than just environmental conditioning or inherent instinctive knowledge. Another remarkable example was born in Lubeck in 1721. This infant could quote the Bible and, by the age of three, talk about world history. It is recorded that the King of Denmark, who refused to believe such a thing possible, was astounded by the child, who incidently also died, according to his own prediction, at four. While such cases are extremes, there are still many remarkably gifted children like Mozart who played and composed music at the age of four. He was clearly drawing upon the experience of previous lives. This dimension, added to the factors of genetic background and social environment together with coping with a new body, must be taken into account.

Seen in terms of the Tree we have the gradual intermeshing of the physical and psychological organisms, as practical skills and the ability to act, think and feel come into relationship with one another through the offices of the ego. However, this interpenetration of the lower face of the psyche and the upper face of the body does not always coordinate correctly, and sometimes not at all when development is retarded. This is observed in autistic children where the processes of the psyche's form, acting as a mould for the body to fill are not complete. Another instance is where the connection is not established is the phenomenon of cot death when a child dies for apparently no obvious physical reason. This suggests that the individual involved is withdrawn from being incarnated for some purpose that is not always apparent to the parents. A recognition of this situation is found amongst primitive people, who do not give a child a name until it has been firmly established that it will live. In the Jewish tradition the Kabbalistic reason for circumcision is not only the naming of the child after seven days have passed, but the fusing of the body with the psyche through the symbolic operation upon *Yesod* which is traditionally associated with the genitals. This ceremonial act also confers a personal and family identity as well admitting the infant into the community of Israel. Seen this way the ego is recognised as the personal element by which one is differentiated from others in that it is the image by which we are known. This is important for the ego which is the combination of the body's *Daat*, the psyche's *Yesod* and all the paths and triads adjacent to it. It is also the non-luminous mirror, as it is called in Kabbalah, by which we orientate the outer and inner worlds and ourselves.

17. Ego Formation

The *Daat-Yesod* complex of ego placed at the centre of the electro-magnetic triad of the body, and the action, thinking and feeling triad of the lower psyche can be seen as a facilitator to everything that passes between the two levels of reality. This ranges from the most gross sensory impressions and motor reactions, through the current preoccupation of the attention, to the finest and most faint influences and recollections of the upper worlds. During the period of infancy the ego is as yet unformed and therefore cannot differentiate between experiences, so that everything is mixed until a recognisable picture of the outer world begins to emerge. As we have seen this is constructed by sensual experience and motor response that is gradually turned into a coherent set of physical and psychological mane-ouvres to solve practical problems and begin to relate to the world.

In the very young infant, the sense of 'me' is almost totally lacking, for everything from bowel movement to the passage of day and night is related to a general impression in which the infant is the centre. Over time, this starts to differentiate into 'me' and 'not me'. The 'me' arises from the fact that, as the infant learns how to live in the physical world, it begins to respond psychologically. In Kabbalistic terms, the action triad starts to fill up with a series of formulae of how to do things, as the thinking triad develops methods and tools of thought, while the feeling triad learns to experience different moods. All these processes occur at the *Yeziratic* level, and so what is observed is a gradually intermeshing set of forms that back up, feed into and absorb what is passing through the ego. Such events, as being burned by a flame, are not only responded to by the sensor motor systems of the side pillars, but are filed in the action triad as what not to do, in the thinking triad as bad but interesting, and in the feeling triad as frightening but exciting. Myriads of impressions of the outside world pour into the ego, but only those of outstanding interest are remembered. This does not mean to say that many things are not unconsciously learned. The *Hod-Nezah-Malkhut* triad of the psyche takes in an enormous amount from the child's environment and this is filed directly into the emotional and conceptual triads as background experience, so that a Moroccan child takes on quite a different cultural view to the Spanish child, just across the straits of Gibraltar. Each will gather much about the customs and values of Islam and Christendom without being aware of more than a series of flickers of consciousness that accumulate in both the individual and collective mind beyond the *Hod-Nezah* threshold line.

As the ego grows it develops a sense of continuity through memory. This means that the forms that each experience generates begin to be stored in some sort of order within the psyche. Thus, while the earliest experience creates certain feelings, thoughts and actions which are unrelated, later ones begin to be connected together by association. Initially, these clusters of memories are very loose because the child has as yet no capacity to co-ordinate its psyche. However, as the mind is based upon the *Sefirot*, an inevitable order begins to prevail as the psyche seeks equilibrium and develops. Thus, experiences that are negative or restrictive accumulate on the left side of the psychological Tree and those that are positive and stimulating go to the right. Those that have a conceptual dimension are attracted to the intellectual triads, while those of an emotional nature congregate in their respective active and passive triads. These groups of complexes are based upon nuclear experiences that form major influences in people's lives which in turn, relate to one of the *Sefirot* that form the archetypal principles, but more of this later.

Through memory, which is based upon all that has passed through the ego, the infant learns to anticipate the future. Slowly but surely the ego recognises when and when not to do certain things. Out of a mass of incomprehensible things that it has experienced there emerges the realisation that it can obtain certain results, if it holds back its impulses, because time has taught it that to do this or that at the wrong moment is counter-productive. Gradually, the confusion of the early months abates as physical rhythms, such as feeding and sleep, give it a sense of time and the focusing image of the world, and especially its mother, give it a sense of space. As the aggregate of thoughts, feelings and actions begins to integrate, so the infant starts to recognise its position of helplessness and dependence. The anger observed in babies, it must be said, may not always be due to infantile needs and moods. It may be the frustration of a mature psyche that periodically realises what it has to go through before it is recognised as an adult. As one great Kabbalist observed, "I was born an old man". Many people have this experience in early childhood. However, all the incarnation processes have to be gone through, especially the development of the ego which is vital if one is to perform well in the World of Action. This is why, in the Kabbalistic tradition, the ego is not regarded as evil, but trained to be a good servant.

The process of learning to control instinctive urges is part of the education of the ego and this applies not only to childhood but to anyone on the spiritual path, because many of these drives become unconscious and unobtrusively influence the view of ourselves and life. In the child, the constraints are applied by the parents, because as yet there is not enough experience in the psyche for it to observe itself. The differentiation between ego and Self or *Yesod* and *Tiferet* comes much later. Until that time, the parents act in the place of Self. Thus modes of useful behaviour are acted out by most parents, even if they do otherwise in private, in order to give the child a model by which they will fit into that family and society. This process of introjection, as it is called, is observed by the growing ego from quite early on, so that it copies acceptable forms of acting, thinking and feeling in order to be assimilated and given what it needs.

Besides learning how to behave in the outside world, the ego also begins to develop an interior capability. When the phase of abstract thought and imagery is reached, so the manipulation of symbols becomes possible. Initially, the individual who has been incarnated has, we are told, quite a clear memory of the pre-natal epoch. This is never forgotten but it is superseded by sensory impressions of the new incarnation and all the problems of adjustment. Thus, there must be a period in which the older memories and the newer ones blend, and this appears to be worked through in the very active imagination of infants. Most young children, for example, take their dreams very seriously and when they are awake often claim to see and talk with beings adult cannot perceive. This may or may not be true , but whatever it is, it certainly has a reality to the child. Seen Kabbalistically, these phenomena occur because *Yesod* is the bridge between two worlds and its screen of consciousness is designed to produce images from either. For example, the sense impression of a room, after being processed by the body and brain, is in its own way no more than a very limited picture, whereas the imagery of many dreams and works of art are sometimes more potent than anything found in the physical world, especially in nightmares or movies. In a mature adult, the ego can separate out either reality. In the case of the child who cannot yet tell the difference, parental care provides both orientation and protection. For the adult who has not learned to differentiate fantasy from reality, life can be very hard as impossible ambitions are thwarted and idealised relationships break down. If these lessons are not learned, then the immature ego can regress in neurosis or psychosis, back to the childlike stage it was stuck or 'fixated' at as it drifted between two worlds.

In the normal ego formation, the successes and failures of adapting to life in the body create a strong and resilient identity. Learning to cope with physicality is not easy, but the struggle to survive develops many useful skills, attitudes and approaches to both external and internal reality. In some cases, conditions are so hard that the ego never grows beyond the infantile reaction of survival often found in deprived families. On the other hand, if a person is over protected by wealth or privilege, this also can produce a spoilt and childish ego that only recognises its own needs. These instances, however, have a karmic factor as does the more normal situation, where the *Yesodic* image of the world is a balance between the level of an individual's development and what they can cope with. For example, a schoolchild is not generally aware of the international political situation, but he or she can deal with a playground crisis or an examination. Out of this comes the image of identity that is based upon what is expected in the child's society and how this is met. Thus, there is usually a school hierarchy for sport, artistry and scholarship and a dozen other sub-systems in which individuals find themselves in a superior or inferior place. This 'role' is an ego image which may or may not coincide with what the person is at a deeper level, but it is what the person takes up and projects in order to hold a place in their world. This assumed personality, moreover, can vary according to different circumstances, so that in one situation the persona or 'mask' is aggressive in a peer group where the individual is predominant, but subservient at home where he or she is the smallest in a large family.

The ego of a growing infant is susceptible to many influences. With the right conditions it can become the perfect servant and foundation of a life. Under extreme duress or excessively easy circumstances it can become crippled. Here, as said we have to take into account the factor of fate. No one can entirely blame the situation into which they were born. There are people who have grown well in the most difficult environment, and others who have failed to make the most of ideal situations, not because it was too easy, but because they were too lazy. This introduces the recurrent element of choice. The behaviourists would argue that there is none and the nativists might say inherent knowledge removes decision. The Kabbalist sees the situation as the interaction of the laws of *Assyah* and *Beriah* with the psyche in *Yezirah* between. Free will is the principle of adjustment, based upon what the ego has perceived in its two-way mirror of internal and external consciousness. However, before the ego can be relied upon to give a clear and undistorted image several other stages have to be passed through before maturity, for at this point *Yesod* is still quite infantile in its perception of reality and its own identity.

18. Identity

In the first two years of bodily growth and development of the psyche we can observe how an individual learns to live within physical limits as they gradually extend their sensory motor range of action and cognition. By the thirteenth month, most babies can stand up and a few weeks later, walk. New skills are added each day and with them the infant's world slowly focuses into an ego-centred existence in which everything is related to what the child thinks, feels and does. This phase of 'narcissism', as it is called, is crucial because it builds up a *Yesodic* body image that gives the individual a sense of independent existence although this, in reality, is an illusion. In a child, this does not matter, because it is not responsible for itself. Indeed, such an egocentricity is necessary in order to find out what and where they are in relation to the 'otherness', as it is sometimes termed, of the rest of the World.

In the so-called normal child, the transition from infant to toddler marks not only the beginning of real mastery of the body and a deeper exploration of the world about them, but a lengthening of the psychological umbilicus that holds the child to the mother. Here, the narcissistic tendency, of wanting one's own way and yet needing and depending upon the mother come into conflict. Such tensions can, under certain circumstances, build up into a major crisis, one of many an individual has to face at critical points of growth. If the balance of the psyche is good, then the Tree can afford to be flexible and adjust. If it is not, because the Tree is too far towards the side of structure, then a harder set is made within the emotional and conceptual complexes building up there. If, in contrast, the Tree is inclined too much the other way, towards the dynamic pillar, then a tendency to lack of control and impulse may be seeded in the growing psyche. This may, despite a docile persona, surface in later life in a crisis when regression to this earlier stage can occur in order to avoid reality. The alcoholic returning to the bottle is an instance of this.

Here it should be realised that while the psyche of a child is immature at the lower face level, its middle and upper face levels are still adult. This is borne out by recollections of childhood in

81

which people knew what was going on about them, even though they may have been inarticulate children. This adult outlook comes from the Self, that is, the *Tiferet* that oversees the psyche from its pivotal point on the Tree. In most cases, memory of previous lives and their past relationship with members of their current family are forgotten, that is they become unconscious. This, however, does not obliterate their reactions to these individuals. This is seen clearly in young children before they have acquired a well-developed ego to contain what they think, feel about, and would like to do to certain people.

In the early days of Freudian psychology many were shocked by the notion of infantile sexuality. The idea of a child desiring its mother sexually and hating its father, or any other rival was unacceptable to nineteenth century society that regarded psychology as unscientific. Today such a view is not so shocking because we see sexuality in a climate of acceptance, created ironically enough by Freud's work. However, what is not taken into account is the fact that the child may be expressing an adult desire through an infantile body that has not the constraints of a mature ego. While a baby's body might be quite sexually inadequate, the adult psyche that inhabits it is not, so that the relationships between sons and mothers and daughters and fathers with all their Oedipal and Electral complexes, so beloved by Freudians, may be more than the infantile sexual label hung on them. Seen Kabbalistically, the infant psyche is an entity half way between two worlds. It still reacts, even if unconsciously to the karmic relationship it may have had with the family it has been born into. Even if they had had no previous relationship such a highly dependent position must generate a sexual attraction that is often responded to by mothers and fathers who treat them quite differently from children of their own sex. While this can no doubt be attributed to the normal processes of parenthood at one level, at another it is sometimes quite noticeable how the rival parent is excluded from such intimacy. As one oblivious father remarked on his relationship with his very young daughter, "It is like having a love affair". Many of the old taboos to prevent such things were set up in every culture because the adult element in the child had been recognised. Child seduction and incest are more common than is generally acknowledged and not always initiated by the adult. The relationship between the child and its parents and the way they work out these sexual tensions have a profound effect upon the formation of the ego and its attitude towards the principles of male and female. Such factors as a male psyche in a female body or vice versa are bound to be an influence, as are those involving previous and present karmic relationships that are to be worked out.

Besides the issue of sexuality, which is traditionally associated with *Yesod*, both in the body and psychological Tree, in that one presents a masculine or feminine image to the world, there is the generation of identity. This is formed by the processes of introjection and projection. In the former, the *Yesodic* faculty of the ego to perceive images, observes and imbibes from its birth the various qualities of its parents. This is seen in the ephemeral likeness to one or the other that the child takes on as it grows a personality. Certainly, there will be particular genetic characteristics, but what is more often noticed is the exact mimicking of parental expressions and movements that reveal a remarkable level of imitation.

Clearly to imitate a beloved person is quite natural, but so too is the tendency to echo those we fear and hate, in order to acquire their power. This characteristic is part and parcel of the highly imaginative process at work in the young *Yesod* which then projects what has been observed into play as the child learns to be an adult. Such introjection and projection not only go into the more superficial structure of the ego but also deep into the unconscious to form a whole series of complexes made up of myriads of tiny experiences of the world about them.

Added to the personal level of identity are not only parental characteristics, but the absorption and acquisition of a whole culture represented by the family that they live in. Thus the little Jewish boy remembers the Passover ceremony in his parents' home with all its customs and atmosphere which form the model for when he has a family of his own, while the little English girl will reproduce in later life every detail of how someone of her class entertains her husband's professional colleagues. Grandparents play a particularly important part in the making of a cultural identity. The phenomenon of the special relationship between grandparent and grandchild occurs because neither is so deeply preoccupied with life as the parents, so that they can communicate directly, soul to soul. This connection is enhanced by the fact that a child is not fully incarnated and the old are slowly discarnating. Thus, it is possible for their psyches to connect more easily, to transmit and receive at the deeper levels of the family and its collective experience. The wise old man and woman in a child's life always leave a profound impression of roots and destiny.

The Freudian view of infantile sexuality could be seen Kabbalist-ically as the period in which the *Daat-Yesod* of the body and psyche unite and co-ordinate the muscle, nerve and organ triads with the psychological action, thinking and feeling processes. In this, the oral, anal and Oedipal phases, that are passed through, from the first to around the sixth year, reveal a distinct progression up the Tree. First the body's *Yesod* or autonomic system, uses the oral senses of touch and taste to explore world; then the body's *Tiferet* or central nervous system which is also the *Malkhut* of the psyche learns to control the anal processes in an act of will. Finally the *Daat-Yesodic* level of ego, where sexuality and identity are established relates to the Oedipal connection with the parents. The oral stage of biting or sucking the breast which is said to generate, in deprived cases, such attitudes as sarcasm or never having enough, might, however, be considered in the light of a past life relationship. So, too, could the anal battle over the potty, in which the child first exerts its will against the parents who perhaps represent an ancient conflict with power and authority that has been carried over to this life. Likewise, the Oedipal problems of boys and the Electra difficulty for girls may go back to now-forgotten fates that have to be worked out in this life.

All that has been described of these earliest of years must be seen against this wider background of fate. Too many psychologists focus upon a particular level. The Aristotelians only see the effects and the Platonists only the causes. Somewhere in between lies the most comprehensive picture. In Kabbalah, we take into account the interaction of all the Worlds, even though we may be examining one particular point or level, function or stage of activity. Thus, for example, the withdrawal of infantile sexuality into a state of latency is seen as the shift of emphasis from *Yesod* to *Hod*. The Lunar stage of babyhood with its mother-orbiting ego now gives way to the age of Mercury or true childhood with its intense activity and insatiable curiosity. Here begins the coherent use of symbols that have slowly been accumulating in the infantile ego. This is when a baby's gurglings move into words and phrases and then on to become language. Let us trace this development from its inception in order to gain an insight into the *Hodian* process of learning.

19. Learning

During the first year of incarnation an infant makes many noises. Initially, they are simply the vocal chords being used instinctively to register pleasure or discomfort, but later distinct sounds are used to express this or that mood, or to pass some comment upon experience. Some psychologists call this 'babble' and consider it an inarticulate form of running commentary. Seen Kabbalistically, it could well be a highly sophisticated stream of observations, as the *Yesod* of the psyche and the *Daat* of the body strive to master the art of language. The fact that an adult psyche may find it difficult to operate within a baby's rudimentary ego is a hard one for those who only perceive the physical level to accept, but many people can recall moments in the infancy when they tried to tell cooing parents round their cot that they were people who wanted to communicate.

Towards the end of the first year, the babbling phenomenon increases as the infant explores the full range of sounds it can use. During this period, it has been noted, sounds related to many languages are detected, as if the child were learning some primordial scheme upon which all tongues are based. This observation is not as strange as it may seem, because every esoteric tradition has maintained that there is a universal language. Some say it is Sanskrit, others Greek and of course, many Jewish Kabbalists and not a few Christians maintain that it is Hebrew. While all these languages are very ancient and contain root meanings of great profundity, the reality is that the universal speech is exactly what it says, that is, it is beyond any particular form. This means that there is a level of existence where the essence of all language resides, because, it has been noted, every one of the several thousand different tongues spoken on the Earth has the same basic structure; it is only the particulars that are different. A man is a man in every language, and so is a woman, whether they are aborigines or jet-setters. Life presents the same basic problems, whether in the desert or a high-rise tenement. There are terms for every human situation, although not for every object, because such things as three-pin electrical plugs are not universal and names have to be invented for them. The level we are talking about is essential and belongs to the realm of Creation or *Beriah*, which is sometimes called the place of ideas. Tradition states that the angelic beings use this universal tongue; so do discarnate humans. Thus when they are born there is already a inherent basis of speech that is adapted to whatever language group they find themselves in.

It has been observed that when the babbling has reached a peak, it suddenly decreases as if, like a kettle about to boil, a new process has begun. By the end of the first year the infant begins to produce sounds in the language of those about him. By the time the child reaches eighteen months there may be several dozen words being used. At the end of the second year these may be paired in various relationships like 'my ball' or 'more ball', which indicates both a sensory-motor and ego development. Moreover, adults can ask questions which will be clearly understood, although the reply may not always be coherent. This again suggest that the intelligence of a child is much higher than its capacity to express itself. By the third year, a child has a modest vocabulary and begins to apply grammar, as thoughts and feelings are articulated with increased precision. By four years the child can use phrases in the future tense, revealing the development of abstract perception.

According to some, we learn by trial and error. If an action is repeated often enough and we avoid making the mistakes made at the beginning of an operation, then we take into the memory a pattern that the becomes a skill in the sensory-motor response to the same situation. This is a very mechanistic view. Initially an infant learns this way. Later, the process of learning by insight comes when simple, and then later, more complex problems can be solved by experiment and thought. Many of the higher primates can do this. The next stage is by association and here is where the human mind shifts into another realm as the *Yesodic* ego collects experiences and files them in loose collections within the psychological Tree. At first, these memories are unrelated, but as time goes on connections are made, such as realising that sand is often on the seashore, that shells and seaweed are also found there, as are ships and lighthouses. These images or forms move through distinct phases, passing from isolated incidents into associations of great complexity which then begin to work and develop into highly structured organisations that can be used by imagination or reason.

The above process is also seen when training adults. First, the apprentice plays with tools and raw materials finding out what they can do, then simple exercises are performed to see their interaction. Later, as skill increases, so the apprentice can forget the process of the operation and concentrate upon the job. When a certain level of proficiency has been reached, a different quality of work emerges that has the competence and reliability of a journeyman. Mastery comes when there is a complete command of all the techniques and the attention can be given to imagination and the development of originality, which is the hallmark of a master. All these phases can be seen in language from the single intelligible word that emerges from a baby's babble, to the sonnets of Shakespeare which in a few lines, conjure up a cloud of associations to move our hearts and make our intellects ponder profundities. This is why the 'word' is so powerful. It keys us into the universal language.

Some psychologists see the learning process as a perception of the total situation in which we respond to the particular configuration of a 'field' present, according to our selected reactions. Thus, two people in the same environment will not see or learn from it in the same way, because their attitudes and objectives are not identical. This is a description of the interaction of the lower two worlds, and as such is greatly influenced by the 'set' of the psyche at birth defined by astrology. An example of this is a child born with Moon in Gemini, whose *Yesod* picks up everything immediately and retains an overall but superficial image, in contrast to another child with Moon in Capricorn, whose mode of learning is extremely slow but very deep. The first child may appear to be the brighter, but as years pass, the latter may surpass his brother in understanding, although he may not compete in articulation. These factors, plus the position of the Sun and all the other planets as well as their placing in the Mundane House system, will give each individual a specific screen of perception, granting this one insight into the mechanics of a situation while another sees a psychological ebb and flow of which the first is oblivious.

Such differences of temperament may account for why some learn from observing details and then build up an image and others from what is termed 'global learning'. One can be trained to work from either extreme, or even combine both, but there will always be a distinct tendency to learn in a particular way according to one's physical and psychological type. The action individual, for example, will understand things in a practical way, while the feeler and thinker will respond in their own modes. Moreover, the extrovert will absorb experience in an open way, while the introvert will tend to reflect upon what has been learned. In the case of a child, all these processes occur, for the most part, unconsciously as its experience of life flows through the lower face of the psychological Tree to fill out the by now interacting collections of associations in the upper side pillars that in turn begin to influence the reactions of the ego and colour the response of the action, thinking and feeling triads and the body.

An example of the foregoing can be seen in the learning of manners which are based upon a cultural background. These influences the way we think, feel and act. Thus, a Hindu child and an English child brought up during the British Raj in India have two totally different outlooks and modes of expressing themselves. This collective unconscious theory is opposed by some psychologists who maintain that the individuals response to circumstance is what generates character. An example of this is the intelligent child brought up in a rough criminal family who adopts their speech and manner and becomes a Mafia-type godfather. A third view is that a child's innate capacities are the principle factors in the development of a personality and their background has only a minimal influence. From a Kabbalistic viewpoint, they are all correct if they are seen as applying to their respective levels of evolution. We are not all the same. Some people are born with their centre of conscious gravity in the body, others are stimulated by the dynamic side of their Tree, yet others operate primarily from one of the lower or side triads and others from the soul or spirit. It depends which stage of development has been reached and what lessons have to be learned in that particular life. Some people, for example, pick up the skills of the World very quickly because they are very familiar with its ways, while other learn to operate just as efficiently because they are highly advanced individuals and need to accomplish a certain task by a particular time.

By the time a child can dress itself, it has a rudimentary and narcissistic image of the world it lives in. This egocentric base is, however, vital for the next step, that of relating to others in the wider field of family and beyond, for without a strong ego it would 'lose' its identity in the greater and less protective society it is about to enter. This process is examined in our next chapter.

20. Society

In the first phase of infancy, the psyche's lower great triad, composed of the acting, thinking and feeling sub-triads creates the mechanical level of the mind which gives the child an established and stabilised ego. If some flaw is incurred in the early processes of development, like maternal deprivation or lack of instruction, then there is a distortion in the psyche's patterns. This means that the paths between the *Sefirot* and the triads will malfunction and seek to compensate their imbalance, leading to psychological disorders in later life. The viability of the *Yesodic* ego is vital for it prevents the outer world from excessively intruding into the psyche and swamping it, and protects others, for example, from the impulsive and irrational aspects rising up from within the person. These checks are part of a complex system in the ego (which will be spoken of in detail later), that defend it from either external or internal threats when the child encounters the larger world outside the home.

The first experience of extension beyond its mother was for the child to relate to its father. Here the child had to learn to differentiate between the two, and to deal with feelings of love and hate as the taboos that control close relationships are imposed by family life. Crises of desire and jealousy are usually contained and absorbed into the unconscious levels of the psyche as *Yesod* learns to conform. Gradually limits are set by daily routines and periods of trial and error which show what can and cannot be done. All this training, however, is more than just experimentation and the establishment of social order. It is also the exercise of free will which is present from the day of birth, even though it may not be articulated. For example, a child soon learns to choose this or that, and is perfectly capable of playing one parent off against the other, revealing a very subtle comprehension of psychology and sometimes mastery of a situation. As one woman observed in adulthood, "I could manipulate my parents because I was more intelligent than they". In contrast some parents recognising this factor, deliberately seek to break the child's will. This does not eliminate free choice for the child often merely chooses to retreat and appear to be obedient. In most cases, a balance of *Gevurah* or Severity and *Hesed* or Mercy by the parents builds up a set of rules that can stop a child from tormenting a cat or encourage a talent for painting, as well as give it a sense of support as its parents' views are introjected. This means that both the individual and cultural values present are taken into the psyche and absorbed by upper side triads of emotional complexes and concepts, according to their left or right pillar orientation. As such they eventually form what some psychologists call the ego ideal and the super-ego. The former is focused around *Hesed* on the dynamic column and the latter around *Gevurah* on the structural side. As these associations develop, so all subsequent experience is referred to them. Later these become crucial factors in the individual and collective unconscious.

The ego ideal is a formation composed of all the ideas and emotions associated with concepts such as freedom or helping others, and being the good guy, according to the criteria of the parents' world. The super-ego is more concerned with maintaining standards, restraining impulse and avoiding anything that might upset the family and the society it belongs to. These *Hesedic* and *Gevurah* elements in the psyche become a social conscience for the child. Individual conscience is another matter. This requires a high degree of self-consciousness which is the quality of the soul.

At this point in development the soul, defined on the Tree as the *Hesed-Tiferet-Gevurah* triad, is dormant for the most part because the psyche is too preoccupied with processing experience. However, from time to time there are moments in which real moral issues come to the fore in a child, as against matters of social customs. One man recalled how as a boy, he stopped killing frogs for amusement because something very deep within said, "This is wrong". It was quite a different inner voice from that which echoed his parents' approval or disapproval. Such moments of true conscience originate from *Tiferet*, the *Sefirah* of the Self, in contrast to the reactions of the super-ego-ideal complexes that make us heed authority figures even though we know them to be wrong. On the positive side, 'Black is beautiful' is a useful ego ideal within limits, as is the collective inspiration 'Britons never, never, never shall be slaves.' Conversely the super-ego of Moslems and Jews will always resist eating pork, even though they may not have been brought up in an orthodox family, and American super-egos have a similar reaction when the institution of free speech is threatened. All these collective notions and much more are interjected by the child as it learns about its society.

Besides beginning to absorb the cultural values of its world the child now starts to relate to others. First of all brothers and sisters present the ego with problems. For example, another baby in the family is a direct threat to any narcissistic *Yesod* for suddenly it has to compete for love as the parents give special attention to the new arrival. Here the powerful animal and vegetable drives of the body's *Nefesh*, called the 'id' by Freud, rise up and disrupt the routine rhythms established in the lower face of the psyche's Tree. The *Daat-Yesod* basis of the ego can be thrown into disarray on such occasions if the psyche is not inherently balanced. However, while jealous dogs have been known to savage new-born babies, young children, having a primitive super-ego and fearing their parents' anger if they throw the baby out of the window often find a substitute for their fury by battering a doll, or in some cases regress to an earlier state of development in order to get the same attention as their younger sibling. Here we have the start of suppression, one of several defence mechanisms in the ego that deal with unacceptable situations by forcing them out of ego consciousness. However, unpleasant and violent thoughts and feelings must go somewhere, and so they will be passed through the liminal line between *Hod* and *Nezah* and into the upper side triads of the unconscious. These will attract and extract the various elements of the experience into related associations of thoughts and emotions that will make up the left side of the individual's unconscious. As such they may influence the rest of the life in attitudes based upon perhaps a crucial incident in childhood that makes them fear and hate all rivals. The converse is true if the problem of siblings is resolved by good will and love.

Such early encounters with family and later friends and schoolfellows will build up a massive host of negative and positive associations in the side triads. The problems of having to accommodate others, finding oneself in an inferior or superior position, defend possessions, share and co-operate must be a profound trauma to a *Yesodic* ego that is insecure. Most children get through this crisis and begin to develop an awareness of a new dimension. After the initial period, in which each child attempts to impose its image of the world centred by itself upon others, it has to adjust, or be left out of all the exciting things that can be done together. This requires a major shift in the psyche in which all the egocentric associations are overlaid or made to conform to the local social order which is based upon the model of the family and society they live in. However, the drives of the id-*Nefesh* and the super-ego-ideal break out from time to time. For example, in the games that are played, imitations of father and mother are acted out with little subtlety, especially when a doll or younger child acting as the infant does something naughty. The combined power of super-ego and id chastises the evil doer as the ego checking systems are as yet not developed enough to restrain the violence which can erupt when feelings of hostility unconsciously held about some rival can be projected into play.

Here we must remember, in order to keep the wider and deeper picture, that not all that is observed going on between brothers and sisters is just local or psychological. People are not born into families at random. There is the factor of karma that gives rise to particular relationships that have to be resolved or lessons that one person may act out for another. Thus a brother and sister's feelings for each other of love, hate or even indifference are not just the result of family conditions. They may have something to work out, not only with each other but with the parents. The problems of favouritism or incest are not just those of sexuality, but also of fatal origins. The loves and hates within a family are the most intense, and these are often seen very clearly in childhood before the mitigating mask of the persona hides them. At this point what is called the shadow of the psyche emerges as socially or personally unacceptable impulses of the body and psyche. These are bridled or hidden by the ego which is reinforced by the strict rules of the games that are learned by children at this *Hodian* stage of development. This stringency comes down from the super-ego of *Gevurah* and into *Hod* as the child imitates the form of the society about it and strives to be as close to the ego-ideal of *Hesed* as possible in order to get approval and benefits from their peers. This need to be loved, and later respected, is also projected upon elder relatives as the process of introjection and transference, moves away from parents and onto other authority figures like teachers at school. Such a process gives the individual a sense of independence from parents while still needing their support as they explore the larger world. Seen Kabbalistically, the psyche is extending its range in *Assyah* and penetrating the greater dimension of *Yezirah* as it encounters society beyond the family.

The introduction of the child into a school widens the horizon even further. Here, the collective experience of the society is reinforced by the way things are done, and by what is considered important. Thus, an Egyptian child learns about the Koran while the Spanish child is taught the rudiments of Roman Catholicism. Some schools emphasize a science curriculum, others politics, in some others good manners will be at the heart of the teaching while somewhere else teaches the arts of war. Wherever it is, that child will take on whatever it can learn, because it needs to become an accepted member of that community. Rebellion at this stage as the result of physical or psychological disturbance or some fatal pattern is usually contained, because the child cannot support itself, even though it can be disruptive to those who have it in their care. Fate working through our environment and temperament holds us to our course during this period, which is why it is sometimes said that 'Heaven protects children'. Providence puts a great deal of thought into a person's life and nothing happens by accident. Parents, siblings, relatives and society are all taken into account so that the maximum may be learned, even in what, for example, appears to be a disaster area. Many people have noted in later years, "If I had not gone through that crisis, I would not have grown". The way that a crisis is dealt with is crucial, and it is here that the factor of free will is critical. In the next chapter, we will examine some of the early major turning points and their relationship to the cosmic rhythms that affect the individual and the collective unconscious.

21. Circumstances

In Kabbalah, everything is part of a unity. Nothing happens in Existence without it affecting everything else, no matter how large or small an event might be. Thus a human being's actions alter the balance of the Universe to a greater or lesser degree, even as by the same law events in the macrocosm of the Milky Way and the Solar System influence mankind to produce history and the fate of individuals who are highly sensitive to the harmonies and dramas of the universal dance. However, as each person is composed in a unique mode, so they react in a different way to the situation being created by cosmic forces which affects them and their society.

Taking the larger scale first, there are periods in history when great activity occurs and others when hardly anything happens. Likewise, there are epochs when exploration is the preoccupation, and others when art is to the forefront. There are also times of mass migration or stagnation, of rigidity or revolution with social changes sweeping whole continents. Modern science has not yet explained this phenomenon, although it has many statistics and observations, because it cannot see the interaction of different levels of reality and only perceives the physical data. It was only when the discovery of the unconscious aspect of human existence was generally accepted that another dimension revealed itself in the hidden forces that work upon society. Alas, most of this knowledge is applied to the mass psychology of propaganda and marketing. It is only recently that social trends are being thought of as expressions of some greater pattern in the rhythm of history.

Before the so-called Age of Reason, the Universe was seen as an interrelated whole, with events in the upper levels having a profound effect on those below and vice versa. Some cultures symbolised the macrocosmos as a hierarchy of gods, others as planets and the Kabbalists the reciprocation of the four worlds. Taking just the lower three levels, the cosmic processes of *Beriah* precipitate shifting patterns in *Yezirah*, that is, the psychological realm. These movements are transmitted by the celestial bodies which, as we have seen, represent archetypal principles that act upon the psyche of humanity in an unfolding stream of trends composed of the various combinations of Sun, Moon and planets. This ever-changing situation is due to the different factors and rhythms of the Solar System as they interact in relation to the Earth. For example, the Sun has a daily and an annual cycle and the Moon a monthly pattern which, together with the three-monthly and six-monthly orbits of Mercury and Venus and the longer cycles of the outer planets, make up a complex system of effects as they pass through the twelve divisions of the Zodiac. These combinations create the psychological climate of mankind. For instance, if there is a conjunction of Mars and Saturn in the sign of Aries, this can precipitate a dramatic war crisis as it did in 1940 when Germany invaded the Low Countries and France, threw the allies out of Europe and blitzed Britain. The result of this continental and later global conflict was to disrupt work and domestic patterns and to displace millions of people as they were caught up in collective events. In the case of the individual, the effect is more specific as they have a particular part to play within the general scheme. For example, supposing a man was born in the year 1900. He would have been too young to have fought in the First World War and too old to fight in the Second, but just the right age and temperament to be useful in the inter- and post-war peace. In contrast the fate of someone incarnated a few years either side of that date might be totally different, because they could contribute something that was needed in time of war. This is the work of Providence which organises the best time and place for the personal and collective experience to interact.

Seeing the individual in this larger setting is most important, for the general atmosphere of a society may be lax, balanced or stringent depending upon the state of the nation's Tree. In one country, individuality for instance may be highly cultivated; in another, close family ties may be the rule. In certain cases, education can be prevailing interest of the community; in another money. A child born into any of these situations must inevitably absorb them into the collective level of the psyche as it passes through its various stages of development. However, not every person will react in the same way to his background because some are constituted to fit well into that particular society and others are not. A thinker, for example, would have no problems if brought up in a university town, but he might have great difficulty as a labourer's son. Likewise, a feeler could have a hard time in a household of intellectuals, while a family of musicians would suit him well. Of course, Providence might set up a difficult situation in order to work out some karma and this will be directly related to the collective situation. Abraham Lincoln was not born on a frontier farm without good reason. It trained him for the tough role of President during a most terrible civil war.

At the level of the individual the factors of time and place in the general circumstance are also governed by the planetary-*Sefirotic* sequence. Some people, as we have noted, react to being incarnated and get stuck in the gestation and birth process resulting in a stunted physical or psychological *Malkhut*. Others, unable to come to terms with life of Earth during the *Yesodic* period of forming an ego, are marred by inability to cope with the outside world. None of these difficulties are accidental but situations provided by Providence to help psychological growth. Free will, however, gives the right to accept or reject the challenge. Many people have early memories of such moments of choice, like the child who decided not to grow up and remained a physical and psychological dwarf. This is an extreme case, but it is only a question of degree.

An example of a *Yesod* crisis-growth process occurs when a child has to deal with not being totally independent of parents. Out of this emerges a healthy ego or the need to remain a psychological infant, if this Lunar stage is not completed. Such people can remain in dependent orbit even in adulthood because their *Yesod* cannot fend for itself. Providence usually comes up with a parent substitute like the State until the person can work it out. *Hod* growth crisis can occur in the form of school examinations or the inability to think coherently which has to be mastered in order to communicate with others. However, for some people this mercurial facility to talk and collect data can be the problem that cuts them off, like the scholar who never related to people unless he was lecturing. Fate fortunately sent him a lovely Venus to teach, who took him through his difficulty. There is always a solution offered if we can see it. The Venusian *Nezah* crisis comes with adolescence and the onset of powerful feelings. These have to be handled skillfully or the individual will run wild and lose all they have learned like dropouts who remain adolescent. Maturity marks the shift from the active right position of Venus to the central column position of the Sun of *Tiferet* where a person reaches their physical prime. There they fill out the full form of their *Yeziratic* vehicle which has been present since birth. At this point a discerning eye can perceive what an individual was like in their last life and what they might become this one.

All the processes spoken of are subject to a myriad subtle influences, ranging from the physical situation through family attitudes and the values of their society to the ever-shifting celestials that express the climate of the Upper Worlds. For the child who is still very susceptible to events in the non-physical dimension, life is lived between two regions. On the one hand, he or she is being taught to live in an elemental environment, inhabited by people who project many moulding factors upon them; and on the other, the child exists in a dimension in which memories of a former life, dreams and fantasies play an enormous part. The quality of this inner life is watery, but day by day the growing body immerses the psyche in Earthy reality. Many people recall this 'floating' time with a sense of loss but it must pass as lower psyche and body become firmly interlocked.

All this conditioning by circumstance is, as said, subject to choice. By this we mean that there are certain decisions that are not part of the routine physical or psychological processes. Seen in terms of the Tree, free will operates from the *Gevurah-Hesed-Tiferet* triad of the soul which hovers between the upper and lower faces of the psyche. As such the soul has the freedom to manoeuvre, because it does not come under such laws as physical growth and decay or automatic obedience to spiritual injunctions. People can, for example, choose to submerge themselves in materiality or raise themselves to Heavenly heights; they can refrain from participation in events, such as condoning or condemning, or join in. Many people choose, for instance, to spend their lives devoted to social status, while some, by choice, retire from the World and become recluses. Yet others choose to remain where they were born and do nothing with their gifts, while some go abroad or start great enterprises. Many choose not to choose, and waver in psychological limbo as others decide to rule everyone but themselves.

Everyone has choice. It is with us from the moment we are conceived. Our circumstances and stage of development physically, psychologically and spiritually may vary but the possibility of free will does not. The various crucial points in infancy and childhood are not dealt with by the ego, but by the Self which operates from its pivotal position on the Tree. It is cognizant with every situation, even through it may appear to be deep within the unconscious. In fact, as many people recall, such crucial moments of decision have that extraordinary quality and clarity of consciousness. This is quite different from the general process of education in which we learn the rules and skills needed for the circumstance that fate has given us.

22. Education

In the process of incarnating we have seen how there are several stages of cognition. The first is the sensory-motor phase, in which the infant discovers and moves within the physical world. Some psychologists, like Darwin, have related this stage of development to the archaic period of mankind, when human beings were learning to live under the most elemental conditions. Life was almost entirely materially orientated and the chief concern was to learn how to move about in physical time and space. While an infant is only concerned with a day at a time the infantile human race had to deal with the annual cycle of the seasons in order to survive, for nothing was as readily supplied as mother's comfort. This archaic stratum is seen by some psychologists in our most primitive instincts which later become the mainspring of the id-*Nefesh* level of our being that rises up through the *Malkhut* of the body.

The next phase is seen as the *Yesodic* mastery of symbols. Here the child learns to articulate and play with abstracts. Nursery stories and pictures, games with imaginary people and toys take on powerful significance which feed the fantasising that goes on in the child's mind. This stage is related in history to the time when men saw gods and ghosts everywhere. Many peoples never got beyond this epoch, but some did develop this imaginative capacity to a high degree, producing myths like the Greeks. The phenomenon is common to every nation and is part of its folk lore education system. The tale of George Washington who as a boy never told a lie, and the courage and skill of William Tell are classic examples of mythical heroes, as are the animal symbols of the various nations, like the Russian Bear or American Eagle. The Nazi party applied this level of folk symbolism to stir the German people's *Yesodic* ego into the state of playground bully, while the British Empire was founded upon the desire to please mother, who was well disguised in the collective image of Britannia and embodied by Queen Victoria. All this roots back to the individual situation, when children play out their *Yesodic* fantasies, according to the values of their society, be it of the back street or palace yard. This phase is usually complete before the final stage of education has begun to grip.

To educate is to bring out the latent talents of a child as the analytical qualities of *Hod* combine with *Yesod* to emerge as a capacity for imagery and invention. Symbols joined with facts become, as they are absorbed and integrated into the psyche, the chief mode of perceiving the world. Symbols overlay the senses with highly subjective filters that convert the dark, for instance, into a space for devils and a sound in the night into a sinister or reassuring noise, just as it might have done to our remote ancestors. Abstracts like as letters and numbers, learned at this time, open up entirely new dimensions, stories about far-away places and the mysteries of measurement take the child into, what is in fact, the World of *Yezirah*, where imaginary problems can be set and solved by mental manipulation and calculation. Here is the basis of all magic, as children perceive, like their remote ancestors, the world of formulae and spells. This level is still with most people, as is witnessed in the great interest in fantasy. There is not a great deal of difference between ancient folk stories and modern science fiction. The saga of King Arthur's knights and the 'Star Wars' movies about the Jedi knights of the future come from the same level of *Yezirah*, as does the mythology about medicine and psychology.

Around the age of seven all the *Hodian* skills that have been acquired, like physical competence in gesture and handling and symbolic manipulation in imagination and problem solving, begin to be rationalised. Language and memory are refined and manual skills applied to many operations. More complex games are played and a deeper interest in the greater world emerges in the investigation of natural and human history. Science starts to take the place of fantasy and practical experiments at school and in the home with plants, animals and machines develops an appreciation for concrete operations in which logic is used to determine results and create desired effects. The irrational *Yesodic* factor is still there in day and night dreams, but slowly the logical method of *Hod* takes charge. Historically this corresponds to the period of the great stone circles, like Stonehenge, which are practical as well as symbolic structures, built to plot and calculate the movements of the stars, Sun and Moon. This is also the period of ancient Egypt whose culture was a blend of high magic and precise calculation. However, we still see *Yesod* present at examination time when children take their mascots into the examination room to bring them luck. Magic is not dead.

The acquisition of concrete skill allows the psyche to develop the *Hod-Yesod-Malkhut* triad to its operational capacity. This is seen in the exacting demands of children in their rules about life as they start to apply the limits imposed upon them by the super-ego on the pillar of structure, onto those about them. It is not permissible to cheat, nor should a toy tank or doll be inaccurate or badly made. Adults are expected to behave as grown ups, or there is no trust or respect. All these are qualities of the left hand column of the Tree. Games become highly organised and talents in art and sciences are developed to a fine degree. Cleverness is admired and tales of bright children outwitting adult villains are popular, although the style is now the young computer genius.

As a child approaches eleven or twelve the qualities of *Nezah* are aroused, although not as yet sexually. This brings about the next phase of what is called 'formal operations'. Here the completion of the great *Malkhut-Hod-Nezah* triad with *Yesod* at its centre gives a power and feeling dimension to the psyche. By this time, a school is not just a place in which to study. It has a well-organised social structure with a strong system of relationship. Thus while the *Hodian* activities are brought to an optimum peak, in which all the general skills needed in life have been learned so there is a corresponding intensity of *Nezahian* passion, as strong feelings about friends and enemies emerge. Hero or heroine worship occurs, as do crazes for this or that. While it is true to say that the psyche can now handle such subjects as geometry, foreign languages and even abstract ideas with remarkable skill, the ever-increasing presence of awakening sexuality also arises. This is the time when homosexuality also occurs as the *Hod-Nezah* axis begins to resonate prior to puberty. Schoolgirls have passions for each other and schoolboys find themselves intrigued or obsessed by their fellows. Difficulties arise because such feelings are incongruous and taboo. Work suffers and friendships undergo tensions that test long-established patterns. In some societies such behaviour is accepted and it runs its course before being transformed into normal sexuality, but in other communities it is forbidden and many people pass through their homosexual phase in private. Some individuals, however, do not manage to shift fully from the *Hod* stage to *Nezah* and retain an androgenous duality of immature sexuality. Historically, the classical Greek period corresponds to this epoch, with its brilliant, clever, logical and mercurial homosexuals who produced schools of ultra-*Hodian* drama, philosophy and an exceptional refinement in art and science based upon measurement, mathematics and the human form, especially the masculine.

With the completion and activation of the great vegetable triad, as the *Malkhut-Hod-Nezah* is called, comes adolescence. Here the Venusian power at the base of the right pillar of dynamics comes into operation with the resultant effect of an abrupt decline of interest in the mercurial activities. Suddenly, an acute sensuality is aroused as the body begins to undergo a transformation. *Nezah* stimulates new growth as body hair and breasts emerge, and the male chest and female hips enlarge. Over a very short period, the psyche, which has been living a relatively quiescent sexual life, is confronted with desires that it has not experienced since early childhood. During infancy such impulses were checked and trained by parental figures and the *Yesodic* ego learned to control and hold the id-*Nefesh* until the right moment, or push it into the unconscious. In adolescence these desires arise with increased force, but the individual has to cope largely on their own. Some adolescents retreat into the feeling triad, in a variety of moods while others let their passion out in *Nezahian* uproar. Parents repeat holding manoeuvres, but they no longer have someone who is completely dependent upon them. The feeling triad of *Hod-Yesod-Nezah* oscillates violently as quarrels and disruptions in the home and between companions occur, until the adolescent begins to relate the triad to the *Malkhut* of the body. When this done then they are ready to produce the next generation and all interest becomes focused upon the art of courting. In left pillar societies this is controlled by a strict code; in others, where the right side of the Tree is dominant, courtships are acted out and sometimes end in pregnancy or even violence as *Nezahian* energy is expressed in positive and negative forms. From the point of view of the human race, this is the oscillating pattern of history between the extremes of Puritanism and Bohemianism. For the individual, here is where he or she begins to become an adult as adolescence shifts consciousness slowly out of the vegetable triad, which is concerned with reproduction, and into the human-animal triad of *Hod-Nezah-Tiferet* known as 'The Awakening'. As the person moves out of the binding hold of the *Yesodic* ego and into contact with the Crown of the body Tree, which is also the *Tiferet* of the psyche and the *Malkhut* of the spirit, so they approach physical maturity and the possibility of individuality symbolised by becoming their 'own' man or woman.

23. Maturation

In many societies puberty is marked by a ceremony called by some the 'rites of passage'. In Judaism, the *Bar Mitzvah* celebration marks a boy's coming of age, when he is called up in the synagogue to read a portion of the Law. What is being symbolised is that he is no longer the responsibility of his parents, that he knows the rules of conduct as set out in the Torah and can take on the role of adult. In early Middle Eastern society, where maturity occurred with greater rapidity, it was not unusual for a youth or maid to be married at fourteen, but this was within a strong family situation in which the couple were still protected by the clan. Today in the West, the situation is quite different. At this pubescent point, we see the onset of the search for identity as the person moves into the *Hod-Nezah-Tiferet* triad of awakening.

By the time an individual has passed into full adolescence there is a massive shift in the balance between body and psyche. The physique is sexually mature and all the physical systems are working up to their maximum efficiency. The psyche, however, is often still that of a juvenile. This causes, at times, much conflict, as adults begin to expect the person to take on some adult burdens. In so-called less sophisticated societies, the boys are sent out into the fields or the world by themselves to prove all the skills they have learned, so that it will be seen that they can survive and support themselves and thereafter a family. When this is done, they are accepted as men and will be treated as such by the adults of the community. In western society no such equivalent exists. The examination system and apprenticeship schemes do cover some aspects of the problem, but unless a person is part of a tight-knit community that holds to ancient traditions, there is no way the transition from childhood to adulthood can be guided, for the side pillars of super-ego and ego-ideal are at this point often rejected. This creates an instability, for the *Yesodic* ego is rarely strong enough to hold the shuddering psychological Tree during this critical period.

The reason for such disruption during the process of adolescence is that all the experience acquired in childhood is under pressure. In

103

some, the impulsive energy of *Nezah* is held by the rules of *Hod* in repression, which gives rise to nervous tension. In others, it is the reverse, with an opposition to anything rational or conformist. In some cases, the *Nezahian* pursuit of pleasure and excitement takes over completely as the *Yesodic* ego adapts the latest fashion and does everything to reject the super-ego-ideal values of the parents. This pursuit of a new image seeks not only to be outrageous and attract attention from the opposite sex, but find a persona that the individual can identify with. In some, several different masks are put on over a short time, in others there is still a holding on to the conservative mode, but with a view to changing it. Here we see the active and passive pillars at work according to the loading of the psyche. With the intelligence of *Hod* enhanced by the power of *Nezah*, curiosity widens out and becomes charged. Wit and novelty emerge and everything is done for effect. Relationships become hyper-sensitive and intense as the feeling triad is fully activated, with each person seeking a companion to mirror the *Yesodic* view they have of themselves. Indeed, the phenomenon of narcissism returns for a while as people look for their own kind or that which is the total opposite, to complement their image, such as the mutual attraction of blondes and brunettes or a refined girl taking on a crude lover, or the reverse, as the shadow side of their *Nefesh* id is released in a *Nezahian* affair. The same can be said of young people who break out of the bonds of a conventional upbringing and take to drugs and crime. This is the violent oscillation of the psychological Tree as it desperately searches for a new equilibrium in the dynamic period of youth.

The *Hod-Tiferet-Nezah* triad of awakening that is now being activated brings about an acute awareness of the world around and its imperfections as *Tiferet* is touched upon. While the great vegetable triad, dominated by the *Yesodic* ego pursues its new thoughts, feelings and actions on the personal level, the path between the ego and the Self, called 'Integrity' in Kabbalah, is alerted. This gives rise in many advanced adolescents to a profound hunger for the truth because of the contact with their *Tiferet*. Thus besides the passionate encounters between the sexes there is a preoccupation with religion, politics, philosophy, psychology, and indeed any subject that can explain what is going on in the World and within oneself. In such a period of confusion, if the background is not secure in belief or discipline, the adolescent will be prone to try anything that offers promising answers. This could mean exploring ideas or modes of living as far from home as possible in order to establish individuality. In most people's cases the pull to extremes is often no more than a protest against the conventions of their time and a passion to put things right. Such people come through this highly disturbed age with just a few physical bruises and maybe a psychological broken nose. Some, however, are lost and others even killed in youthful foolishness or adventure, even as some young tribesmen never return from their initiation because they went too far into strange country.

The irony and test of the adolescent situation is that it is concerned with finding oneself. At this point, however, there is not enough life experience to differentiate the ego image of education from the Self that hovers just beyond the liminal line of consciousness stretched between *Hod* and *Nezah*, and so the attention is usually directed down to *Yesod* and what adult image to acquire. This is often perceived in the form of ambition and the animal drive of the *Nefesh* id produces the most glamorous projections from pop stars to Nobel prize winners. Those who work best through action will see themselves as great sportsmen or dancers, while the thinkers will want to be esteemed scientists or philosophers. The feelers will yearn to be famous poets or musicians. For a period these fantasies will be held as real possibilities, until the young person realises the work involved may be more than they are prepared to do, or beyond their talents. This is the first sign of maturity as the process of development brings them closer to *Tiferet*, the place of Truth. In some cases, the image is not seen as an impossible ambition and the ego clings onto it long after physical maturity has been reached. Fortunately, life chips away the fantasy, which is often based upon an infantile desire for attention rather than a real search for Selfhood. Most people find their proper level, accepting that to be a good number two, three or four, is the best they could ever do, as they see the stress such top positions carry. A few do hold on tight to their *Yesodic* dream and if it is not a true vision they can become neurotic and then, in extreme cases, psychotic, as they live their fantasy and neglect reality. Kabbalistically this is when the path between the ego and the Self is blocked by a delusion and integrity is lost.

This path between *Yesod* and *Tiferet* is maintained by most people to a greater or lesser degree. In some it is no more than a dull recognition that honesty exists, although it may or may not be practised at work or in the home. In others it is important enough to check their conduct at work or in personal relationships, and in yet others it can generate a desire to guide the community into what is right according to the code of that society. In a few, it is more than just obeying the conventions. They will seek to know what is right for them in terms of self-development.

The perception that there is more to life than begetting families or becoming successful holds such people at a certain disadvantage, because while they are still preoccupied with what and who they are, others who have now filled out this triad of the human animal level, forge ahead, and make their way in the World. Here, we see the fully developed natural man and woman who want to be the kings and queens of their generation until they are displaced by the up and coming of the next. The seeker, of sometimes he or she knows not what, is somehow never fully involved in these games of material possessions or social status. They are what has been defined by some as 'outsiders'. Of these, some are simply seeking to avoid reality and to disappear into the dream existence of an eccentric recluse, if they can manage it, or of a vagrant if they cannot. Most other seekers, it must be said, can be quite competent artisans and professional people, or may be found in the home, office or factory. They occur in the boardroom and on the farm, in the studio and in the military. These people are not outwardly that unusual, but they differ from the rest in that they recognise a sense of an inner or other life. In most, it is just a dim memory of coming from somewhere else. Many, alas, over the years, forget, as they become deeply enmeshed in work and family, but some still hold on to this belief, seeking people like themselves, who ask the same questions and feel that deep sense of being in exile, from where, they do not know. A few know why they are here. They have either not forgotten their instructions, before they came into incarnation, or have slowly recalled that they had something to do, while here on Earth.

This phenomenon is not uncommon and indeed statistical researchers into social trends actually use such terms as 'inner directed' along with 'conspicuous consumers', or animal people, and 'survivors', or the vegetable level of humanity. These categories relate to the lower face of the psychological Tree. After spending their youth in the awakening triad in which the opportunity for further development is offered, most people fall back to an optimum position to become fixed in one of the three sub-triads focused upon *Yesodic* ego. Thus, after their wild days, they sink below the *Hod-Nezah* line of consciousness and live life out at the vegetable level of routine. Only the animal people and the inner-directed operate in what is called in Kabbalah, the *Gatlut* or greater state. This *Hod-Tiferet-Nezah* triad however can be used either to exploit others or be applied to self-development. The choice as always is there. Those in the *Katnut* or lesser state are those who prefer to remain in ego. Only a major crisis will shift them upwards to *Tiferet* like a pit disaster or personal shock that makes them awaken and start to ask questions again. This can also occur to the animal person if they are traumatised by being displaced or find that success has a hollowness. Such a realisation may move them into the position of seeking the Self, like the 'outsider' who knows that there are other stages of development beyond the Crown of physical prime. As the place where the Worlds of Action, Formation and Creation meet, the Self allows the higher vehicles of psyche and spirit to fully engage with the physical. It is then that the physical organism is complete.

24. Completions

According to esoteric tradition, the three lower organisms of the material, psychological and spiritual are not all fused together at birth, but are loosely related, hence the frailty of life during the earliest years. As months and years pass, the tenuous hold of the vital body, governed by the *Nefesh* id, increases as the dynamic and structure of the upper face of the body accumulate and bind into the lower face of the psyche, so that by the age of about seven years the *Daat-Yesod* of ego has generated, in the average child, an operational personality. At puberty, the middle levels of the psyche are engaged. With the release of sexuality and the awakening triad brought into action, the active and passive emotional triads and the soul become consciously accessible. At around the age of twenty-one, the body reaches its maximum extension of growth and development. At this time the Crown of the physical Tree interlocks with the *Tiferet* or Self of the psyche and activates the lowest *Sefirah* of the spiritual organism. Here begins the contact with what is called by some the 'mental' body and by others the transpersonal and truly intellectual level of an individual. At this point embodiment is complete.

All the foregoing summarises the process of incarnation from the moment of conception, through gestation, birth and early development to a point when the body, psyche, and spirit are brought together. This situation grants extraordinary capacities, as revealed by the great ones of the human race. However, most young adults on maturing usually only apply themselves to surviving in the physical world and to outdoing each other. For the mass of humanity this is quite acceptable, and many are content to live relatively comfortable and secure lives, while they let the more assertive compete amongst themselves for leadership. The 'outsiders' are different, but we shall deal with them later.

Having reached their prime, most people see no further than to earn a living, mate and fit into their particular society. The working man does what his father did, unless he is exceptional, and marries a girl who lives the same sort of life. The son of a professional will probably go to university, unless he is unusual, and espouse a woman of similar background. The daughter of an aristocrat, after reacting against her class, unless she is very different, will more often than not, finish up with a man of the same rank, running a household not all that different in essence from that of her parents. This, it must be repeated, is a generalisation and does not always apply to the kind of people who read books like this, being outsiders for one reason or another.

Having reached the peak of physicality many people no longer seek further. Family and occupation absorb most of the energy available and there is a flattening out of the field of activity. The intense curiosity of childhood and the vitality of youth start to fade and many brilliant and beautiful young people become quite ordinary by the time they reach thirty. Some, of course seek to retain their cleverness and desirability, but it has not the freshness of youth. The wild and often painful and but sometimes wonderful epoch is passed, and early middle age which is so concerned with finding and establishing a place in the world has to be endured. This, it will be recalled, is the period of Mars and *Gevurah* where tenacity and courage, discipline and discrimination are brought into action both in private and public life. Job satisfaction and personal fulfilment are very important to people between thirty and forty. A good marriage and a respectable social position are seen as a valid objectives. Over this period, experience ripens the skills acquired when young, and life widens as material wealth increases and work, either in the home or in the world, opens out as children grow and promotion occurs. By late middle age, the hard grind is over for most people, and they begin to slow down and enjoy what they have earned. The interpersonal crises of family and profession that go with the thirties and forties have passed, and love and wealth can be generously given, unless the arduous years have left the person withdrawn and bitter, because they have been defeated, not by life, but by their own illusions. This is the point where the soul triad begins to consciously emerge, as the Self of *Tiferet*, the Judgment of *Gevurah* and the Mercy of *Hesed* start to work in unison and people begin to evaluate their performance.

For most, middle age is when they begin to descend from the physical plateau of an active life. Gradually people can no longer do what they could nor do they wish to, unless they are still immature or feel they have failed. It is quite natural to begin to ponder death at this time as contemporaries start to die more frequently. This consideration of one's time on Earth continues from the fifties onward, as the senses begin to dim and there is a feeling of a closing down of the radius of physical action. To those who are only centred in the body, it is the beginning of the end, and they will seek every method to hold back the process. Those who have developed some insight into the purpose of life now begin to reflect even more seriously and give out and back much of their experience and material possessions, because they realise that the body has already started to detach itself from the psyche. As early old age approaches, so the shrinking body cannot recall yesterday, because its systems are not as efficient as they were, although images of yesteryear may be remembered with extraordinary clarity. Long-vanished scenes of childhood, moments of youth and the dramas of young adulthood return, as the loosening ego frees the unconscious from its hold. Many hours are spent pondering deeds and attitudes as the super-ego and the ego-ideal are separated out by the emergent *Sefirot* of *Binah* and *Hokhmah* that give understanding and wisdom to those that heed their deeper levels of the mind. Thus, this person may realise why they succeeded, and that one why they failed. Another may see the meaning of a particular relationship and yet another the problems they themselves had created. Certain patterns will recur during these reflections, until the reason for their appearance is solved and some vital key is given to their psychological *Daat* of knowledge of themselves in some important realisation.

The final stage of old age increases the separation of the physical from the psyche, so that the level of psychological and spiritual development reached in the life becomes increasingly apparent. Those who have spent their time devoted to possessions will cling onto the *Malkhut* of materiality, while others solely concerned with a *Yesodic* image of the persona find that this fades as the id-*Nefesh* drive behind the ego emerges in a childishness that many old people exhibit. Only those who have moved beyond the dominance of physicality, who have learned that the personality is only a medium to operate through, come to see the lesson of their lives, and moreover, perceive death as a welcome door to deeper experience. Those still centred in the material world cannot see anything else, and death is for them a total annihilation. The hallmark of these two states, observers have noted, is dignity and integrity in those who have learned their lesson from fate, and despair and disillusionment in those who have not. This may seem a hard conclusion to the end of so brief a sojourn of life on Earth, but we must also remember that from a Kabbalistic viewpoint, this is not the finish of existence, and that many more opportunities will be given to the person to develop and perfect their being through incarnation.

As death approaches so the id-*Nefesh* begins to withdraw the vitality of the body and there appears that strange luminosity of skin, as the eyes seem to be gazing into another world. This is borne out by the fact that many dying people report seeing dead relatives about them. Some sensitive or advanced individuals can pick up these presences who appear, like similar entities present at birth, to be watching over the mortem operation. The moment of departure comes at a crucial point in time and space, even as it does at birth. Sometimes, as in the natal operation, nothing obvious appears to be happening. Here we have to remember that while the body and lower psyche may be old and inert, the higher levels are anything but as they ease themselves free of the physical vehicle. When the ebbing vitality of the ego finally loosens the *Yesod-Daat* connection then death is imminent. However, some dying people still hover within the body through force of habit. This delays the departure as the person hangs around the corpse after clinical death has occurred. When the moment of decease comes, the processes described in the chapter on Death begin, and the whole post-mortem/prenatal cycle starts over again, but this time a stage further on.

We have now mapped out the general developmental cycle of life from conception to death, bearing in mind that everyone has deep prenatal memories stored in the psyche, which profoundly affect the particular fate and psychology of each individual. These are in turn related to environment and the people he or she will encounter, as well as what work is to be done and what opportunities will be given. All this adds up to a much more complex situation than most psychologists take into consideration. The next stage is to examine, in detail, some of the main components and processes of the psyche, especially the ones observed by the two major modern schools of depth psychology and relate them to the Kabbalistic scheme. Let us begin with the Freudian view.

25. Id-*Nefesh*

Sigmund Freud was born in 1856 and died in 1939. Most of his life was spent as a working psychologist in Vienna where he introduced some fundamental contributions to the study of western psychology. Many of his original ideas have been modified and several schools, based upon his view, have emerged to form the middle ground between the body- and reflex-oriented psychologists and the Jungians who, following their founder, explore the middle and upper zones of the psyche. Freud's main discovery was the recognition of two levels of psychological activity: the conscious and the unconscious. The latter, he maintained had a far greater influence upon people's lives than they realised. Most people, he observed, were manipulated by powerful instinctive drives that were held in check by their education and social customs. The ego or conscious mind acted as the facilitator between the id impulses and the constraints of the super-ego-ideal which punished or rewarded one's performance, according to its often quite unconsciously acquired opinions. This tripartite system forms the basic model of Freudian psychology and can be seen, from the Kabbalistic standpoint, to relate to the body and the lower part of the psychological Tree. The focus of consciousness resides in the *Daat-Yesod* ego, while that which is unconscious lies beyond the liminal line between *Hod* and *Nezah*. This hidden zone contains a distinct structure and dynamics of its own and many new terms have been added by Freudians to differentiate various functions. We shall begin by examining the basics first.

Like the embryo body, the psyche builds slowly up from a primitive general scheme that over time becomes more refined as the processes of inner growth and experience fill out and integrate. However, before the psychological organism can begin to function it has to have a massive input of energy and sensory impressions. This is provided by the vehicle of the body that has been grafted onto the lower psyche at birth. From that moment on a flood of impulses rises up from the physical Tree and passes into the psyche which is initially swamped by the experience. One reason why an infant has to sleep so much is in order to allow the as-yet unprotected psyche to adjust to the impact of the *Nefesh* or vital soul, called the id by Freud.

The id, which draws its energy from the mineral, vegetable and animal levels of the body's mechanical, chemical and electronic systems follows a basic law of primitive life. It seeks relief from any tension it might experience, such as hunger or excessive light. That is, it will attempt to find whatever is pleasurable and avoid what is painful. This is an instinctive reflex that drives all its activities, such as the withdrawal of its finger from something that is too hot, or the seeking of the mother's nipple for sustenance. Such reflexes operate at every level of the body and the newly-incarnated psyche initially has no control over them, because the connections between the physical and psychological organism are, in the infant, quite tenuous and unrelated. Because of this, there is no restraining factor and the immediate needs of the id are sought with a degree of ferocity that one would associate with the *Nefesh*, that is a synthesis of the animal, vegetable and mineral levels of body consciousness. An example of this in Nature are wolves who have eaten nothing for days and who will attack anything. Another instance are elephants that will trek hundreds of miles for a lick of rock salt. The id has the same powerful drive, because it knows that if its needs are not met it will die.

Because an infant's needs are not always met instantly — it may not be convenient for the mother to meet them — there arises, Freud observed, the phenomenon of frustration. Normally, the sense organs and motor functions respond instantly to such situations, like something in the eye, but there are times when even they cannot solve a problem. A child may want to be picked up, but nobody is there, or it might wish to touch an object out of reach. This generates a tension that cannot be released, and without the governing experience of a developed ego, the intensity of the charge is reinforced by all the energy available being focused on that incident, resulting in a passionate response that cannot find satisfaction.

Added to this is the frustration of a psyche which is still adult in its outlook, but which can do nothing with so primitive a body. Here begins what is called the 'primary process' that begins to connect the body and psyche through the *Daat-Yesod* of the ego.

Over the first month of life, the infant slowly builds up a series of images through the senses and the perception of the *Yesodic* ego of, say, the mother's breast that gives sustenance. With the constant repetition of feeding, memory beings to develop, so that the baby can recall the object that gives it satisfaction. As the ego is not sufficiently evolved to differentiate time or space, it cannot tell the difference between the image and the reality of its source of nourishment, and this can cause further frustration and distress, until the child realises there will be times when it is and is not fed. Here we see the beginning of a process in which the psyche starts to relate to the body, as sense impressions and reflexes are recognised and synthesised through memory into imagination. Imagination in turn is used by the infant to help reduce its physical tension as it conjures up the object in an attempt to satisfy its need. This gives the infant the illusion of reality because the id-*Nefesh* cannot tell the difference between an objective perception and a subjective memory. In Kabbalah, this is the difference between the *Daat* or knowledge of the body, which only relates to sense data and *Yesod* which is concerned with images. Many people will recognise the phenomenon when they see a distant bus and the number they want quite clearly — until the bus comes close and the number is not what they imagined. Babies have the same problem, but do not know it, until they develop the secondary processes of identifying reality, that is realising that the imaginary breast, for example, is not really there and a nearby object that is desired does not come closer unless the infant extends its hand or cries out for it.

Until the first and secondary processes start to become operational, the id energy has no form to fill and be channelled by. Because the psyche belongs to the *Yeziratic* World of Formation, these processes have to built up in order to make conscious links between body and psyche. However, until a well-organised system is established the id will go wherever it wants. As such it will infuse the psyche with two powerful *Nefesh* urges that remain always in the individual, no matter how educated or sophisticated they may become. The positive aspect is called the 'libido' and is related to the merciful right side of the Tree, as an active, creative process. The negative aspect of the id is called 'mortido' and this is identified with the left pillar of Severity. These two poles of life and death are necessary because in Nature, the power to kill, in order to defend or eat is as vital as the power to propagate and create. In a human being, these two faces of the id-*Nefesh* are usually contained and controlled by the ego and later by the super-ego, but their presence is always there in what some psychologists call the 'subconscious', or that which is *below* consciousness. The 'unconscious', according to the same view, being *above* the ego. Here is the distinction between the Tree of the body and the Tree of the psyche as they meet and operate below and above the *Daat-Yesod* of the ego.

The power of the subconscious levels wells up in all of us, and in some people, where the ego is not sufficiently strong, the conflicts of neurosis can set in, as powerful instinctive drives oppose the standards set by the super-ego. In occasional cases, where *Daat-Yesod* is not well founded the ego is overthrown and psychosis will occur as the id-*Nefesh* bursts out in a psychotic episode such as stealing or suicide if the mortido turns back upon the person. This is seen in the larger scale in time of war, when nations suffer a mass psychosis, and even in peacetime, when for example, white Australians went out on weekend hunts for black aborigines who they raped or castrated before killing. Here both the libido and mortido were used savagely by so-called 'civilised' human beings in a way no animal would. The function of the ego is to check these primitive urges and convert, not pervert, their raw vitality into a higher order of activity. The factor of free will is quite crucial in such matters if we remember the infant has an adult psyche that is not as yet unconscious.

The id-*Nefesh* is wild and untamed in the infant's body. As such its energy flows freely into the lower face of the psychological Tree until it is bridled. The clinical terms used, as the ego begins to contain the id, is 'binding'. This means the setting up of patterns of thinking, feeling and acting, that is the triads that overlay the upper face of the body Tree, are brought to bear on the *Daat-Yesod* that will generate the ego. This process, Freud noted, was helped by the ancient memories of previous generations in which the experience of mankind was passed on perhaps by the genes or perhaps held in the older parts of the brain. These archaic forms were, however, still quite primitive inasmuch as they were preoccupied with seeking pleasure and avoiding pain. They were also quite irrational and perceived the World, like the infant, as centred upon itself. He also observed that capacity to make images of wish-fulfilment was very similar to the basis of primitive magic which related to an infant's belief in its own power to get what it desired by moving its limbs or calling in a certain way. This is a very Freudian view of Existence. The sense of omnipotence that a child experiences may well be its perception of physical reality, but not all its dreams and fantasies are about food and comfort. Many people recall the pre-natal state in the upper worlds and they retreated there during their sleep periods while their infant bodies remained in the cot.

Returning to the id-*Nefesh*, what can be said is that it is the physical basis of the psyche's activity; that is it anchors the overlay of education, custom and even spiritual development. As such it plays an important part in life as a source of power that can elate or deplete the psyche, according to how it is handled. As a largely hidden factor, the id infiltrates the psyche to aid or oppose conscious and unconscious events such as so-called accidents, that prevent or initiate certain actions. It is often symbolised as the nocturnal animal in many dreams or day fantasies that carry the person on through dark or hard times. The id-*Nefesh* is the power-pack of the physical Tree. When the skills and intelligence of the psyche can convert its vital energy then much can be achieved. But this capacity is as yet a long way off in the infant who first has to learn how to relate its psyche to the new body.

26. Ego-*Yesod*

According to many psychologists the infantile ego is created by the interaction of the outer and inner worlds. The astrologer takes this further by saying that the position of the Moon, in Sign and House, gives the ego a particular character. The Kabbalist sees the ego as the focus of many processes, between the upper face of the body and the lower face of the psyche as sensory impressions and psychological activity ebb and flow along the paths and around the sub-triads centred on the *Daat-Yesod* of ego. The Freudians see the ego as an executive function that emerges from the frustrations of the infant as it learns to control and discharge the sensory-motor stimulus. It produces images of reality and fantasy which govern the exchanges between the consciousness and the unconscious levels. The fact that there are different views of the same reality is in itself an example of how the ego perceives according to its disposition and training.

The ego's chief duty is to give continuity to what it experiences. This is done by memory, which is the recording of myriads of perceptions that form patterns in the mind and brain. Out of this process comes recall of the past and imagination about the future, when seen in the light of the present. Initially, the ego cannot tell the difference between inner and outer worlds, but as the infant becomes familiar with its body and the environment, it develops what is called the 'reality principle'. This enables the infant to see what is feasible and what is not, and much time is spent in testing this principle to find its limits. In Kabbalistic terms, the ego-*Yesod* starts to differentiate from its *Malkhut* through experience and to distinguish between body and psyche as it acquires the ability to control the impulses of the id-*Nefesh* and segregate the psychological processes of thinking, feeling and behaviour. Because of the Tree mode Kabbalists argue that a *form* already exists, with inbuilt tendencies, which are simply filled out by experience and that the ego-*Yesod* is the non-luminous mirror that reflects an image according to its particular constitution which is governed by factors such as karma and stage of development. It is not just a virgin wax to be worked upon as many psychologists believe.

The delay created by the ego of immediate reaction to a situation, because the baby recognises it will not get the desired result, turns the primary process of perceiving an object into the secondary process of negotiating with the outer world. Over time the picture of reality is built up and finer powers of discrimination and manipulation are acquired as the paths and triads of the lower face of the psychological Tree become more and more fused into the upper face of the body Tree. Accuracy of perception and precision of response are enhanced by the learning and use of symbols, which become charged with meaning in a moment of consciousness and then pass across the liminal line between *Hod* and *Nezah*, to take up a position with others, of like kind, in the unconscious. An example of this is learning to tell the time. There is a moment when the numbers and hands on the clock-face cease to be just objects and become images of certain hours and minutes of the day. When this occurs the clock is no longer seen objectively. Thus, nine o'clock is when one should be in school and noon is the time to go home. All these associations, and myriads more, pass through ego consciousness and disappear into the unconscious, where they are stored, according to classification in the triads of concepts and emotion. Some of these early memories will be pleasant and some otherwise, and this will determine which side of the Tree they will be drawn to. Meanwhile the ego-*Yesod* slowly constructs a general image of the outside world and where the person fits into it.

Here it must be said that a simultaneous capacity for imagery is also built up in the ego which clothes the impulse of the id-*Nefesh* and the activities of the unconscious in forms that occur in dreams and daytime fantasies. These will be dealt with in detail later, but it should be noted at this point that such internal imaging occupies much of the time and energy of children, and not a few adults. In some cases, as in children, it is just play to pass the time or enact a situation that is not possible in the outer reality. In others it is a way of obtaining a release for inner tensions that cannot be met otherwise, and in yet others it is simply a form of escapism. Conversely this is the mechanism by which creative people invent new forms of art, science, business or what you will. Most people have their day dreams. Some use them to relax in mental reverie and others to do an action replay of what they should have said and done in this or that situation, while others employ this *Yesodic* faculty to plan strategies or anticipate what has or will happen. All this inner ego activity, in many individuals, is related to outer reality, so that for the most part it does not interfere directly with their perception of the external world. However, in cases of trauma or fever, the *Yesodic* capacity for imagery can take over and appear quite real in illusions. In more serious situations of psychological disturbance fantasies can become delusions that totally blot out external reality in transient or cyclic periods. When a deluded ego cannot perceive the difference between internal or external reality the state of insanity reigns.

The reality principle is crucial in the development of the ego. From the Kabbalistic view, it anchors the *Yesod* of the psyche to the *Daat* of the body and makes the *Malkhut* of *Yezirah* lock into the physical *Tiferet* of *Assyah*. From the Freudian view, it enables the person to make use of the id's vitality and convert it into whatever practical application is needed. An appreciation of outer reality also brings about a sense of identity that over time establishes a recognisable place in the World. As the ego-*Yesod* learns about what is real, so its capacity enlarges in both the inner and outer realms. This means that an increasing exchange of experience is processed and related to the acquisition of knowledge and skills which greatly influence the person's outlook and personal values.

The persona or mask an individual wears over the face of the ego is the image that is required by circumstance. These however can change radically, as in time of war or personal crisis, when there can be moments or even long periods when none of the masks a person has acquired can shield them from what is happening, and the naked ego has to deal with things directly. In many cases, like in military combat, only discipline applied by others can prevent breakdown. In equally strenuous circumstances, like failing an important ambition, the initial shock can generate great confusion, until a new mask is put on, to protect the ego. The widow donning black and the rejected lover putting on a brave face are examples. There are those, however, who do not have a strong ego that can withstand the knocks of life who crumple because their sense of ego identity is basically insecure. They often not only fear the world at large, but also themselves, as they cannot always contain the powerful id-*Nefesh* urges that arise in a crisis such as, for example, panic. Some people cannot cope, as infantile drives that have never been quite bridled by the ego, burst out. The reality principle is lost in anything from a childish sulk to a psychotic suicide or homocidal episode.

Such incidents are often the work of the shadow side of the ego.

As the persona is the front of the ego's image, so the shadow is that which is not seen, at least by ourselves; because most of us hide our less desirable traits behind what we project in our ego image. These unacceptable elements of our nature have their roots in the primitive power of the id-*Nefesh*. Fortunately they are usually held in check by the ego and the individual's social personality. However, such potent drives arising from the body, and not a few from perverse elements in the psyche, do penetrate through the ego under certain conditions such as, for example, the stress of a marital breakdown when terrible things are said and done. When Freud introduced this dark dimension he hit an enormous resistance in the very prudish but sensual nineteenth-century Viennese society of his time. Two horrific world wars revealed this shadow side of thousands of so-called decent people on both sides, when the veneer of civilisation was peeled off in combat and millions died most violently. This sinister element, Freud observed, may be well concealed by pleasant manners, but the ego does not always succeed in stopping it from filtering through in unconscious slips of the tongue and actions that avoid *Yesod* and come down or up the side pillars between *Malkhut*, *Hod* and *Nezah*. More on the shadow later.

The ego is the outer reception centre of the psyche, inasmuch as it acts as the screening consciousness for the moment by moment perception of life as it interprets sense data and operates the voluntary and motor systems to respond to physical reality. It also checks and balances moods, thoughts and behaviour of the lower psyche. These manifest as various personae that make up a personality from what has been introjected or absorbed from the parents in particular, and from the environment in general. Thus, a combination of external influences and individual tendencies, based upon genetic and inherited qualities, together with the karmic and cosmic set of the incarnated psyche are synthesised to make up the distinct character of an ego. Being essentially a facilitator, the *Yesodic* ego has the faculty of adjusting to circumstances. This in most people is often limited, once the personality has become fixed, for few people are prepared to change after maturity, although the ego can be forced by dramatic circumstance, like becoming a prisoner of war, to cope with changing conditions. This, however, becomes increasingly difficult with the years as many middle-aged people discover as they find the World begins to regard their values, skills and manners as old fashioned.

In Kabbalah, the ego is regarded as a talented steward who serves the master of the Self. With its vast array of skills, it can perform and protect, provided it does not seek to steal the Self's role. One of the first lessons in inner development, is to perceive the *Yesodic* ego as an entity within the psyche and not, as most people consider it, one's identity. The ego is the instrument by which we can see the interior and exterior world. Its capacity, as go-between, is not to be underestimated, but nor should it be given credit beyond its scope. In some spiritual disciplines, the ego is denigrated, because it is considered to be inferior and gross. In Kabbalah it is seen as indeed the Foundation of the psyche and as such it should be encouraged to perform well. This leads up to the third component of Freud's basic system: the super-ego-ideal which counterbalances as the ego and the id within the psyche.

27. Super-Ego-Ideal

At the moment of birth, the psyche is not, as some believe, a blank record. It is a complete organism with memories of previous lives and a consciousness of what is going on. However, upon the fusion with the infant body, its experience and capacity is greatly limited, and it has to learn, from that moment of incarnation, to live a new life. Over time the consciousness of the pre-natal state is buried beneath the preoccupation with physicality, as the psyche adjusts to the laws of the natural world. It is also overlaid by the intake of new experiences that enter the psyche through the *Malkhut* of the body and *Yesod* of ego. At first the ego is developed in order to contain and control the primitive drives of the id-*Nefesh*, so that it can get the best out of the situation, as any animal will do. Thus, the child learns how to please its parents, and thereby gratify its needs, and avoid pain, because it recognises that food or love can be withdrawn if it does not comply with their will. This process builds up over the early years of life and forms what Freud called the super-ego and ego-ideal which we here combine into 'super-ego-ideal'.

According to the Freudians, the super-ego-ideal is the influence of the parents that emerges out of the ego's experience to act as an image of morality. Seen Kabbalistically this is *Binah-Hokhmah* or the interior mother and father in conjunction with *Gevurah* and *Hesed* and *Nezah* and *Hod*. Thus, the rewards granted by the parents accumulate around the right column of Mercy and their punishments focus on the left column of Severity. These aggregations are purely psychological, for it will be seen that the side triads have no direct contact with the physical Tree. As the emotional and conceptual elements of the psyche, they hold the individual and collective values of the person as passed on by the parents. The super-ego-ideal, however, is not the same as the soul which is composed of *Gevurah-Tiferet-Hesed*, constituting on the central column, the organ of conscience.

In most people, the introjection or absorption of their parents' values becomes their model of good and evil. For example, in some primitive tribes certain actions are taboo like not speaking to their mother-in-law, while in other communities it is considered bad taste if you are not courteous to your wife's mother. Many of these customs have lost their original purpose, but they form, along with those which are still practical, the rules of personal and social conduct. All this is imbibed by a child and reinforced in adulthood, so that a large reservoir of do's and don'ts is formed in the unconscious. These dictates are not to be confused with conscience, which means 'with knowing', whereas the super-ego-ideal is largely unconscious. Here it must be said that various schools of psychology use the term differently. In this work the above scheme will be used.

It is clear that what is introjected by the child is a mixture of what the parents say and what their society demands, which is not always the same. Thus, instead of having a well-integrated system of interrelated emotional complexes and concepts, there will be many clusters of associated positive and negative experiences that are not only unconnected but even opposed, which can create powerful tensions within a person's psyche. These can be quite unconscious conflicts that nevertheless influence an individual's thinking, feelings and actions. Moreover, while the innocence of childhood may be lost when the discrepancies between parents and society are perceived the super-ego-ideal still has its effect in adulthood. The ego-ideal aspect will manifest in high expectations of performance and ambition, while the super-ego element will chastise if the local values are contravened, because the deeply laid foundations of the early years are the bedrock upon which the structure of the psyche is set. This leads to the fact that if a psyche is well balanced, then a sense of certainty and confidence is established. If not, Freud observed, there is always a feeling of insecurity in the person, no matter how successful or affirmed the individual may be in later life. The Freudians see the solution to such problems in psychoanalysis where these early distortions are identified and resolved. Kabbalists use the same principles, but apply them in the world rather than in the consulting room so that a problem is solved by direct action.

The power of parental influence is enormous in a child, and while it may react this way or that to its upbringing, it will nevertheless transform his outlook into an interior authority and later project his values onto social authories, like teachers, police and political and religious figures. Under ordinary conditions, this is useful, because it controls the id-*Nefesh* impulses and helps a person integrate with his society. If, however, the inevitable rebellion of youth against parental authority is not contained by the individual's super-ego-ideal then the society will react *Gevuricly* with its social and penal laws, even as its *Hesed* rewards good conduct, according to its criteria, with wealth and honour. This mixture of personal and collective checks and balances is the basis of civilisation. The acquisition of manners in a primitive society or the notion of chivalry that expects a gentleman or gentlewoman to behave as such are more, however, than just veneer. Such things can produce events like the abolition of slavery, or create communities where people behave according to political or spiritual codes. The super-ego-ideal of some societies can, of course, be perverse, as in Medieval Spain, where it was an honour to be a member of the Inquisition that burned and tortured thousands of so-called heretics and apostates. Here we see the difference between custom and conscience; the former being the accepted norm, the latter based upon an eternal morality. This often causes a split between conformists who usually live in the ego, and individuals who see from the level of the Self and are no longer under the domination of the parental super-ego-ideal of the side pillars.

For those who are unaware of the difference between the ego and the Self, the substitute conscience of the super-ego-ideal operates unconsciously. For example, if such a person does, thinks or feels something socially improper, then a sense of guilt will arise from they know not where. Likewise, if they are performing well, according to their society, then a sense of well-being will arise often without their realising where it comes from. Further, sometimes if a person is deliberately breaking rules but refusing to acknowledge it, which is not uncommon, then the super-ego will impose its judgment down the side pillars and paths to affect *Malkhut* in an incident that punishes or draws attention to the misdemeanor. Such incidents can range from a small but significant mistake to an accident that spells out that something vital is amiss. Conversely, luck or good fortune can be attracted by the ego-ideal, which will create the psychological conditions for, perhaps, promotion because the person conforms to that society's model of what is right. This, of course, is contingent upon the values of that community, for reward has been known to be the privilege of being a human sacrifice. It depends on where you are fated to be incarnated.

Conscience is quite different from what is generally understood. It may be, as in most people a blend of custom and a genuine comprehension of morality. All religions have sought to raise their followers by instilling certain ethical tenets that lift local practices above the social level. For example, the Ten Commandments are a code that considers all the Worlds. The first three Commandments, which are related to the supernal *Sefirot*, are about God while the seven below *Daat*, the place of Knowledge, are about human conduct. *Hesed* and *Gevurah* speak of remembering the sabbath and honouring one's parents, while *Tiferet* talks of not murdering. *Nezah* and *Hod* are concerned with adultery and theft, and *Yesod* and *Malkhut* with speaking the truth and not coveting one's neighbour's property. The position of each Commandment on the Tree and their specific order form the basis of a morality that is concerned with the Divine, spirituality, the psyche and issues of the practical world. As such, they have a bearing upon a human being's place in the Universe and his relation to others and to God; thus they are the laws that apply, not just to this or that time and place but to all conditions and levels of development. Real conscience is concerned with these laws and is expressed in a saying found all over the world: "Do unto others as you would have them do unto you". Which is to say, you see them as the same Self or *Tiferet*.

The super-ego-ideal is the accumulated overlay of acquired experience and introjected authority. It acts within the psyche as the counterweight to the id-*Nefesh*, with the ego holding the balance between. As such it fills out the side triads of the psyche with a complete system of attitudes that governs the conduct of the individual in public if not in private. On the more sinister side it must be said that the super-ego-ideal is the basis of the psychological shadow that aids and abets the shadow of the id. For example, distorted values can can justify murder such as is found in the mafia's code when someone betrays the clan. It can also operate within so-called nice people who deliberately ignore someone in need of help, because they disapprove of them.

The super-ego-ideal is by no means a cohesive element. Indeed, some individuals have quite lop-sided Trees with too much emphasis on this or that triad or *Sefirah*, as groups of dominant emotions or ideas distort the person's view of reality. Many petty officials, for instance, suffer from an excessive super-ego and not a few do-gooders are so full of ego-ideals that they cannot see that their efforts could upset the balance of power and precipitate war. In most people, these discrepancies are not obvious, until they are placed under pressure. For a few, unfortunately, the imbalances are too great and the splits generated in childhood emerge in later years as personality disorders or psychological disturbances. However, as a Tree always seeks equilibrium so the id, ego and super-ego-ideal will compensate as interdependent operations. Let us now look at the psyche as a working system.

28. Working System

By the time the id, ego and super-ego-ideal complex are operational in the psyche, the individual is well, if not completely, incarnate. This means that the person has a relationship with the inner and outer worlds and can operate in both. However, it should be remembered that the psyche still only sees external reality in terms of sensual images, and most of what is seen is a very subjective view, according to personal temperament and culture. Thus, the Bedouin in the desert will see things no town-dweller would notice and vice versa. All that we perceive is greatly modified, moreover, by the interaction of the three systems we are about to examine.

According to many psychologists, the energy of the psyche is derived from the body. This one-world view is held because they do not recognise the existence of other dimensions and cannot grasp the reality of different worlds, each of which is a complete structure-dynamic cosmos. The truth is that physicality is confined to its own world and can only reach, in terms of the interpenetrating Trees of psyche and body, the coarsest level of the mind. No doubt exchanges and conversions of energy between the two organisms occur as thought and emotion are transformed into action, but these processes are communications through the *Daat-Yesod* connection of ego rather than massive interflows of energies. The brain is a highly complex mechanism compared with the stomach, but it is quite crude in operation next to the subtlety of the psyche.

Taking the lower level first, the energy generated by the body is used by instincts to keep it alive. According to Freudians this energy has a distinct characteristic in that it flows through an aim towards a specific object. Thus hunger in the body sets up the desire to eat and therefore to seek food. This process is basic, inasmuch as the id-*Nefesh* will always try to relieve any physical tension. When relief has been obtained the aim vanishes, and equilibrium is re-established until the next need arises. This continuous process that drives the organism is annotated as 'source', 'aim', 'object' and 'impetus' and sub-divided into 'internal aim', that is, equilibrium, and 'external aim', that is attaining the objective, such as food or sex. In itself, this process is quite repetitive and compulsive and corresponds to the vegetable triad of *Malkhut-Hod-Nezah* and *Yesod* in the body Tree.

Because the id-*Nefesh* has no discrimination, it can and will often produce, in the imagery of *Yesod*, a picture of what it desires. This is based upon the body's experience and the symbolic form the ego places upon such things as apples, which evoke all the qualities of the fruit and how it can satisfy. Such images, of course, cannot fulfil the need of the id-*Nefesh* and so action is planned to possess and eat it. This process can equally apply to acquiring a car or a sexual partner, the image of which is charged with what is called 'object-cathexis'. This means the object desired by the id becomes loaded with psychological interest or energy which originates in the *Yeziratic* vehicle of the psyche, not in the body. It also illustrates how many things are imbued with a dynamic that we give them, because of memory, desire, projection and many other associations that attach themselves to whatever we see or what the id-*Nefesh* targets. The reality is that psychological power is projected into any object that resembles what is in our mind at the moment. Freud argued that sex, for example, was projected into all sorts of objects, and this was because the id-*Nefesh* will seek release anywhere if it cannot be relieved by the normal means. This gives rise to the notion of displacement or energy taken away from its prime object and projected into another as a secondary release. The childless woman doting upon her cat, illustrates this. Indeed much of life is influenced by the association of common characteristics, which may not, in essence, be related. Once upon a time a suntan in winter was associated with the rich, as is a Rolls Royce thought of as synonymous with success, although in fact neither may be true. It is just a collective association. There are myriads of such things that are charged with psychological cathexis that stimulate interest. Advertising depends on it. Indeed the words 'new' and 'free' when applied to most objects will set the id-*Nefesh* working on finding a release and a sale for the producer who has stimulated the desire in the market place.

The ego's task in this tripartite system is to differentiate reality from fantasy. Experience shows that not every image of food, for example, can be eaten. It may just be the id using the ego's *Yesodic* imagination to say that it is hungry, if a picture of a hotdog comes to mind. The ego has the capacity to identify the difference because it refers to memory based upon experience that is filed in the psyche.

As the door-keeper between the inner and outer realities it will advise the person to hold on to the instinctive impulse until the moment is right to eat, for an adult cannot always just yell for food and get it if he wants it. This restraint is possible because of the many anti-cathected associations, as they are called, within the super-ego-ideal, that oppose the id-*Nefesh* even though it may have a delicious meal in front of it. Here we see how positively or negatively charged elements work to counterbalance each other. The function of the *Yesodic* ego is to see that the person relates their instinctive needs to what is socially acceptable. This gives the ego the crucial role of pivot between the side pillars and the upper and lower faces of the physical and psychological Trees.

The super-ego-ideal exists in a purely psychological world. As such it has little common sense, because it has no direct contact with physical reality. However like the id-*Nefesh* impulse the super-ego-ideal has its compulsions. From its unconscious pillars of Severity and Mercy it will relentlessly give out punishment and rewards based upon the thousands of cathexed and anticathexed charges that hold the emotional and intellectual associations in their active and passive side triads. These opposing and complementary galaxies of complexes are a fusion of the person's individual and collective experience which add up to a considerable influence. Most people are unaware of this until their psyche is perhaps momentarily unbalanced. An example of this is when a man picks up a lost wallet. The temptation to pocket it and thereby gain something somebody would have foregone anyway (id), is countered by the feeling of guilt and the thought, of what would happen, if he were found out (super-ego). The ego, as pig in the middle, might see images of the money being spent in a great splurge on the one hand and the trial scene in court on the other. Being the realist of tripartite system, the ego would then conclude that it would be best to take the wallet to the police station. Now while the id has been held in check by the super-ego, the ego-ideal then prompts the man to celebrate as a reward. This however may be countered by the ego which knows the man cannot afford it and he is merely deluding himself that he is honest, because for a moment his id-*Nefesh* nearly got away with it. Seen in modern mythology the ego has acted like a pragmatic U.S. marshal caught between a puritanical saint (super-ego-ideal) and a bandito (id) in a spaghetti Western movie.

There are occasions when the three part system does not always work so smoothly. Usually the super-ego-ideal will oppose any primitive moves made by the id, but sometimes there is confusion and even distortion. This can occur in personal crisis or in a social context. Take, for example, a country under invasion. The enemy are everywhere destroying not just the fabric of the towns but a whole way of life. The collective mind of the invaded people may then generate an image of the enemy as totally evil. This happens in most wars and soon quite stable and respectable individuals are making the most devastating attacks upon their foes as the mortido aspect of the id-*Nefesh*, backed by the super-ego, uses the ego's practicality to take vengeance on the intruders for trying to destroy their ego-ideal. Such things as freedom and religious or national identity are used to fan the wrath of the super-ego and spur on the id, as the ego image of people, fighting for whatever they believe in, obscures what they are actually doing. The same occurs at the personal level, when a man has his sense of reality disturbed by drugs or stress. If the ego is disabled by physical or psychological trauma, it may allow the id and the super-ego-ideal, both of which are irrational, to run riot. This can precipitate a violent outburst or a total mental collapse until the ego re-establishes stability and then supremacy over the uncontrolled interflow between the upper face of the body Tree and the lower face of the psyche. The normally conventional man who frequented brothels after losing his wife until he realised what he was doing is an example of this.

In less dramatic circumstances, the combination can be manipulated by any one of the factors. For example, the *Yesodic* ego, on seeing a particularly delicious cream-cake, can obliterate the super-ego's advice and enjoy it with the id. Likewise the passion of the id-*Nefesh* can be used to overcome the common sense of the ego, when courting a girl, who the ego-ideal usually mistakenly believes is perfect, because she conforms to its criteria. Many works of art have been created by the combining of *Nefesh* energy, *Yesodic* imagination and the super-ego-ideal's pursuit of excellence. These masterpieces, however, always have a feeling of unreality about them. The works of creation have another quality, and that is the dimension of the Self, which as *Tiferet* or the conscious arbitrator of Truth and Beauty introduces something of a higher order by its connection with the Worlds of Creation. That is why original art is so rare. The *Yesodic* ego is designed to manage everyday reality. As such it is supreme but it cannot see as deeply as *Tiferet* or create like the Self. It can only imitate, although superbly.

The power, structure, complexity and subtlety of the ego, however, should not be underestimated. It is the crucial clearing house between psyche and body. Its development and education, especially during the early years, will determine its capability in processing all the paths and triads convergent upon it, through which flow the impressions and drives of the id, and the dreams, projections and inspirations of the unconscious. A weak or narrowly focused ego is like a poor valve that controls very powerful forces that ebb and flow at many levels and in great variety. Consider walking down a familiar street. Many things are taken care of by this automatic pilot, as it reads a shopping list, ponders a professional problem, tries to deal with an unconscious worry or nagging leg pain, as you dodge through the traffic while talking politely with a friend who wants your attention. All this and more is going on at the same time, and the reason the ego can cope is because there are several psychological devices which prevent it from being overwhelmed by the outside world, the id-*Nefesh* and the unconscious. These are called by the technical term 'defence mechanisms' and they are vital in preserving the balance of the balance of the psyche.

29. Defence Mechanism

While an incarnating psyche may be advanced, it is still a shock to be born into the physical world. Initially the only way a baby can protect itself is to retreat into sleep or into what Freudians see as fantasy. Seen Kabbalistically, this is the withdrawal back into the realm of *Yezirah*, and some people can actually recall leaving the infantile body only to return when the new situation was acceptable. However, there does come a time when the individual has to cope with life on Earth. Here begins the battle between different realities that causes the phenomenon of anxiety.

One of Freud's most important observations was the effect of anxiety of the psyche and the way the tripart system of the ego, id and super-ego deal with them. For example, he noted that the id generates anxieties which distort the infant's picture of reality as it is dominated by its needs. In this context anxiety can be seen as a biological or *Asyyatic* tension affecting the psyche. But Freud also observed that some anxiety states were quite different from organic discomforts which arose and disappeared according to their fulfillment. These were disturbances which had no obvious source. Freud eventually defined three basic kinds of anxiety which relate to the three lower levels of reality.

The first was a general anxiety that had its roots in the external world. This was quite natural because it was created by the instincts to protect the individual from physical danger. Thus, being frightened of the dark or snakes was normal and formed the basis of a bio-psychological defence system which in Kabbalah relates to the World of *Asyyah*. The second type of anxiety was termed 'neurotic', and this was precipitated by an individual's own id-*Nefesh* drives. Here, the ego is not strong enough to hold the libido and mortido impulses firmly in check. This creates a feeling of insecurity in *Yesod*, the foundation of the psyche. An example of this might be the tension of sexual frustration or deep-seated anger or fear based upon some early experience. The individual in the wild can do many things to relieve such pressures in the dramas of survival, but the person in civilised society cannot obtain so easy a release, unless he or she finds a way acceptable to their super-ego-ideal. Such inhibited drives can build up enormous heads of energy that distort the lower face of the psychological Tree and threaten its efficiency. However, as the Tree is a self-regulating system, so it can adjust, at certain cost, and hold tensions in check until they can be released. The most obvious device for releasing pent-up forces is sport , which is a contained mortido operation seen at any Cup Final or World Series. In many cases, the mortido impulse that is not discharged may generate a neurotic fear of or love of destruction. This is witnessed in a pathological fascination with war and crime movies in which the death instinct is played out in *Yezirah*. Those who are obsessively opposed to such preoccupations are often applying another defence device to block the same drives in themselves. Here it must be noted that the mechanism is usually unconscious. This occurs because the super-ego-ideal, operating down the side pillars, allows *Yesod* to justify aggression in protest meetings which are often as militant as those who support their tribe or local football team. Many people, it has been observed, find great relief in the release of marches and matches.

The third form of anxiety is moral. Here, the super-ego-ideal brings pressure to bear on the ego from the unconscious. Values taken in from parents and society create pressure when the person thinks, feels, or does something contrary to their upbringing. The ego may make excuses, but the super-ego-ideal does not take these into account because it exists in a reality based upon collective laws. Having an illicit love affair can be rationalised by the ego, but the super-ego-ideal will still transmit its disapproval and give rise to deep unease in the lower face of the psyche. This is a phenomenon that has driven some to drink, which is a very practical form of ego defence. Moral anxiety is particularly common in spiritually-oriented people, who suffer the pangs of guilt without apparently having done anything evil. This is the result of a complicated situation for the Self, as *Tiferet* may be protecting the *Yesodic* ego to preserve its viability. If this were lost before the person was ready to cope with whatever the problem was, then a shattering of the psyche foundation could occur. An example of this was the man who was illegitimate and could not accept himself until he had found his inner identity. His unconscious guilt felt that it was his fault. From a karmic viewpoint he may have been right, but he was not yet ready to accept this. Few psychologists would take this dimension into account whereas no Kabbalist would leave it out.

There are many defence mechanisms. Some operate upon principles called 'displacement' and 'sublimation' in which the tensions are referred to somewhere else in the psyche or body or converted into something different until it can be resolved. In the normal process of psychological development personal quirks or minor illnesses indicate and alleviate tensions within the structures and dynamics of the psyche, while quite primitive impulses like obstinacy and competitiveness are transformed by the side *Sefirot* into quite harmless and indeed constructive modes, such as stamina and initiative. The conversion of id-*Nefesh* energy that is not used for sex, bringing up a family, or making a living can go into many kinds of activity ranging from playing games to pass the time to disciplines of self-development. All these processes draw upon energies that could disrupt the ego and so destroy its balance if it were not for the defence mechanisms. An example of this is the old spinster who knits socks for sailors because her long-dead sweetheart was a sea captain. She is guarding her mental equilibrium from emotions, thoughts and actions that could destroy her if she allowed them into her ego consciousness.

'Repression' is another form of defence system which operates by withdrawing the ego's attention from any difficulty it cannot cope with so that it does not disturb the *Yesodic* picture of the world or the person's image of themselves. The problem, however, remains and may return in another form out of the unconscious. This occurs because while the ego may have avoided the issue, the Self cannot. Moreover, fate often intervenes like the woman who crossed an ocean to avoid a sexual problem, but quickly set it up again with a new lover. This indicates that some devices do not block the side pillars or *Malkhut*.

'Reaction formation' is a term used to describe something that is repressed by being covered over with its opposite, so that *Yesod* presents the very reverse of what the psyche thinks or feels. An example of this is feigned love for someone the individual loathes because the social situation demands it. This process can also occur deep in the unconscious which seeks to counterbalance the ego's view. An instance of this is the double-talk of religious fanatics who preach love, but desire to dominate. Seen in Tree terms these are the outer pillars and upper and lower faces overcompensating for some excessive function.

The phenomenon of 'projection' is when something going on beyond the liminal line between *Hod* and *Nezah* but denied by *Yesod* is projected out on the world. This device gives free passage to many shadow aspects of the psyche that come down one side pillar so as to avoid going through the ego. An instance of is the puritan who sees dirt everywhere because he cannot acknowledge his own inner corruption. Projection can be used by either the id or the super-ego-ideal. It is seen most obviously in war propaganda that rejects the enemy as all bad while ignoring the home nations evils. The U.S.A. and U.S.S.R. see each other as imperialists, yet both view themselves as upholding revolutionary ideals.

'Introjection' is also used by the psyche as a defence mechanism in that it can absorb what can protect the person. For example, the ego may adopt the *Yesodic* image of a peer group in order not to be victimised by them. To wear the same outfit is to be safe in the clan, and the man who concurs with his boss's will, until he finds a more secure new job, is doing exactly the same. Here *Yesod* with its chameleon qualities protects the person by physical and psychological camouflage.

'Regression' is a mode by which the ego avoids a difficult present by retreating into the past. This may take the form of returning to, for instance, a state of childhood when life was less complex. The *Hodian* pastime of sailing toy boats is not just a hobby but a serious business for those who wish to escape reality. Many people regress without realising it when they smoke or take a drink in a tense situation as they unconsciously seek the security of the nipple, according to Freud. However, this release may be vital in order to protect them from what they really think and feel about their situation at that point. Here is where *Malkhut* takes over from the ego in sensual stimulation and relaxation.

Humour is a useful device that deals with awkward situations like the story of the rabbi whose brother was dishonest. The rabbi avoided him until he was confronted with the words "So who are you that you should avoid me? You have a brother who is a thief whereas my brother is a rabbi." This is the manipulation of *Yesod* and the super-ego-ideal in order to avoid a *Malkhutian* reality. The same is true of the man who said, "My wife divorced me for religious reasons. She worshipped money and I had none". Here reality is contrasted with fantasy in order to protect the ego of the husband. Such jokes are designed to devalue issues that could impair the psyche's balance. Abraham Lincoln was asked why he always told jokes during the worst moments of the American Civil War. He replied that he would break down under the strain if he did not. He was a depressive anyway and desperately needed to offset his left pillar of Severity.

'Fixation' is an important defence mechanism. It occurs when the psyche is retarded by some unresolved developmental problem. Thus, while the body and ego may appear adult, the psyche may be quite immature. For example, some women play the eternal girl, even when youth and beauty have gone, and some men will always behave like boys, though they may be six foot three or run a huge commercial company. This occurs because a vital stage of inner growth has not been completed. Such individuals often have a well fortified psychology that refuses to acknowledge what it cannot deal with, but this can lead to disaster. Many dictators have the fixated quality of still playing juvenile games in their public and private lives. Hitler's invasion of Russia was a childish fantasy. Napoleon's failure would have warned off most adults, but he went ahead and millions died. The eternal youth and maid may play the field, but at some point they meet their Waterloo as fate confronts them with a major crisis that forces them to grow. Such crises, be they national or individual, are designed by Providence to dissolve the defence system and prevent the fortress mentality from turning into a prison or asylum.

All the foregoing are but samples of the many defence systems that the psyche uses to protect its viability. Their function is to maintain the equilibrium of the psyche until the problem can be solved. Most of these mechanisms are quite unseen as they operate in the unconscious which we shall examine next as a general principle.

30. The Unconscious

The Freudian view of psychology lays strong emphasis upon the id-*Nefesh*. Indeed, Freud argued that the energy of the psyche was derived mainly from the id, which is why there is such preoccupation with satisfying the basic needs of a life, so that a person can survive and propagate. This is a specific standpoint and one that relates particularly to the body and lower psyche; the unconscious being largely, according to Freudians, concerned with id drives. The ego and the super-ego-ideal are seen as developments of the id that emerge to control the instincts, so that the most favourable conditions for fulfilment can be obtained. For example, people will not support someone who only considers himself, because society is a balance between personal necessity and communal needs that aid all. This means that socially unacceptable behaviour is repressed. It is nevertheless still at work in the unconscious of both the individual and the community. The recognition of this hidden dimension was Freud's chief contribution to psychology.

However, it must be said that Freud's discovery of the unconscious was not new. He himself acknowledged that the arts and philosophy were well aware of it; but it was he who brought it to the attention of the scientific world, although he had a difficult time getting them to accept its presence and power to influence. Later, his valuation of the unconscious, and the part it played in his scheme of the psyche, became less important, as his emphasis focused upon the id, ego and super-ego-ideal. This reveals the range of Freudian perception which, when placed upon Jacob's Ladder covers the body Tree and the lower face and middle zone of the psyche; the unconscious being a grey area above and beyond *Hod* and *Nezah*. This is where Freud and Jung parted company, for the latter was more interested in the higher dimension of the psyche and in the subdivisions of the unconscious.

Freud saw the archetypal levels of the mind, but he considered their symbolic imagery as mostly instinctive and sexual in origin. Here we see how even a great man's perception can be influenced by the astrological set of his psyche, for it is interesting to note that Freud had a Taurus Sun at his birth, which inclines a person towards the sensual and earthy, and a Gemini Moon, which gives an extremely analytical ego that is forever probing what the fixed sign of the Bull is absorbed in. Moreover, his Scorpio Ascendant not only gave rise to an acute sexual consciousness, but inclined him towards an in-depth investigation of the hidden. This combination of Scorpio *Malkhut*, Geminian *Yesod* and Taurean *Tiferet* is the essence of Freud's vision and preoccupations. Because he had such a temperament and was born at a specific time, he was in the right place to carry out his investigations and present his conclusions. These have evolved over the years, in conjunction with those who followed him, into a general plan of the unconscious which still varies in detail according to school. In Kabbalah the laws of the Tree indicate a distinct system of structures and dynamics and it is interesting to see how clinical observation matches what has been given out by esoteric Tradition regarding the anatomy of the psyche.

Now while Freud thought that the psyche's power came from the body, Kabbalah indicates that this is only true where the upper face of the body comes into contact with the lower face of the psyche. This means that the central nervous system, at the *Malkhut* of the psyche, is affected by the id-*Nefesh* as is the *Daat-Yesod*-ego, and to some degree the Self, which is at the *Keter* of the body Tree and the *Tiferet* of the psyche. The fact that the two Trees interconnect at the same level does not mean that they share the same reality, and indeed Freud's observations clearly differentiate between physical and psychological perception. It is the *Daat-Yesod* function of the ego that negotiates between the two worlds, and this suggests there are two quite different kinds of energy. In Kabbalah the body Tree would certainly contain the more obvious dynamic, but physicality cannot enter a more subtle order of reality, any more than a chimpanzee can comprehend the meaning of Hamlet, no matter how many performances it might see. The nature of the psyche is much finer and its form more delicate than any physical process or instinct. The conversion of practical experience through the *Daat-Yesod* interchange into the lower psyche is a quantum jump facilitated by consciousness which can move between different worlds in the ever-moving moment of 'now'. Thus, the continual screening of imagery in the ego is the place where physical and psychological realities can meet, as the person reacts to an exterior and interior situation. The effects of such transient moments, however, are not lost, but disappear across the liminal threshold into the unconscious which is a vast and complex library of experience distributed around the pillars, *Sefirot* and triads of the psychological Tree.

Those memories which can be retrieved into *Yesodic* consciousness of the ego are called 'preconscious'. These may range from what one was doing a moment ago, to events in the distant past. They can be fine details of information and mood, or general principles, the profound complexity of a relationship or the simplicity of a single action. All the *Yeziratic* forms of memory are charged with some emotion or idea. Some retrievable moments may be pleasing, others unpleasant, some will be highly infused with energy and others weak and just on the edge of recall. The chief characteristic, is that they can be brought across the liminal threshold and placed in the general sequence of thought, feeling and action that goes on in the *Yesodic* ego. As such, they are considered rational, even if incongruous at times, like the incongruous juxtaposition of two elements that occurs in all humour. The irrational begins on the margin between the preconscious and the unconscious. Here forms that have no bearing upon what is being done, thought or felt, flit across the ego's screen. For example, sometimes an idea will arise with such force that it makes one start, as if something were trying to intrude, and indeed this may be the case when the unconscious prods the conscious about some repressed issue that has been activated, such as the name of someone we prefer to forget. Here it must be said that repression in the general sense is an absolutely necessary function, or the *Yesodic* consciousness would be over cluttered and the beam of ego attention distracted by too many diversions. Sometimes the unconscious will draw attention to these repressed elements via dreams.

According to Freud's findings, day and night dreams reveal a kind of activity not unlike that within the body. Kabbalistically, the parallel is exact. These psychological processes of digestion assimilate material taken in by the ego and distribute energy and matter throughout the psyche. When the ego's attention is withdrawn from the issues that have preoccupied it, the residue is deposited behind the liminal line, some in the pre-conscious zone and the rest in the unconscious which Freud came to see as the reservoir of psychic energy and the storehouse of personal and archaic material that maintains the unseen life of the psyche. Seen in terms of the Tree, the side triads of complexes and concepts, with their positive or negative charges are like the hidden organs of the psyche, continually regulating the psyche's balance, in relation to ego consciousness. Thus, in the course of development, certain adjustments occur as the psyche's capacity enlarges and it shifts its equilibrium. If this does not happen, like a refusal to move from childhood to adolescence then the psyche becomes unstable and the unconscious has to regress in order to cope with and hold onto a familiar centre of gravity. Thus, for example, the *Sefirah* of *Hod* would became overactive as the person sought out the company of children or played childish pranks while his or her peers moved on. The correction of such fixations could be accomplished, according to Freud, by penetrating the unconscious and bringing the key experience that had stopped the processes of maturation into consciousness. This he argued would release the various cathexed and anticathexed charges and allow the delayed adjustment to occur. This was the other major discovery he made while mapping the lower psyche.

An example of this technique was the examination of dreams, because Freud thought that the unconscious often indicated by a dream's content what was the analysand's real difficulty. The problems of most psychotic patients were relatively easy to see in dreams, but with neurotics or people who were only temporarily disturbed this was not always so apparent, and much skill and patience has to be used to discern what is really going on within the psyche. For instance, a man might continually dream about knives. This could be symbolic of hate or judgment, a mortido impulse or sexual frustration or guilt. The Kabbalist would see it as a manifestation of *Gevurah* in whatever context it might occur; but Freud would probably have seen it as a strong id-*Nefesh* wish that sought to be fulfilled when the restraint of ego removed by sleep allowed some unconscious desire to express itself. Unfortunately the psyche as we have seen is a highly complex organism and it is not always clear where such symbols originate. This is made yet more difficult because the *Yeziratic* world of the unconscious does not obey the laws of physical reality. Time and space are quite different, as any dreamer knows and such processes as 'condensation' can for example, compress complicated problems into simple ciphers or even reverse unacceptable emotions like hate into their opposites, as the cathexed memories are checked and counter-checked by the super-ego-ideal, distort the material stored in the unconscious. Over a lifetime layer upon layer and larger and larger groups of associated concepts and complexes accumulate in the unconscious to give an individual a distinct character. This can be seen by the perceptive observer in the form of the body which expresses the nature of the psyche that inhabits it. This is because of the law that the lower world always conforms to the higher. In Kabbalah the reading of character by the face was considered an important art, for by its features a person's state of soul and level of spirit, that is, the unconscious, could be discerned.

Now while the unconscious may appear to be an incoherent muddle to the untrained eye it is, as we can see by the way it fits into the Tree, a well-ordered scheme that absorbs experiences and processes them at various levels before integrating them into the psyche. An exact analogy is the way an embryo takes in all the elements and builds up a highly sophisticated system of cells and organs which operate at many different levels as a unified whole. In the case of the psyche, however, the process of growth does not cease on attaining physical maturity, but goes on all through life. Freud, who could not take into account the occult or spiritual dimensions, because he wanted to address a purely scientific audience, only considered the development of the psyche up to adulthood, which he saw in the physical and social terms of his time. Indeed he was extremely pessimistic about mankind as an evolving species, because he would not go beyond the id-*Nefesh* and the lower level of the psyche. The unconscious was too intangible and bound up, he argued, with early memories and instinctive needs. While this may be true of much of humanity, it is not so for many people who have reached their prime and want more out of life than having their material and egocentric wants satisfied. For such people the unconscious is often the spur for further inner development, because it contains all that has been experienced and constitutes the story of their fate so far. This state usually occurs when the individual has reached a certain level of adulthood. But before going on to this, let us take a more detailed look at what Freud meant by maturity.

31. Maturity

From the moment of conception, when the psyche becomes connected with the fertilised ovum, the individual has to cope with physical reality. This begins with the growth of perception and learning how to exist in the environment. Later the family and the cultural situation in which Providence has placed that individual has to be accommodated. From birth to puberty the speed of growth is rapid, each day bringing a new experience and phase of development. From time to time major changes occur, as the body reaches a frontier of competence and the psyche uses what it has learned to negotiate an ever-widening world. From puberty to bodily maturity the rapidity of development slows down, although the process of transformation is no less dramatic. By the time a person reaches his prime in the twenties, a certain stability begins to assert itself as personal habits become set and a place is found in the world. All this applies to the average human being who lives a conventional life. There are, of course, exceptions where people leave their locality and break out of the pattern, but on the whole most of the people stay stays within their cultural orbit even if they migrate like gypsies. This stability is usually maintained for the rest of life unless some major event, such as a war or economic recession disrupts it. But even then most people will seek to recreate the established mode as a father becomes like his father and the mother acts out her own mother's ways after they mature.

The Freudians recognise little change after maturation except under unusual circumstances. Thus, having reached a physical peak, the psyche ceases, in most cases, to develop. This viewpoint is based upon the idea that the mind is a part of the body and has no independent existence. Many psychologists hold this belief, as there is much evidence to prove the case that most people do not go beyond physical and social maturity. Indeed many individuals start to regress in midlife, before lapsing into infantile senility in old age. Because this is the rule rather than the exception many psychologists have related the psyche to the physical phases of early development. Freud's observation of the oral, anal, phallic and genital stages of consciousness led him to believe that these were crucial in the developmental process of the psyche, because their arising and resolution formed the basis of maturity, or immaturity if the process got stuck at certain points in their unfoldment. For example, an incomplete anal stage could, it was felt, generate a pathological meanness, while the Oedipal stage of an infant and how it related to its parents profoundly affected its adult sexuality. These conclusions would be valid if only the id-*Nefesh*, *Daat-Yesod* ego levels were involved. However, here we must apply the esoteric maxim of 'what was said, by whom, to whom and and for who else to hear' because Freud had to formulate his conclusions very carefully for an openly hostile audience. Therefore we must give him the benefit of the doubt and suspect there was much more to what he thought then he let out into the public domain.

The 'classical' picture of a mature and stable personality is that all the psychological systems are more or less operational. The id is contained and channelled, the super-ego-ideal is relatively balanced, and the ego maintains a sense of reality. However, this picture does not mean that the person is mature. It is quite possible, for example, for someone who is quite juvenile to find a niche in life that does not require him to take on adult responsibilities. Some people get by, playing games, like the 'broken wing' act that evinces help, which allow them to live quite securely provided they are supported just as some nymphomaniacs are quite stable as long as they have lovers. So the obvious criteria of maturity are not valid. For example, many people can operate, because there is a massive compensation in one of the triads or *Sefirot*. The minor official, for instance, with an overactive *Hod* can be protected by the rigidity of a bureaucratic system while the aggressive persona of, say a sergeant-major, over-laying a weak ego will preserve it from internal or external assault by military discipline. Such compensated imbalances are not uncom-mon in apparently quite socially acceptable people such as the cool airline pilot who was totally irrational in his private life.

What could be thought of as a truly mature and stable psyche is when the loading of the two sides of the Tree is roughly equal. Thus the positively charged cathexis of the dynamic concepts and emotions are held in balance by their anticathexed counterparts, thereby allowing the Tree a certain flexibility of movement which is not possible if one of the pillars is strongly predominant. The Freudian definition of 'repetitious compulsion', for example, is a

Nezahian cycle that maintains the momentum of many of our routines, while its *Hod* counterpart adjusts the fine focus of the operation, such as driving a car while map-reading. Likewise, the problem of tension and its release is accommodated, in the mature psyche, by the channelling and dispersal of id-*Nefesh* drives into the many skills and interests that an adult develops. Thus through displacement and multiple differentiation, for example, energy, that in childhood or adolescence would have burst out of a limited repertoire of controls in some violent episode, is held and directed into a more diverse and useful form of activity. All this suggests that the psyche is capable of developing a highly refined and complex internal organisation. The essentials for this are there at birth in the *Yeziratic* vehicle, even as the embryonic nervous system exists in the infant. Over the years of growth and education the form of this *Yeziratic* body is evolved by, for instance, language which takes an experience and divides it into the subtleties of thought and feeling that feed the conceptual and emotional triads. These in turn form complex sub-systems which can carry and absorb a very powerful shock such as the breakdown of a marriage and hold the psyche in a secure posture until the crisis has passed. An unstable psyche cannot cope with such traumas and will regress, for example, to an infantile state, such as violence or self pity, taking to drink or sex in order to obliterate reality. The mature psyche can grieve deeply, but ride out the storm of failure, because the balance of the mind is basically sound, which means the Tree is well established in the *Malkhut* of the body, secure in the ego of *Yesod* and has the two outer pillars, symbolised by the super-ego-ideal, in a flexible equilibrium.

This stability is only possible when the infrastructure of the psyche has been filled out, so that there is a reduced chance of a massive disruption, like a psychological burst blood vessel. For instance, the processes of introjection and projection do not distort the ego if the super-ego-ideal is sufficiently modified by experience not to expect impossible standards, based upon a childhood model which may well be redundant. Situations are handled in a mature compromise between what *can* be rather than what *should* be. This realism arises out of the emergence of the *Gevurah-Tiferet-Hesed* triad of the soul, which through moments of Self-consciousness, perceives what is really feasible for that person. The Self at *Tiferet* acts as the balancing pivot or the 'Watcher' in most people's unconscious, which alerts us, often by dream or omen, to shift our attention to something that needs correcting. The mature psyche will recognise such a sign and take action. Here begins the possibility of further development, yet few people heed the instruction of the Self and most will revert to a habit-oriented view of life and the world. This is why fate sometimes sends the shock of crisis in order to move the psyche on from a comfortable but slumbering state of stagnation. This is where some knowledge of astrology is most useful.

In the process of maturation, the experience gained from the moment of birth is slowly worked upon deep in the psyche. For most it is a completely unconscious procedure as thoughts, feelings and actions which have been, if only for a moment, in the ego's spotlight are sorted out and related within the structure and dynamics of the Tree, into their respective orders and relationship. This differentiation and integration begins to manifest, in Kabbalistic terms, as Understanding and Wisdom, as the two *Sefirot* of *Binah* and *Hokhmah* at the head of the left and right columns process experience. As such they give an intellectual weight to the comments of mature people who acquire, over the years, an increasingly broader and deeper view of life. It has been said that by the time one reaches forty, one is either a fool or a scoundrel. Such an observation, however, can be taken many ways. To the worldly oriented, it means you have or you have not 'made it'; but then many who have fulfilled their ambitions are often no more than overgrown children playing with expensive toys. To be a scoundrel could also mean that one is a master of one's situation and can manipulate events. It might also be said that to be a fool indicates that one still retains one's innocence and has not been corrupted. These different interpretations suggest that there are different levels of stability and maturity.

According to Kabbalah the psyche contains the Soul and the lower part of the Spirit, as well as the Divine connection in our being. For most, these hidden levels belong to a mysterious zone deep within the unconscious. Sometimes, however, people do remember, as they move through the phases of life, that they came from another place, to which they will return on death. This realisation is announced by the occasional experience of being a stranger to the Earth, suddenly seeing a different reality in a flash of illumination or through dreams. Here is where psychologist and Kabbalist can meet at the door which opens out on the inner and upper worlds.

32. Dreams

In the midst of routine and rationality is the realm of the dream. No matter how well ordered a person may be, or how controlling of their thoughts, feelings and actions, there is that strange space in which the irrational manifests and sometimes intrudes with enormous power, as the unconscious fleetingly touches, pervades or even invades the processes of the ego with its world of imagery. All people day dream; for most it is usually in the form of reviews of past events, or projections into the future, with a touch of fantasy added to distort reality in this or that direction. Many recognise this as wishful thinking and regard them as controlled fantasies. Others just drift off into make-believe, living out some idle story that may relate to reality or be totally remote from anything in their outer life. Some people have been known to spend more time in this zone between two worlds than they do anywhere else. These people can range from lunatics to luminaries.

Seen Kabbalistically, dreaming is when the *Yesodic* screen of the ego receives an irrational input from either the side pillars or *Tiferet*, as against a rationalistic one from the body's *Daat* or sensory-motor impressions of *Malkhut*. At such moments, there is a slight separation of the body and psyche, which loosens the ego's hold on the outer world and allows the unconscious to override the normal perception of reality that keeps the person in touch with the mundane. In sleep this separation is increased, as the reticular formation of the mid-brain that governs the flow between the higher levels of cerebral activity, cuts off the impulses coming from the rest of the nervous system. The result is not less activity, but an altered state of consciousness which is not dependent upon the sense organs. In other words, the *Malkhut* of the psyche is separated, but not disconnected, from the *Tiferet* of the body. During sleep the brain appears to modify its pattern of rhythms generating periods of great activity which are associated with dreaming. Biologists have not yet determined what exactly sleep is, even though they can monitor its mechanical, chemical and electrical manifestations. Psychologists see sleep as a period of unconscious work in which many psychological

146

processes go on. This conclusion is based upon the phenomenon of dreaming.

Freud saw dreams as a way of gaining a deeper insight into the structure and dynamics of the unconscious. Indeed, he called it the 'royal road' into that realm. His first conclusion was, as said, that most dreams were wish fulfilling and that many were sexual in origin. For example, the resolution of tensions that could not be satisfied in outer life, such as making love with unattainable people or succeeding where only failure could be expected. This occurred, he concluded, because the rational ego was dormant and the super-ego-ideal appeared to be partly disabled, although it was observed that it could take part in the strange symbolic plays that the unconscious put on. Such dramas were seen by Freud as having an obvious or manifest content, and a latent or hidden meaning, as well as being a condensation of what was going on in the unconscious. He detected, moreover, much distortion and many contradictions in the format of dreams in order to cover or indicate the meaning being communicated to the ego. Over time certain principles emerged so that he began to recognise key elements common to all dreams. He discovered that certain symbols invariably, but not always, said the same thing. The image of a king was often a picture of the patient's father and being drawn out of water usually touched on events related to birth, even as trains in dreams appeared to be concerns about death. These later became useful for decoding what was going on in the unconscious.

In Kabbalah, the World of *Yezirah* is the realm of forms and symbols. Moreover, its traditional element is water, and indeed the dream dimension has that fluidic quality as it adopts whatever thought, form or emotion that impels it. Freud recognised the language of symbolism, but he related it to things and situations that the person encountered in his life, arguing that the unconscious used whatever was to hand to express this or that issue of the moment. Thus he would analyse a dream according to the person's background and relate it, after seeing what associations it connected with, to the problem that was making itself apparent in the dream. From here he would probe to find the knot that was seeking to be untied. Once identified, he would try to bring what was inaccessible in the unconscious into consciousness and so resolve, perhaps some old difficulty with the patient's father. In terms of the Tree he was adjusting the balance between the emotional and conceptual triads of structure and dynamics, through the medium of the *Yesodic* ego, having been given a series of clues as to what in the aberration might be. An example of this was the recurrent dream of a woman about a benign despot who she sought to overthrow. Analysis of the dream and her situation eventually led this seemingly, well-controlled person to the realisation that she resented her husband, even though they were on the most polite and even affectionate terms. Twenty years of habit, social appearance and material security might support the ego image, but it did not fool the Self deep within the unconscious which expressed a nagging dissatisfaction with a marriage in which she felt a kept adolescent.

Jung's view of dreams was somewhat different. While he agreed with Freud that many dreams were concerned with unresolved yearnings, he did not see them as predominantly instinctive. He perceived the more memorable as being related to the person's psychological development rather than to the unsatisfied drives of the id. Such dreams he called 'numinous', because for him they had the quality of another world. He recognised the distinct difference between the body-psyche levels of the unconscious and the purely psychological. Indeed, he went further and detected the spiritual dimension of these 'big' dreams as he called them. He saw, like the ancient esoterics that he studied, that the symbolism of dreams was not always related to the personal, but could be archetypal, that is purely psychological or spiritual principles, and so he related the dreams of his clients to mythology which describe in story and symbol the processes of the collective unconscious of mankind. Seen Kabbalistically archetypes are the forms of *Yezirah* and the creative modes of the *Beriatic* World.

Such a view, along with other factors, divided Freud and Jung, and they went their respective ways, with their schools, to differentiate the various levels of what Freud called 'dream work'. Jung, for example, examined the dreams of a person over a long period, in order to see if a sequence unfolded, because he believed there was a distinct progression to be observed. To him it was not just a question of detecting and releasing fixations, but of helping the person to develop their psyche through what he perceived as archetypal situations, which when brought into consciousness aided them to become individuals. Jung saw the symbolism in dreams not as disguised representations of id drives, but as a method by which the person was shown a way of being truly themselves. This was quite different from the *Yesod*-ego orientated view of Freud. Jung's psychology was pivoted upon the *Sefirah* of *Tiferet* or the Self at the centre of the *Yeziratic* Tree. He saw dreams as an attempt by the Self, which could perceive the psyche as a whole, to differentiate and refine its disparate elements into an integrated unity. This is why he found so much in common with the discipline of alchemy and many other esoteric traditions including Kabbalah.

In Kabbalah dreams are divided into three categories. The first is concerned with immediate events. This means those involving the three triads centred upon the *Yesodic*-ego that often carry over into sleep the momentum of mundane activities, such as dreaming that one is still driving a car after a long journey. The second order is of a deeper nature and is focused upon *Tiferet*-Self. Here issues of the soul and the individual's integrity are brought out of the unconscious and projected onto the screen of *Yesod* during sleep so that the ego's attention is awakened to the problem. An example of this might be the dream about a wedding in which the individual is seen espoused to the right or wrong person, and the result of the marriage to whatever the partner symbolises internally or externally. Such dreams are considered in the light of the symbols used for the various *Sefirot*, which are in essence the archetypes of Jung. Reflection upon, say, the relationship between the traditional image of Adam and Eve, associated with *Hokhmah* and *Binah* will tell much about the state of the animus and anima, if they, or something of the masculine and feminine principles, occur in a dream.

The third order of dream, in Kabbalah, is called prophetic, and Jung had experience of this when he observed, between the world wars, how various German patients spoke about 'the blond beast' coming out of its underground prison in their dreams. Here is the voice of the collective unconscious, defined by the upper face of the psychological Tree, speaking through, what is called in the Bible, the 'lesser prophecy' of sleepers. The greater prophets were considered to be awake when they were given these visions. These insights belonged to the *Beriatic* dimension and the upper central column whereas most dreams originate in the side triads or the *Tiferet* of Self, to be seen fleetingly in the sleeper's *Yesod*. By combining Freud, Jung and Kabbalah we have a more coherent picture of the World of *Yezirah*, as experienced by the individual, when detached from sensory consciousness. According to tradition, the soul, during sleep, is free to wander about in the World of Formation, although the physical connection is never broken. Many dreams have the quality of 'astral travel', as some call it, for the psyche 'floats' during sleep in a zone that is of a quite different order of reality. Such unearthly experiences are not uncommon, as the psyche, being without the weight of physicality to hold it down, seeks its true level in *Yezirah*. For sleepers still at the stage of the ego-*Yesod* the lower, more mundane stratum of *Yezirah* will be their area, while those who seek the Self will rise to less dense altitudes where a purer form of psychological symbolism will occur. Individuals of a greater development ascend to the upper face of *Yezirah* and the lower face of *Beriah* or the transpersonal realm of the Spirit. Here the most highly evolved individuals commune with the Divine during deep sleep and receive revelations 'face to face', as the Bible puts it. However, as in everything Kabbalah urges balance, for to become too preoccupied with dreams is to live in the wrong world. We here on Earth must work with the World of *Assyah* and therefore only those dreams that are naturally remembered should be noted. This was the psyche's original intention. To examine every dream can become obsessional, like X-raying our alimentary canal every time we have a meal. Excessive scrutiny of dreams can lose the emphasis and, therefore, what the unconscious is telling us, which could result in an unnecessary crisis. This brings us to the theme of imbalance in the mind and the problems of psychopathology.

33. Psychopathology

Everyone is familiar with the phenomenon of the phase just before one falls asleep or wakes up. It is a twilight zone of consciousness where dream and reality blend. At such moments sense impressions can trigger off fantasies and images from the unconscious and generate sensual experience. This area lies in the psycho-physical space between the *Yesod* of the psyche and the *Daat* of the body, just before they separate in sleep, or fuse, prior to becoming fully awake when the distinction between the worlds is resolved by outward orientation. In some abnormal situations, this process may be retarded, so that it becomes an area of confusion, such as in the delirium of fever, or a refuge from reality, as happens in schizophrenia. The reason for such events can be simple or complex, but whatever it is, it indicates an imbalance within the body or psyche or both.

In body-based disorientations purely physical conditions can alter the brain's chemistry to produce delusions. Alcohol poisoning, for example, or excessive malnutrition will distort the ego's perceptions and allow the id-*Nefesh* or unconscious impulses to flood the screen of *Yesod* to confuse the person. With psychologically generated situations the disability is not so easily identified and corrected. Here is where therapists divide into Aristotelians or Platonists. The pure mechanist naturally sees the problem and solution in the body and perceives all mental disturbances as entirely organic. This may be true in some cases, but the question is, does the body create or respond to a psychological disorder? The very word 'dis-ease' gives a clue, in that something is out of its proper place, which is compensated by the malfunction of something else. Seen in terms of the Trees of body and psyche many diseases can be seen as referred malfunctions, at the corresponding level, above or below the seat of the trouble. For example, the feeling triad of *Hod-Nezah-Yesod* relates to the organ triad of *Hod-Yesod-Nezah* in the body, while *Hod-Yesod-Malkhut* triad of thinking corresponds with the body triad of nerves, so that any difficulty in one will generate a resonance in the other. For instance, excessive worry can start stomach disorders,

151

and panic thinking makes people physically nervous.

Psychological disturbances can be permanent or transient. An accident, for example, often disorientates the body and psychological Trees for a day or so as the *Yesod-Daat* connection is lost and the ego is deranged. Sometimes months are spent in this state after the end of a deep love affair. It is well known that divorce can disturb quite balanced people for several years, so that their perception of reality is quite distorted, as their egos and emotional and conceptual triads take their time to steady and reorganise a traumatised Tree. In most cases the psyche will eventually bring itself back into balance, providing there is not a deep-seated lesion in the person that goes back to their early years or beyond.

As we have seen, the moment of incarnation is a traumatic one. Suddenly one is confined to a small and ineffective body after being in a relatively free space and time dimension. The impact of the elements, gravity and the fierce demands of the id-*Nefesh*, that cohabits the body with the psyche, must impose an enormous strain, which is initially offset by the physical and psychological support of the mother. This backup is crucial and must have a profound effect on the totally dependent infant. If the vital needs of those first few hours, days and weeks are not met, however, then the lower face of the psyche is often not properly welded into the upper face of the body Tree. This could create an incorrectly fused *Daat-Yesod* or ego so that the person is never quite earthbound or sees the world through a deformed *Yesodic* screen. In many cases, there is a correction, as the individual's early life usually provides the solution to the first problem that fate has set it. The extra care given to most ailing children is an example. Not all deprived infants become crippled in mind.

The factor of fate does not come into many psychologists' consideration, even though it is the groundbed of life and explains why this person behaves in this particular way and that person in that, although they may be born within the same environment. For instance, even identical twins, who are rarely born at exactly the same time, are subject to quite different fates, in that they have to work out some ancient relationship in a new way, with each reacting according to their understanding of the situation. Here, we have the factor of free-will and different levels of development. For example, one twin might be only concerned with the material, while the other is preoccupied with the moral, so that one responds to their common situation by becoming a policeman and the other a criminal as they take up the light and shadow of each other's super-ego-ideal. The place of birth is not accidental, nor are the problems encountered therein. The fool might well be born a king, and the genius into a merchant's house, or even in the jungle. One spiritual giant was born into a carpenter's family and another began life as a prince. Parents and environment play their role, but more important is how the individual reacts to his or her lot.

Keeping the dimension of fate in mind, and the facility of free-will, which operates in the infant, as well as in the adult, there are the various phases that everyone has to go through. Failure to complete these phases can be the source of mental sickness or psychopathology. The first process is that of symbiosis with the mother. This critical period of infancy can produce, on the one hand, an over-protected situation, if taken to one extreme, or naked deprivation, at the other. Both will leave their mark on the individual, so that as adults they will either expect the world to give them what they want or believe the world has rejected them. Both types, under stress, can revert to having an infantile tantrum or resort to sullen retreat. This is a regression back into a condition of narcissism in which they become the egocentric pivot of their own universe. Such a state might be shallow or deep, depending upon choice and circumstance. Fortunately the laws of karma provide many opportunities to break what could become a psychopathic pattern. At first, fate is often very gentle in setting up a situation that could solve the problem, such as meeting just the person to help. This is often seen in the archetypal 'rescue' relationship of the saint and the sinner. If this chance is rejected then the pressure is increased, so that a progressively more difficult life circumstance is met, where people become increasingly less sympathetic to the child's psyche in an adult's body. It is interesting to note that such people often know exactly what they are doing, but choose not to stop their games because it brings their ego much solace. One sign is that they frequently move from situation to situation endlessly recreating the same egocentric result until they come to a crisis point in which fate usually gives them the possibility to dissolve the problem and move on into maturity. Many recognise and seize the moment to cut the fixated knot that binds them, but some wishing to hold onto their narcissistic view of life seek to maintain it by entering a twilight zone in which fantasy and reality merge. As such they are trapped between *Assyah* and *Yezirah* like early morning dreamers who are not sure which world they are in. In ancient times, such people were called lunatics, because like the Moon, which is the symbol of *Yesod* and the ego, they circle and hang between Heaven and Earth without being in contact with either. In Kabbalistic terms they are caught in the world of *Yezirah* without any contact with the worlds above and below.

All the foregoing applies in principle to each stage of development. The problems of identity, relation to parents, sibling rivalry and social relationships arise in a definite sequence and are dealt with by adjustment, expansion and absorption. If this does not occur, then the process is locked into a retarded configuration, until the imbalance is resolved in the normal course of life, or with help. If the difficulty is not recognised then the problem can deepen with time, as flexibility is lost and the Tree becomes distorted and compensated by patterns that could generate symptoms of stress and then disease. In some cases, a fixation may show up as no more than a quirk in the personality, like collecting teddy bears which could represent the lack of a loving father. In another, it might be noticeable enough to be classified as a phobia of basements which could be rooted in some early experience of being crushed in an air raid shelter. A very common neurosis is evident in a person who is continuously but not seriously ill, which can be a way of getting the special treatment they were deprived of as children. The problems of newly-weds often, for example bring up the issue of parental models that each partner projects onto the other. This can cause a crisis in the spouse who cannot break out of reinacting what was introjected as a child. Here is where the archetypal mother and father images inherent in the super-ego-ideal can shatter in the face of reality, resulting in the collapse of all marital expectations.

Most neuroses are more than just anxieties. They are often the sign of conflicts within the psyche that deplete a person's ability to live their life normally, whatever that may mean. In Tree terms it is when one group of complexes or concepts, blocks the flow of another, or constrains one of the triads or *Sefirot* to such an extent that it cannot function properly. An example of this is an over-judgmental *Gevurah* which constricts any allowance made by *Hesed* and its associate triads of intellectual stimulation and emotional expression. This could produce a neurotic tendency to be hypercritical or pernick-ety, so that the cleaning of a house or office becomes more important than its being a home or place for creativity. Such a tendency might go back to pot training, but it can also be argued that an obsession with purity is already inherent in the psyche, and therefore built into the fate, which is designed to meet and deal with a problem that perhaps dominated the last life. One person, for example, remembers being a nun and was obsessed with keeping her house clean. Fate gave her an untidy but affectionate husband to teach her balance.

Some signs of a psychopathology may not manifest until well into adulthood when a person becomes responsible for themselves and perhaps others in work or partnership. In such cases the sense of unease is often present long before odd behaviour indicates something is amiss. Frustration, disappointment and setback are the usual triggers which start the process of regression that takes the person back to where the problem began. If this is not seen and resolved then symptom formation begins in the Tree and the malfunction of the psyche increases as the three triads around the ego start to break down. For example, in excessive moods or lack of feeling, thoughts can become obsessive or scrambled and action inappropriate or disproportionate. Very often dissociation from people and external events occurs as the *Daat-Yesod* components of ego begin to fracture. This may be no more than a neurotic reaction under a specific tension which may pass when the stress is eased, or it might be more serious, in that the individual is oblivious to what is happening and, indeed, believes wholeheartedly that their distorted experience is reality. This is where the twilight zone becomes the battleground between the id-*Nefesh* and the super-ego-ideal, with the ego betwixt the two trying to keep some kind of working stability. If it fails and chaos ensues, then psychosis takes over, profoundly disrupting the overall balance of the Tree of the psyche. If the situation is fundamental then madness can eclipse the life.

34. Madness

The difference between neuroses and psychoses is that the neurotic is aware of a psychological conflict and the psychotic is not. This marks a quite different order of psychopathology. Conflict within the psyche is not unusual, as various elements struggle for ascendancy, balance and compensation. In most people the tension between different needs, ideas and emotions can be accommodated, but in those who have a basic imbalance because of a trauma or fixation, the situation can approach a critical point in which the psyche cannot maintain an operational level. 'Symptom formation' is a warning that such a possibility is present. For example, most phobias are devices to avoid facing a breaking point. Fear of dogs, for instance, may guard the person from their own savage anger which they refuse to acknowledge, while agrophobia, or fear of open spaces, might relate to the feeling of being exposed and therefore highly vulnerable — which could lead to an uncontrollable panic. The list of phobias is enormous, but their function is the same: that is, to protect the person from themselves. Seen in Tree terms a phobia is when the left-hand side of the psyche holds the right in check. For example, an exacting *Hod* restrains a wild *Nezah*, while a severe *Gevurah* ties down an over-expansive *Hesed* and a heavy *Binah* blocks an erratic *Hokhmah*. If the left pillar did not have the power of fear then the right column might explode in a disintegration of sanity, so the person believes, hence a phobia which means 'fear'.

Between the neurotic and psychotic is the hysteric. In such individuals internal conflicts are relieved by 'conversion reaction'. In this process, the problem is relayed, by sympathetic resonance, from the Tree of the psyche to that of the body so that psychological blindness or deafness becomes physical. Here the *Yesodic* ego transfers what it cannot face, through *Daat* and the side pillars into the corresponding triads of the body Tree. This has a twofold 'payoff'. First, the individual avoids the problem, and as a 'secondary gain' special concessions are evinced from others. This is the pattern of many hypochondriacs whose symptoms often have no physical reality. Such a discovery gave rise to the notion that mental illness was not always organic, as had been believed.

Madness is a relative term. For example, there are many people, who although quite insane, can nevertheless run a job or even a country, provided that they are not placed under stress. If a critical situation does occur, it can break the *Yesodic* defence system and precipitate a psychological crisis. An example of this is the manic-depressive who oscillates between the side pillars. As long as neither extreme is reached, the integrity of the Tree is maintained, but should circumstance decree an excessive dose of success or failure, then one side of the Tree will overthrow the counter-balance of the other, perhaps triggering a period of uncontrollable mania or deep suicidal depression. For example, an eminent scholar with a very clever *Hod* was humiliated in a major intellectual battle. This caused the loss of his *Yesodic* image of himself as a brilliant academic. He was so unhinged that his left pillar collapsed and he broke down in wild outbursts that released all the power of an unrestrained right pillar in an insane orgy of sex and drink before he burnt himself out. In some cases, the breakdown could occur in the vertical balance of id and super-ego-ideal, when a person oscillates between ultra-introversion and extraversion. Such instances may be just personality disorders or they may be deeper and pathological. Here it should be noted that not all psychopaths are in asylums. Many quite famous people come into this class. The highly-decorated soldier could be a homicidal killer, while the sex symbol film star might be a nymphomaniac, who, like the hero, was in just the place where their madness fitted in with what was needed. Many historic and renowned figures were psychopaths. Hitler's megalomania was not recognised until it was too late.

Psychosis appears at the point when the ego no longer relates events in the exterior world to what is happening in the psyche. This might take the form of inflation, in which the *Yesodic* image is blown up to be the King of the Universe, or deflated into being a non-person. The mechanism of this is that, when an inner conflict occurs, various aspects of the psyche split off in order to avoid a major confrontation within the Tree. Such an operation, however, cannot be successful if the *Yesodic* foundation of the ego is impaired. In this situation, the Tree is distorted as the flows between the pivotal position of *Tiferet* and the adjacent triads and side *Sefirot* are pushed out of balance. Over a long period, this can cause a gradual fragmentation or, in some circumstances, a dramatic loss of the cohesiveness of the psyche in psychotic breakdown. In this the pillars, *Sefirot* and triads release their hold and the id-*Nefesh* and all the energy locked up in the complexes and concepts break out or implode within the person. If the process of disintegration is not fatal then a partial recovery can be expected, as the Tree will always seek to heal itself by finding some lower point of operational equilibrium such as is found in many vagrant personalities. If, however, the madness runs its full course, then sometimes only a fragmented shell of the person will be left with unrelated parts of a burnt-out psyche ticking over, which express themselves in strange gestures and speech, until death intervenes and grants the possibility of a new start at a later point in history.

The various kinds of psychosis indicate which pillars, triads and *Sefirot* are being affected in the psychological Tree. Paranoia, for example, can be a heavy combination of *Gevurah* and the super-ego triads. This imbalance allows the mortido impulses into the ego which diverts the threat to its stability by projecting it out on to others. Some paranoid people hear voices abusing them. These come from beyond the liminal line *Hod* and *Nezah,* and arise from the split-off and conflicting segments in the side-triads. Catatonic schizophrenia is a clear example of being locked on the left-hand pillar as the person takes up a stiff and often bizarre posture in order to check to violent dynamic that could be released with devastating effect by the right-hand column. This occurs because *Yesod* is out of commission and very little contact with reality above or below is perceptible. Indeed, it has been noticed that such inaccessible patients have an eerie other-world atmosphere about them. From a Kabbalist view, this is because the *Yesod-Daat* connection is loosened with the inevitable loss of physical vitality and substance as the lower face of the psyche separates out from the upper face of the body, leaving an empty ego that lives at the ethereal level and only responds mechanically to external stimuli.

Taking a specific case, let us look at the process in detail. 'X' was a young woman who feared engulfment should she become involved with anyone. Retreat protected her from the outer world, but this led to an impoverishment of the psyche which created a vacuum in an already sparse inner space. In Tree terms *Yesod* prevented the emotional and conceptual triads from being filled out by experience. Lack of external stimulus depersonalised her because there was nothing to keep the lower face of the psyche active. Slowly a kind of petrification occurred in the persona which was compensated for by a build-up of fantasy. That is, the body's *Daat* started to separate out from the psyche's *Yesod*. This gave rise to the symptom formation of feeling disembodied. The trend was countered by the ego which constructed an acceptable picture of her situation. This was quite satisfactory, for she was the narcissistic mistress of her *Yeziratic* world. However, the Self at *Tiferet* saw the danger and she had many dreams about dying, being on a desert island and disintegrating. She ignored the warnings. Meanwhile, her *Yesod* built up a quite false image of herself and her place in the world. This was the beginning of insanity. Such people have been known to get well if they can recognise their situation, but, alas, many wander between the worlds, often quite wilfully asserting that their image of existence is correct, until at last fate brings them to crisis and they are given the choice to be healed or to become fully insane.

From a Kabbalistic view, madness is seen as a rejection of how things are. Indeed, the hallmark of many neurotics and psychotics is a willfulness that must have its own way, even if life is telling them that they are wrong. The phenomenon of madness is the result of a process, not its cause. Providence designs each life to develop an individual and insanity may be a last resort of fate as it attempts to prevent damage to the spirit. Many psychotics deliberately disregard life's laws in order to impose their egocentric version of reality. The Kabbalist perceives such events as the result of free will being misused even though the side pillars continually edge the individual back into the centre of their Tree. Everyone has to learn their lessons in order to develop and play their part in the universe correctly. Some choose not to and they accumulate a massive karma resulting in the hell of madness, called in Kabbalah the Pit of *Gehennah* where all those (dead or alive) who deliberately oppose reality reside. Most of us do not get to this point, although we may come close in the major crises that always occur at crucial moments in our lives. This is the theme we will look at next.

35. Crisis

An encounter with neurosis and even psychosis is not uncommon. Most people know someone under strain who has been unable to cope. Everyone, if the truth be known, has had personal experiences of a crisis at some point. Indeed, to be born is to enter a situation in which the individual is periodically faced with change and adjustment. This is one of the chief characteristics of life. Why, one may ask, do these crises occur? From the point of view of Kabbalah, they are seen as opportunities for development, in the process of evolution, as the Divine atom of consciousness in each person learns to expand in experience, yet remain contained with limits of balance. Here is the gradual spiral upwards, as an individual shifts from right to left columns in an ascent of Self-realisation. Seen psychologically, crises check growth and ease limitation, as the person moves through the progression of expansion and consolidation in the process of becoming a full and whole individual.

An example of crisis and its function is the arrival of a new baby into a family of three. Suddenly the pattern that has been perhaps well established between the first born and the parents is disturbed. The elder child's sense of being the focus of love is threatened as the younger initially takes precedence. The security, taken for granted, is jeopardised and an instinctive rising up of the id-*Nefesh* generates jealousy of considerable power. The parents may understand the situation and go to great lengths to reassure the child that their love is constant. But the animal soul with its fear that the new baby is going to thwart its needs will assert enormous pressure upon the elder child's psyche. In most cases, the crisis is dealt with by the ego when it realises that it would lose out if any hostile action were taken. This is the act of coming to terms with reality as the ego holds back a considerable feeling of hostility. However, although this impulse is repressed it is nevertheless still present and has to be periodically mastered in the conflicts of sibling rivalry. This struggle, like the exercise of learning to walk, strengthens the structural side of the psyche so that its wilder dynamic pillar is tamed and then controlled. Such a capacity is very useful in developing resilience in later life. It might, for example, stop a person from behaving in an infantile way when thwarted in love or through professional rivalry. It also helps the person to contain the super-ego-ideal which is sometimes quite irrational, especially during periods of crisis when collective views oppose individual development, as when a man has to choose between social custom and what conscience says is correct.

Crisis is observed in a child's developmental shift from motor-sensory perception to abstract cognition, when the old mode of operation has to be discarded and a new method acquired. This principle applies to most critical situations. The same moment of hesitancy and fear of risk and adventure occurs in the change from infancy to childhood. The first day at school leaves a deep impression on the psyche, and the way it is handled by the *Yesodic* ego is crucial in forming social attitudes. Here the expansion and limitation of the side pillars, when entering a wider world, must come as a shock to the egocentric image that has been so carefully nurtured up to that time. If the narcissistic view is not dissolved and re-formed to accommodate others, many crises will arise to push the person through that initiation. If this is not done at the right time, it can become quite a problem in adulthood as the psyche continually generates the same situation in order to move the developmental process on. If such crises are not faced and overcome then the person will remain fixed at that stage. Some individuals try to deal with it by taking on some evasive mask, like being a joker. Other people, who are temperamentally on the left pillar, simply retreat into a passive mode, while those inclined to the right column will seek to avoid the problem by excessive action. However, sooner or later fate will organise yet another crisis to solve the difficulty, such as a love affair in which these opposites are attracted to each other as they unconsciously seek a solution.

As we have seen, a person's fate is set out in a progression, so that the growth in body and mind is matched as each supports the other in the developmental process. However, besides these phases and transitional crises, there is the more subtle infrastructure noted by astrologers who have thousands of years of data to draw upon. For example, it has been observed that, as well as the planetary ages and stages of life, there are the periodic rhythms and their side effects. The Moon, for instance, generates in the body and lower psyche, especially the ego, a monthly pattern of ease, tension and equilibrium, as it moves in relation to the natal Moon of the horoscope. Thus, a person with the Moon in Aries in her chart will feel full of energy when the Moon conjuncts that sign, but frustrated when it is squared by the Moon passing through Capricorn. Moreover, they will be irritable when the Moon is in Cancer, and perhaps a little over-confident when the Moon is in Leo. When the Moon is in Libra, then the tension in the ego on that day can go either way, according to how the person uses the energy. These changing states of ego consciousness (the Moon is usually two days in each sign) mostly go unnoticed because they are so ephemeral. Nevertheless, they have a bearing on the moods of the psyche, for they can sometimes be the trigger to some deeper situation brought about by the longer but more subtle rhythms of the Sun and planets.

According to astrological tradition these cyclic patterns create an ever-changing configuration of influence that profoundly affects the state of the psyche. For example, Mercury and Venus have short rhythms, and their various inputs, in relation to the other planets and luminaries, are swift and passing. The superior planets, with their much longer cycles, have deeper and more protracted effects upon the psyche. Mars, with its two-year circuit, precipitates moments of sudden conflict as it transits and angles each sign. If one of these happens to be in the House of Partnership of an individual, so confrontations with friends will occur at school when the subject is a child and over matters of love during youth, and indeed at any point in life when Mars is in a crucial position to that person's horoscope. This is equally true of Jupiter which has a twelve year pattern. If that planet passes through the House of Partnership an expansion in that area is to be expected unless, as must sometimes happen, an opposing Saturn retards a relationship in a crisis of prudence versus love. This and many other planetary combinations at work in the subtle backdrop of the cosmos operate mostly through the unconscious, not only of the individual, but for all humanity that periodically has to face such crises as the Dark Ages or Industrial Revolution. These collective crises affect millions, although most people are oblivious to this dimension, either because they are too involved in the personal level or have a reluctance to accept they are not masters of their Fate. Only those who are conscious of these *Yeziratic* forces can manoeuvre within their powerful ebb and flow, and even then it is usually only their attitude to what happens that can be altered, for even fewer can actually alter their fate. Despite their spiritual power even Jesus and Socrates had to go through with their executions. Their triumph was that they chose to do it with grace.

A crisis may be seen as both an internal and an external situation since it is the result of both factors interacting upon the person in that place and time. Such critical moments are not random. Every life builds up to each moment as Fate brings old and new into fruition, before moving on to the next lesson. Many individuals live as if they were the centre of the Universe, and indeed, in one sense, they are, for deep within their being, at the core of their unconscious, is the Divine. But because most of us are unconscious we only see the four worlds from an egocentric viewpoint. This, however, does not alter the fact that everything in Existence is subject to the laws, graphically outlined by Jacob's Ladder, which place us exactly where we ought to be in order to go through our journey of Self-realisation. These may be periods of relaxation, so that we can prepare, or epochs of tension, which build to a breaking up or a breaking through. In between come moments of equilibrium which allow us to perceive what is happening, when the Tree of our being is momentarily in balance and the whole situation can be appreciated from the Self at *Tiferet*.

Such illuminating moments might last a fraction of a second, or go on for some time as the active and passive factors in a situation oscillate before coming to a resolution. Many people regard easy times as good, and difficult times as bad. From a developmental standpoint the reverse is often true. Lack of tension and friction can generate laziness and laxity. This is seen when an empire has touched its peak, lost its vitality and started to decline. The same occurs when a person reaches a point in development when well-established patterns start to stifle creativity. Fortunately there comes a moment in which the forces of the active pillar begin to swing the other way in order to precipitate a shift. This may be applied externally, by circumstance, or internally, by the dynamic side of the psyche. Either way, both are a mirror of the other, because fate is an expression of the balance between the two pillars. Crises of accidents and illness are the effects of the pillars and *Sefirot* at work throughout all the Worlds so as to bring into consciousness that which needs to be done at that point in time and space. An instance of this might be a car crash that showed a person that he was not looking where he was going in more ways than one.

The *Yeziratic* organism of the psyche is watery by nature. It can, however, become too jelly like if the process of growth leans over much onto the side of structure. Likewise, the psyche occasionally becomes excessively fluid if the emphasis is heavily on the side of the dynamic. These imbalances always precipitate their counteractions which continually dissolve and resolve the situation. Thus, a healthy psyche is never too fixed or too free, because excess in either direction will disturb the optimum balance necessary to keep it within its limits. Crises that arise quite naturally in the course of events can usually be contained. The ones that cannot be are often self-inflicted by willfulness or the result of karma.

Taking a more transpersonal view, our examination now moves beyond the mechanics of the psyche to focus once more on the unconscious, but from a different level as we look at individuals who are not neurotic or psychotic, but have a profound sense of something missing in their lives. These people are in often crisis, but not of the usual order. They are the 'seekers' that have been spoken of earlier who wish to find their true Selves. This is where the Jungian approach comes into our study.

36. Jung and Freud

Carl Jung was born in 1875 and died in 1961. His horoscope had Sun (*Tiferet*) in Leo, a fiery fixed sign and Moon (*Yesod*) in Taurus, an earthly fixed sign. Thus his Moon corresponded with Freud's Taurus Sun, which encouraged a close relationship, as long as Jung's ego reflected the light of Freud's Self. However, as their Suns were squared, conflict would be inevitable between equals. This is exactly what happened when Jung went his own way and ceased to be, as Freud called him, 'his crown prince'. The split, it is interesting to note, as an event in Freud's pattern of fate, occurred in 1913 when Uranus, the planet of illumination and sudden change, with Mars the planet of confrontation and decision, were exactly opposed to Jung's Sun, precipitating a revolution in the House of partnership. Their relationship, moreover, was not helped by Saturn, the weighty planet of law, conjuncting Freud's Moon later that year, as Mars did likewise to his Sun. The combination of these cosmic aspects could only bring about a fatal parting, as the principles, represented by the planets, reflected in their psyches brought their differences to a crisis head. Jung, having of a fiery and equally fixed Sun or Self would inevitably turn away from Freud's earthy approach and follow the more inspirational standpoint. This has been borne out by his life and work. This does not mean he was Freud's superior. They simply perceived different levels of reality.

Before we begin to explore the Jungian view in detail, let us look at his general scheme of the psyche, so as to see where he and Freud agreed and parted company. Jung saw the psyche as an organism. He held the view that its structure and dynamics were not built up as a result of experience, but that it was an already existing whole which developed from birth into a well-differentiated system in which the various components sought to operate in harmony. He rejected the jigsaw view of the psyche and the piecemeal development pattern in which autonomous elements struggled for supremacy. The conflicts of neurosis and psychosis were seen as dissociated factions opposed to the essential unity of the psyche, whose normal tendency was always towards integration and a profound sense of oneness with all that existed. This view is Platonic in contrast to Freud's more Aristotelian approach. As will be seen from this opening statement, Jung's standpoint is in concurrence with Kabbalah and with most other esoteric traditions.

Where Jung and Freud did share much common ground was upon the division of the psyche into the conscious and unconscious, although as they developed their respective ways they gave slightly different names to the same thing. For example, the super-ego-ideal of Freud was called the 'personal unconscious' by Jung, while the Freudian id was seen by some Jungians as the 'collective unconscious'. Sometimes the same term was used for different things, which led to some confusion, but considering that both schools were covering new territory, it is not surprising. It is rather like the name of the West Indies deriving from the assumption of the European explorers that they had discovered a new route to India. The same situation occurs when scientists discover new physical phenomena and call them by various names, according to their current understanding. The titles of the Freudian and Jungian methods reflect their different approaches. Freud called his 'psycho-analysis' and Jung his 'analytical psychology'. Kabbalists have not been without the same problem. Some knew the study of the psyche as 'Going down into the Chariot' and others as 'Going up into the Chariot', which anyone in esoteric work will tell you are exactly the same, but approached from opposite directions. The key is to recognise that there is an above and below, and this both Freud and Jung acknowledged in the recognition of the basic division between conscious and unconscious. Jung, however, went further by subdividing the unconscious into an individual and a cosmic level.

Jung, like Freud, defined consciousness as the part of the psyche that is obviously accessible. He believed that it probably existed prior to birth; that is, the psyche is something quite distinct from the body. This appears to be corroborated by his remarks about life after death, and his belief in a grand design. Freud, who, it is said, regarded God as a vast parental projection, could not openly come this far, and indeed sought to eliminate all occult elements from his work, while Jung was clearly interested in this dimension.

According to Jung's observations, an infant's consciousness was not organised. Everything that came into it was transient, and initially there was no particular continuity, as the instinctive processes and the mother took care of its immediate needs. However, as time passed and the developmental process got under way, experiences that passed through the rudimentary ego began to accumulate within the various systems of psyche as memory started to form. Seen from a Kabbalistic view, here is the acceptance of a ready-made vehicle or chariot that selected incoming material and stored it in an appropriate pace. Some of these experiences were absorbed by the triads around the ego; others went into the personal unconscious and yet others to the collective.

Over time, according to Jung, the ego begins to learn how to assess situations and respond. It can in its limited way, focus consciousness, so as to identify external objects or perceive interior events. This ability for the ego to be selective is greatly affected by the infant's physical type, basic psychological condition, education and many unconscious influences that filter across the *Hod-Nezah* line from the personal and collective levels. This all concurred with the findings of Freud. However, what particularly interested Jung was the process of 'individuation'. In this, the ego's development of an identity was not only the start of being recognised as a person, but the beginning of a differentiation of the general into the particular. This was a major departure from the view that everyone is subject to identical id drives and super-ego-ideal pressures which make people conform to a social pattern. While this might be true at one level, many individuals respond in their own way to circumstances. They are peculiar to themselves and their perception of their inner and outer world is unique. These people are those who continue the process of individuation. Usually they have fully matured or fulfilled life's basic needs and ambitions. This in Kabbalistic terms means they have filled out the lower face of the psyche and are ready to go higher and deeper into the Tree. This is why Jung was more interested in his patients' future than Freud, who was more preoccupied with their past.

Jung's picture of the psyche is of a sphere with a bright patch on its surface. This spot of light is seen as the centre of the field of consciousness, as experienced by the ego, as it moves to and fro over the surface, which may be seen as the *Hod-Nezah* line. In this way, many things that are available in the pre-conscious can be brought up (or down) and projected onto the *Yesodic* screen, although they are immediately forgotten when the attention of the ego passes from them. Below the surface of the sphere (or above the liminal line) are those things that are attracted by the light which rise up from deep down, like long-forgotten memories that are associated with what is going on in the ego, such as recalling the smell of the sea when flicking through a travel brochure. They may not be directly relevant to the ego's business, but they will influence a thought, feeling or action to, perhaps, go to this or that holiday resort, because it reminds one of childhood vacations. These, of course can be negatively or positively loaded or cathexed. Below this deeper retrievable level are those associations that cannot surface because their cathectic charge is too weak or there are powerful anticathexes holding them down. These are the mind's truly unconscious elements composed of suppressed personal recollections, such as unpleasant wartime experiences and memories that have not been relevant to a person's life for a long time, such as 'one's least favourite subject learned at school'. Deeper still, towards the centre of the sphere, are those areas of which few people are even aware, but which are nevertheless there as influences. Here is where archaic experiences reside that belong to all mankind, at the Collective level or the upper part of the Tree. This zone is only accessible to the highly evolved people such as saints, sages and prophets, although it may express itself to lesser mortals in dreams or flashes of deep insight in understanding and wisdom. At the very centre of the sphere is what Jung calls the Self. This is the governor of the psyche and relates to the fullest realisation a human being can attain in both individuation and Universal Consciousness. From the point of view of the Tree, Jung's definition of Self is a combination of *Tiferet*, *Daat* and *Keter* which holds the conscious of Selfhood at various levels on the central column.

As will be seen, the Jungian overview has much in common with the Kabbalistic scheme. Indeed much of his work was based upon years of intensive study of various esoteric traditions ranging from alchemy to Shamanism. Besides spending long hours in his extensive library he undertook many journeys abroad to meet people who practised various mystical and magical techniques. All this experience went into what is called Jungian psychology. He was certainly acquainted with Kabbalah, as indeed was Freud, who had a Jewish background. Neither, however, related this very precise system directly to his work, because during their lifetimes Kabbalah was in disrepute, especially amongst western Jews. Today, because of work done by such eminent scholars as Gershen Scholem, Kabbalah is once more becoming an acceptable mode by which to view Existence. If we place the general Freudian and Jungian scheme upon Jacob's Ladder, we can see exactly how they overlap and divide.

The Jungian diagram of the sphere is like all schemes, including the *Sefirotic* Tree, only a diagrammatic way of describing the indescribable. However, with a synthesis of the two systems, let us look at the psyche so as to see not only how it operates from a Jungian viewpoint but where it relates to the higher worlds of the Spirit and Divine as set out in Kabbalah.

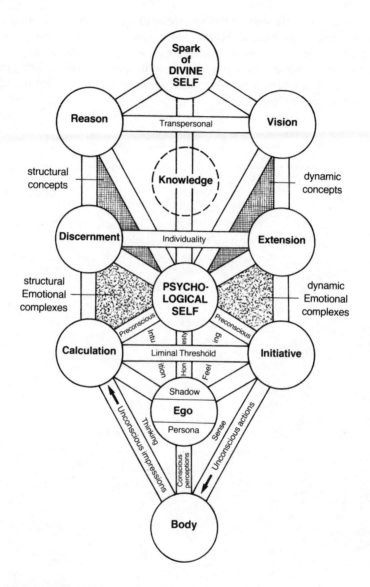

10. FUNCTIONS

Here the Jungian functions are placed within the lower face of the psyche and constitute the psychological, as against the physical types. Also seen are the active and passive functional triads of emotions and concepts, together with the levels and Sefirotic qualities as they flow through Conscious and Unconsciousness. Between the ego and the Self lies the crucial path of Honesty.

37. Functions

Like Freud, Jung saw the ego as the focus of consciousness, though he perceived it not only as the pivot of perception, thought, feeling and action, but also as the centre of several psychological functions. While he acknowledged that the ego played only a limited part in the psyche's total operation, he regarded that role as very important, since it was through the ego that a person viewed both the interior and the exterior world. As such, the ego selects what can be absorbed or what should be rejected from the attention. Thus, for example, as we walk down a street, we notice only those things that are relevant. The rest is screened out; otherwise our perception would be overloaded. Seen from a Kabbalistic view, *Yesod* deals with what is of direct interest, as it comes in up the path from *Malkhut*, while the rest is filed and responded to by the side paths that go up to *Hod* and *Nezah*. This phenomenon becomes apparent when people are asked by the police about what they remember of an incident. Skilful questioning such as what colour was this, or what position was that, reveals that much more has been absorbed than the ego noted at the time.

Of particular interest to Jung was just what was selected and why. This he related to two crucial factors that influenced the ego's outlook, besides the effect of external impressions and the unconscious with all their physical, personal and cultural pressures. The first he designated as the attitude held by the ego, and the second, as the dominant psychological function. These were seen as two interacting sub-systems which applied their emphasis either as transient factors to meet a particular moment, or as a permanent tendency that made the ego see the world in a certain way.

The first system was that of 'introversion' and 'extroversion'. These terms were not new, but Jung used them in a specific mode. Introversion was seen as an inclination to perceive the world in a more reflective way, assessing the interior content of events rather than their apparent form. For example, two men out for a walk at night and trip over something in the dark. The extrovert gropes around to find out what it was, while the introvert might give

171

thought as to why such an event should happen, seeing it perhaps as an omen. The extrovert having discovered the object would then remove it from their path while the introvert stood by ruminating on how fate periodically put such things in one's way. This difference in attitude alters what is perceived by the ego, so that two quite different images are presented of the same scene in the consciousness of each person. The extrovert sees the world in terms of external phenomena, while the introvert perceives the Universe symbolically because his awareness is oriented to an inner reality. There are, of course, gradations of these outlooks. At the extremes lies neurotic imbalance that denies the introvert's relation to external reality and the extrovert's avoidance of inner processes. The cocaine addict's preference for dreams and the Hell's Angels' love of violent action are examples of these. In Tree terms, the extrovert looks out of *Yesod* and down into *Malkhut*, while the introvert directs the ego's attention to the inner world of reveries. Fortunately for most of us, any imbalance between the body and the psyche is held by a relatively competent ego. Nevertheless, in most people there is usually a tendency for one of these two attitudes to be predominant.

The second ego system, according to Jung, was the interaction of the four psychological functions, as he saw them. These were based upon observation of four reciprocating processes centred on the ego. They were named by Jung as *thinking, sense, feeling,* and *intuition.* At first sight they appear to relate to the triads of thought, feeling and action which can be confusing because the names are so close, but if one can see that the latter system relates to the body types of ectomorph (nerve: thinking), mesomorph (muscular: doer), and endomorph (visceral: feeler) then the Jungian system can be seen as indeed a description of psychological functions. Seen in terms of the Tree, the four functions, unlike the body types, fill all the lower face of the psychological Tree. Their disposition is as follows: the thinking function fits into the *Hod, Yesod, Malkhut* triad; the sensing the *Nezah, Yesod, Malkhut* triad; the feeling into the *Nezah, Tiferet, Yesod* triad and the intuition the *Hod, Tiferet, Yesod* triad. All, it will be noted, focus like the body types on the ego at *Yesod.* As a sub-system within the Tree, thinking and intuition are on the passive side and sense and feeling are on the active side of the lower face. Moreover, the two outer triads of thinking and sense have an extrovert tendency by being connected with *Malkhut* and the two inner triads of intuition and feeling are inclined towards introversion because of their attachment to *Tiferet,* This means that the upper and inner pair reciprocate as introverted triads and the lower do the same but in an extroverted fashion. Besides these horizontal and vertical relationships there is a criss-cross process in which the sense triad counter-balances the triad of intuition and the thinking triad complements the feeling. Further, Jung saw this quarternity as divided into rational and irrational, with the sense and intuition triads taking up the irrational axis, because they operate without any obvious logic. Feeling at least has likes and dislikes.

To add complexity but more subtlety to the system, all the various functions could, in fact, be introverted or extroverted. Thus, to give examples, the sense triad, which is usually concerned with action in its extrovert mode, can become reflective so that sense impressions gave rise to speculation. Likewise, the thinking triad, normally only concerned with concrete matters, could be preoccupied with reading such a book as this. Under certain circumstances, the feeling function, which is by nature actively introvert, might switch to applying silent pressure by projecting a strong mood into the World. The intuition triad, also introvert by inclination, can likewise shift from being the hidden, highly sensitive, but passive receptor, into an extrovert posture in which data is actively sought out, like when someone tunes into a situation to perceive what is really going on.

Jung not only observed that one of the functions and attitudes was usually predominant, but that this strong element was often compensating for a weak function. Thus, for example, the extrovert sensor was hiding from his own intuitive faculty, while the extrovert thinker was trying to rationalise her feelings. In contrast, intuitive people often use their delicate and introverted faculty to avoid encounters with practical matters, while the introverted feeler frequently does everything to stop thinking too much about material problems. Seen positively, each function can be developed to a high degree, so that there are brilliant thinkers, talented feelers, stalwart doers and gifted intuiters. These highly evolved functions, however, are usually at the cost of their counterparts, so that the clever mathematician is cold, the temperamental musician has no idea of order, the courageous mountaineer no sensitivity to others, while the mystic poet is unpractical. Jung also saw that any one of these functions could be brought into action, so that a whole and truer picture of both internal and external reality could be perceived. Alas, most of us have only one or two of these functions in good working order and so our view is somewhat subjective.

Seen Kabbalistically, the four functions and their introvert and extrovert combinations describe the dynamics of the five lower *Sefirot* and the triads they compose. The largest triad is the *Malkhut-Hod-Nezah* one that deals with the practical thinking, feeling and action processes. Behind this overlay are the four Jungian functions, which add the psychological dimension to the inflow of material that is coming from the body below and the psyche above the liminal line. The triad of *Hod-Tiferet-Nezah*, or the 'Awakening' in this scheme, is the level where the *Tiferet* connection of the Self illuminates what is going on in the upper half of the functional triads of intuition and feeling. This is when a person is not just dimly aware of a hunch, or something that is hovering around the liminal line, but actually perceives what it is with insight. Such moments separate out ego from Self-consciousness, and the person sees with great clarity exactly what the ego is thinking, feeling and doing, in relation to the outer world, that is, via the body triads. This might be quite different from what is going on in the psychological functions. Such a circumstance could occur in a diplomatic crisis in which the ego has to play a part in order to cover up or distract attention from an awkward situation, or in a personal crisis in which the ego acts out what is needed, while the Self watches for the moment of truth in which to speak. Many people are given such insights but they do not always act upon them, because the momentum of the ego's system is too great to counteract as habit carries them on. In Kabbalah, this is designated as being in the lesser state of *Katnut* as against the *Gadlut* state where one is in control of the functions.

As will be seen, the complexity of the structure and dynamics surrounding the ego can generate many kinds of pattern. Most people, influenced by their innate temperament and stamp of their backgrounds, will develop into a particular kind of 'psychological type' as Jung called it. This typology was a useful way of defining the way the ego reacts and for perceiving its strengths and weaknesses. It also explained why certain people did not get on with each other or their environment. For instance, an intuitive introvert would find life very difficult living in a crowded industrial slum, whereas he would probably be quite happy as a solitary goatherd in the mountains. Here we have to remember the larger picture and see the mechanism of Fate which seeks to balance the individual by placing the intuitive introvert, for example, in a situation which challenges him. The feeler may need to learn how to think and the sense-based person the arts of intuition, while the thinker is given a life where feelings are constantly being provoked. The intuitive might well find themselves in situations that cultivated the other three functions as could the others in order to experience and balance their discrepancies. All the foregoing occurs in the lower face of ego consciousness and on the margin of what Jung called the personal unconscious. Let us look at his view of this area of the psyche which occupies the central zone of the Tree.

38. Personal Unconscious

The personal unconscious is that part of the psyche which contains all of an individual's experience. It holds the memories of what passed through the focus of the ego and has gone into the mind. An example of this is the detailed recall of a love affair; when every sight, sound and smell is remembered. along with what was said, felt and thought. In contrast there are also the recollections of dark moments, such as an accident in which each detail of torn metal and flesh, flashing lights, pain and even oblivion can be remembered. Under normal circumstances memories of the pleasant and good will be stored in the pre-conscious zone of the personal unconscious because their potency does not disturb the ego's equilibrium or give rise to powerful defensive reactions. These acceptable memories can be called forth into consciousness by a melody of that period, a letter or picture that brings back, with astonishing clarity, a myriad other things related to an epoch of perhaps half a century ago. Highly unpleasant memories, on the contrary, because of their painful charge might never surface again into *Yesodic* consciousness, because they are held back by one of the ego defence mechanisms which confines them to the unconscious so that nothing, except some similar event, shock or deep enquiry will evoke their presence. Their power, however, will nevertheless still be an influence which can surface in dreams or in a momentary memory that is immediately suppressed.

The personal unconscious is made up of millions of such positive and negative experiences. Some will be small and insignificant, others of moderate importance and others of major account. All, to a greater or lesser degree, will have their effect upon an individual's life. For example, a childhood incident, such as an incestuous encounter that has been long repressed could unconsciously continue to spoil adult relationships, while a not forgotten professional failure might dog every attempt to start up in that field again. How, one may ask, can all these bits and pieces of memory even begin to influence the psyche, for they appear to enter in a most random way, some passing directly through the ego and others coming in via the side pillars? The organisation of the personal unconscious may be perceived two ways.

The first is based upon Jung's discovery of the emotional and conceptual complexes that relate to the upper side triads of the Tree. During his study of word association, Jung noticed that patients occasionally paused over certain words. Closer observation revealed that these words evoked a powerful response in the unconscious which led to the conclusion that there were associated collections of highly charged memories which appeared to gather around certain nuclear principles within the psyche. Thus, as every experience was processed, so the thoughts and feeling evoked were attracted by similarity, to ideas and emotions which were related by common links. These groups formed over time into various associated complexes. An example of this might be when someone picks up a sea shell from a mantlepiece during a party. As it is turned in the hand, so the memories of times by the sea might come up from the unconscious. Suddenly the room full of people might fade as all the sights, smells and sounds of the seashore return. Perhaps a particular incident is recalled, a sad and poignant moment of parting in the last stage of a deep relationship that held such promise. As the person looks at the shell, he might remember the heartache and what happened after, which abruptly brings him back into the room and the party again. The present might then stimulate a new line of thought as the shell is classified scientifically while the shape of the shell reminds the person of some work of art seen in a foreign country which, in turn, evokes other memories that flicker across the *Yesodic* screen. Such a casual moment can reveal many levels of memory which are part of a great interconnected web of associations. These, in turn, fall into various categories that form the structural and dynamic background of the vast inner Universe of the psyche. Here we begin to see how the psychological Tree is more than just a diagram. It starts to become alive with what is seen in it.

A complex, as Jung saw it, was one particular grouping that had its core a specific theme. One such complex might be everything that related to money, so that whatever touched this area brought a strong or weak response, depending upon the emphasis the person had given this subject. To one individual money might not mean much more than a useful tool, while to another it could be an obsession, resulting from either a current problem or early deprivation. In some cases the loading of a complex might be quite even, so that a certain equanimity would govern the attitude to money, while in someone else this complex might dominate everything. In most people a kind of working balance is struck, although many have their pet loves and fears which may be expressed in day or night dreams and unconscious trends, like the miser who is saving for a rainy day even though he is rich.

Such obsessions or powerful complexes can, it was observed, form quite distinct entities within the psyche, creating what are called 'sub-personalities'. These operate, in certain situations, as independent units that seek their own autonomy. We all have our id-*Nefesh* drives and psychological fantasies, but most people keep them under control or express them in hobbies such as sport and drama, games or art. But some individuals cannot find such outlets because they are simply unconscious of such drives. This sometimes allows the sub-personality a free hand so that a person is driven into a situation against their reason. The man, who appears to be quite normal, can become homicidal if the conditions are just right for such an event and remember nothing of his crime. This is because the mortido impulse and perhaps a hate-loaded complex is too deeply buried in the unconscious to be detected by relatives and friends, even though some odd things done from time to time would have been a clear omen to a trained observer. Such an event might occur when the balance of the psyche was sufficiently disturbed so that it could be triggered by some trivial incident which was the last straw. This could release a festering revenge complex which turns the person into an avenger who kills whoever is nearby. Such is, of course, a psychopathic episode, but many people have these unintegrated elements in their psyche, although not to this degree. Jung observed of this phenomenon, "Such a person does not have a complex; the complex has him".

From a Kabbalistic view the personal unconscious is made up of experiences that cross the threshold line between *Hod* and *Nezah* and are drawn to their respective triads. Some incline to the left, where they build up the structure of the psyche, as they accumulate in the passive triads of emotion and concepts; others do the reverse and add to the triads of emotional and conceptual stimulae. Once in the respective triad they gather about a particular *Sefirah*. Those concerned with general and particular information, such as learning how to drive or calculate will collect around *Hod*. Those drawn to *Nezah* will have the quality of action and rhythm, attraction and repulsion. Experiences that have the element of discipline, discrimination, righteous anger or even hate, will cluster around *Gevurah*, while those associated with love, laxity, generosity and powerful but positive emotions will be attracted to *Hesed*. Likewise, ideas concerned with law, principles, organisation and reason will cluster around *Binah* and those moments that generate inspiration, vision and revelation will go to that part of the psyche governed by *Hokhmah*. In a similar fashion everything that is related to the ego will cluster in the triads that serve *Yesod*, and all experiences related to the individual's essential Self will orbit the central *Sefirah* of *Tiferet*, in the same way as all material concerned with higher knowledge and experience of the Divine will be drawn to the deep and high *Sefirot* of *Daat* and *Keter* that lie beyond the personal unconscious in the transpersonal.

The number of complexes and their components, when seen in terms of the Tree, does not matter, because all will align themselves with the ten basic *Sefirotic* principles and their resultant triads and paths. These fundamentals will always divide whatever enters the psyche into active and passive, dynamic and structure, higher or lower, emotion or idea, in the same way that iron filings will arrange themselves into a force field pattern. This complex may not seem related to that complex, but on close examination, the cores will share a basis that draws them to a particular *Sefirah*. For example, all the thoughts about time, have at their heart the principle of limits, so too does every emotion connected with loss. This would incline them to the left-hand pillar, where they might meet and relate, through *Gevurah*, which would attract everything to do with karma, which contains elements of both. Thousands of such configurations are built up of *Yeziratic* forms which are cathexed positively or negatively. These accumulate over the early years as base layers, rather like the backing cloth of a tapestry that is continually being worked by the psyche. The general pattern of this ever-enriching design is determined by the particular setting of the *Sefirot* at the time of birth, which gives a distinct character to the way the person responds to the fate that these innate tendencies make him or her live out. In most people, the internal build-up of the personal unconscious takes on a conventional form because there is not a high degree of self-development. Thus the ego, which is socially-oriented, generates a type of personality, rather than a distinct individual. This fact may offend some idealists, but observation will lead one to realise that most people conform to what is expected of them by the super-ego-ideal of their particular society. A recent miners' strike in Britain revealed only too well the power of conformity in the mining community. The social condemnation of being called a 'blackleg' or 'scab' prevented many desperately needy individuals from breaking rank and going back to work. Here the personal unconscious is not sufficiently evolved to overcome the super-ego-ideal that holds the ego in place. True individuality is quite rare for the hippy or drop-out are just as conventional in their way as the conformists they despise. They too wear their uniform and have their rigid code.

Here we come to the upper edge of the personal unconscious as it blends into the collective. Below this level, all that has been experienced becomes the matrix for a particular psyche, in which the karma acquired is worked upon by the performance of the person in the present life. This is where Kabbalistic psychology considers what might be taking place in the light of former incarnations, for every life is the result of countless impressions that have been synthesised over many centuries. The woman who looks and lives like a nun is not just a spinster who cannot understand sex. She probably has a whole history of celibacy and purity suffusing her psyche. And the man who is a professional soldier might not be just working out his strong mortido drive, but learning about discipline, having spent his previous three or four lives being a layabout or a libertine. Both Francis and Augustine were sinners before they became saints. Some people require several lives before they learn their lesson; most of us need many. What can be said is that the personal unconscious contains what we are at the moment. This, together with fate, defines the work that has to be done during the present incarnation. However, before we can come to know what we are, we must separate out the collective unconscious.

39. Collective Unconscious

As the body was known to contain all the experience of physical development, so it was believed the mind inherited the knowledge gained by the human race since it inhabited the Earth. Freud acknowledged this archaic level within the psyche but saw it as a primitive vestige. In contrast, Jung regarded the ancient stratum as the accumulated experience of humanity, a collective dimension embedded in the unconscious of every individual. From here it affected the psyche in many ways to influence contemporary affairs. An example is the need to conform to one's social group or professional trade union for protection. This was a reinactment of a prehistoric tribal situation. So too were many of the roles people played from the cradle to the grave. For instance, Jung perceived, in his observations of both primitive and advanced cultures, that parents held much the same position in all societies and that there was clearly a common image of what a parent is and does. It was as if there was a universal archetype that was quite recognisable the world over. Jung perceived the phenomenon as an objective psychological fact that had its own form of reality in the collective human mind, along with many other archetypal principles that have become part of this deep level of the human mind. The recognition of this dimension was of great importance because it separated the lower and more physical and the middle or more personal from that which was transpersonal. Here was an archetypal world in its own right that had little to do with individuals, yet profoundly influenced what they thought, felt and did in both their inner and outer lives. Kabbalistically, Jung had restated and identified the realm of *Yezirah*, known in other spiritual traditions as the Astral World, the Palace of the Gods, Paradise and Purgatory, and many other names that describe the level which is above the physical but below the spiritual. This world is not only the dimension of the psyche but the habitat of angels and demons. It is also the Treasure House of souls where the as yet unborn reside and where the psyche is processed in its post-mortem and pre-birth period. Jung brought into the study of western psychology what the Buddhist monk, Christian mystic,

Muslim Sufi and Jewish Kabbalist had known and written about for centuries. Jung took the scientific community into what, for it, was uncharted waters. In the course of his wide research into ancient knowledge he repeatedly found the same descriptions, stories and principles when this level of the psyche was being described. These he synthesised and related to what he observed in his patients, as he began to discover the same symbolism arising in certain classical psychological and spiritual situations.

As his theoretical and practical work developed, so Jung began to formulate certain conclusions about the collective unconscious. For example, he said that, "The form of the world into which he (the individual) is born, is already inborn within him as a virtual image". A Kabbalist in the thirteenth century wrote, "It is this image which receives us when we come into the world, it develops with us while we grow and accompanies us when we leave the Earth". Jung saw this form as full of latent patterns and archetypes, in the same way as an infant's body has all its various systems in place at birth. These psychological processes become active, he noted, when a person perceives an object in the outer world that corresponds to the archetype of, for instance, a father, whom the child responds to in a certain way because the paternal image already exists in the mind. This archetypal form is so powerful that people who have been deprived of a father will project it upon men who have the fatherly quality and seek to work out that ritual parent-child relationship in order to be able to mature. Kabbalistically, the father figure is the symbol associated with the *Sefirah Hokhmah* or Wisdom. Standing at the head of the right-hand and active column, it is considered to be the male aspect of the Divine, manifest in the lower world of Formation in the image of Adam, the father of mankind. On the opposite pillar is Eve at *Binah*, the female counterpart and mate, who was formed after the spiritual *Adam* of *Beriah* or Creation had been transformed from an androgynous being, like the primordial Adam Kadmon, into a *Yeziratic* or psychological couple. From this comes the Jewish myth of soul-mates in which those of the same Divine and Spiritual root are divided at the psychological level and live in separate bodies while incarnated. Here is the origin of an idea that influences many people's search for their alter-ego in a mate.

Every spiritual tradition, be it of a primitive hunter culture or the highest civilisation, has its mythology. Some are simple stories of how the Universe and humanity came into being, while others are extremely complex, involving elaborate metaphysics and subtle symbols that describe various levels, the way they work and who and what lives there. Nearly all speak of mankind's descent into the lower worlds, and of how individuals can rise to recover their proper place and the Grace and knowledge that goes with it. Jung analysed many of these stories, and perceived a pattern of spiritual development inherent in them. This is where he parted company with Freud and many other psychologists who only recognised the psychological and physical dimensions.

Out of Jung's work on the collective unconscious emerged a general and detailed composite picture based upon folklore, mythology and various esoteric disciplines. This was related to the analysis of countless patient's dreams as well as of his own. From these studies he clarified the concept of archetypes. An archetype means the original model, but in this sense it is the essential principle at the root of certain phenomena. Early man had projected archetypal images upon rivers, mountains and the weather, but these were seen as exterior gods or devils. They were a response and personification of, say, a whirlwind or a waterfall. Jung's archetypes were concerned with identifying social and psychological phenomena. For example, archetypes like the innocence of childhood or the wisdom of the old are quite recognisable as are the hero and the trickster who not only occur in mythology but operate as distinct human characters. One may see the cardsharper in the market-place of a Mexican town or in the back room of a pub in London, and every army, from the ancient Egyptians to the British special air service, has its men of valour. Such individuals are often quite oblivious of the model they are acting out, as are the average mother and father who instinctively follow the directions of the archetypal Eve and Adam.

Jung catalogued many kinds of archetypal principles, ranging from situations like birth and death to objects such as rings which can carry a symbolic meaning and state. Love and hate have archetypal forms as do the events of meeting and parting. These archetypes he saw as pure forms until they were manifested by an actual incident which then took on a poignancy far beyond what people put into them. Any marriage, no matter in what culture, generates an enormous focus of power as people enter into an archetypal celebration of union. Everyone involved draws out far more than they put in from the instant the couple announce they are to wed until they depart on their honeymoon. All the rituals of meeting the family, setting up a home, organising the wedding and buying presents are highly charged social forms that even affects outsiders. The royal wedding between the Prince and Princess of Wales drew a television audience of hundreds of millions. Such is the power of the collective as it generates an interaction between the collective unconscious and the personal unconscious. Even many people of strong republican traditions were deeply affected by the wedding as the fairy tale story of an aristocratic Cinderella marrying a future king was seen on the television screen.

An example of the archetypal on the individual level is the transition from childhood to youth. This is accomplished when the archetype of 'boy' is displaced by the archetype of 'adolescent' which the person adopts with all its dress and attitudes. Here is where we see the archetypal ages of man, planetary principles and the *Sefirot* at work behind the forms. The power of these modes is enormous as can be witnessed every spring when the eternal youth and maid suddenly manifest everywhere to play out the games of love, while the old look on and remember their time of courting. This collective archetype of Venus, Eros or *Nezah* occurs in the primitive Brazilian jungle as well as London's sophisticated Chelsea, in Communist Siberia as in capitalist California. Wherever young people are, so there the archetype of romance will emerge.

At the heart of each archetype is a principle that attracts anything that resonates with it. This follows the laws that operate within the *Sefirot*, sending out and drawing to them whatever is similar to their nature. These processes naturally come under the over-all influence of the Tree, so that all the archetypes are related to this *Sefirah* or that triad or column. This means that there is an ordered basis to myriads of archetypes that correspond to the various aspects of the Tree. Seen the other way round, out of the *Azilutic* Tree's complexity and subtlety arise myriads of possibilities. These are multiplied threefold by the time they reach the world of *Yezirah* because it contains both the Divine and spiritual dimensions as well as the psychological. Thus, the collective unconscious includes many abstract modes, such as the Divine, the polar archetypes of Mercy and Justice, and the spiritual archetypes of Goodness and Evil. These are expressed in the religion, art and literature of every culture. Divinity, for example, is universally portrayed as Light, even as the images of Christ and Mahomet are used by Christians and Muslims to symbolise a fully realised human being. In order to get some idea how the archetypes operate, let us now look at the ten key Kabbalistic symbols so as to see how they relate to the psyche.

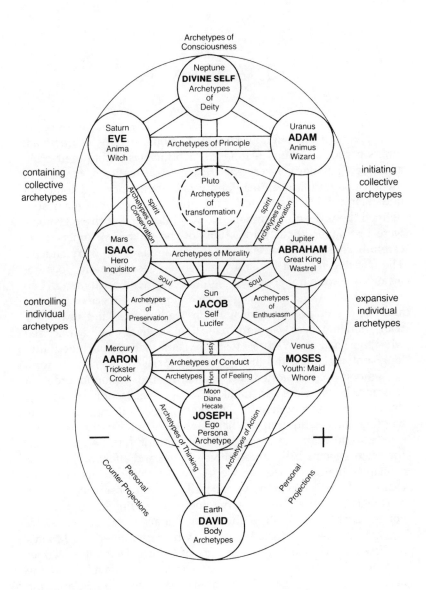

11. ARCHETYPES

In this Tree the many aspects of the Sefirot are shown in their various archetypes. Some are major, some minor with sub-archetypes filling the triads and arising out of the paths. Biblical, astrological and Jungian archetypes are seen, including the negative aspect of each Sefirah.

40. Archetypes

The notion of archetypes is an old one. The personification of principles occurs throughout mythology. Some archetypes are broad, others particular; many include lesser principles within their orbit, and a few personify a very specific aspect of reality or fantasy. In the ancient world, when mankind was in its infancy and could not understand the forces at work in the universe except as magical, it defined the unseen in symbols. Now, while some of these symbols were just superstitious impressions of the unknown, others were carefully considered concepts cast in the language of poetry and art. The fact that most of humanity may have been ignorant does not mean there were not people of high development. Such men as Lao Tsu in China, Akhenaton in Egypt, and Homer in Greece were saints and sages who were responsible for leading mankind towards a realisation that there was more to life than survival. They synthesised what they had received in mystical vision or had concluded after long contemplation, and they presented these concepts in the form of symbols that indicated and explained the profound order of Existence as it related to mankind. These realisations went into the collective unconscious as stories, sayings, buildings, sculpture, painting, dance and drama which contained archetypal principles.

At certain points in history various esoteric schools formulated complete systems based upon the character and effect of the major principles that governed the world. The astrologers produced, for example, five distinct archetypes based upon the observable planets as well as two very complex symbologies about the Sun and Moon. For instance, one aspect of the lunar character was expressed by Artemis the many-breasted goddess, who represented the Moon's fullness and relation to the fecundity of Nature. Diana, the slender maidenly hunter with her crescent shaped bow, symbolised the juncture in the cycle between death and rebirth. As Selene, the Moon was worshipped by Pan, the god of Nature, but she loved Endymion, symbol of humanity, upon whom she gazed with adoration as he slept. This myth spoke of the *Yesodic*-ego level of mankind and its unawakened state. Hecate, the great sorceress, was the symbol of Moon magic which had the power to influence the ego's view of reality and represented the lower mind. Buried in these myths is much information about the workings of the psyche. Artemis and Diana are the light and shadow poles of the ego and the libido and mortido impulses. The Celene principle is the ego's dominion over Nature or the body, while Hecate's capacity for directing highly cathexed images speaks of applied imagination and conscious projection. This and much more can be gleaned by examining mythology, as Jung indeed did.

As regards Kabbalah the same applies, except here a system of anthropological archetypes are used. This is because the characters in the Bible have names that describe their function. Joshua, for example, means 'deliverer' and David, 'the beloved', while Ruth, the loyal daughter-in-law of Naomi means 'friendship' and Ahithophel, the evil counsellor who advised Absolem to rebel against his father David, actually means 'brother of folly'. These and many other Biblical people represent certain principles which act out specific roles, even as Joshua or Jesus of Nazareth embodied the idea of the Divine man who would deliver a Roman-dominated Judea, which represented humanity imprisoned by physicality. In terms of the Tree, Kabbalists placed Biblical archetypes on it according to their nature, so that David, the earthy but Divinely inspired king, represented the body or *Malkhut* the Kingdom, the lowest of the *Sefirot* while Joseph, the dreamer who had the coat of many colours and became the Vizier to Pharaoh, was seen as the symbol of *Yesod* or the minister of the ego. Moses and Aaron were put at the bottom of the right and left pillars as they had to deal with the day to day problems of the years in the wilderness where life was at a basic level. Moses was placed in *Nezah* as the practical prophet and Aaron in *Hod* for he was the silver-tongued speaker and priest. Isaac was placed in the *Sefirah* of *Gevurah* for he feared the Judgment of the Lord; Abraham, the friend of God, was placed at *Hesed*, the loving and forgiving *Sefirah*, while the third patriarch, Jacob, was assigned to *Tiferet* which is the position of the Self, where he was transformed into Israel, which means 'He who struggles with or for God'. The non-*Sefirah* of *Daat* has no human image, although the Archangel Gabriel is said to sometimes be seen through its dark glass. *Keter*, the Crown, has no symbol either, for it was not permitted to have an image of the Divine. *Binah* and *Hokhmah* have the archetypes of Eve and Adam ascribed to them as the female and male heads of the outer pillars. This brings us to two of Jung's most important archetypes — the anima and animus that have their roots in the soul and spiritual mate idea.

The anima and animus correspond to what Kabbalists call the Eve and Adam principles, who represent the passive and active sides of the Tree. According to some Jungians, the animus is the masculine in women and the anima is the feminine in men. In fact, both are present in each individual, but the sex opposite to the person is hidden in their unconscious. A man works from the right-hand column while his left operates unconsciously, and vice versa in women. The anima and animus archetypes play an enormous part in how we act, how we respond in the World and in our attitudes to ourselves and our relationships. In the most obvious and important area, namely the intimate communication between the sexes, the archetypal Eve in the man and the Adam in the woman seeks out its opposite in a mate who is the mirror of their interior image. When there is a sufficiently close correspondence between a man's inner Eve and a woman's inner Adam, there occurs the phenomenon of projection and counter-projection experienced in love affairs that raises the relationship out of the mundane into another world. Kabbalistically, this is quite precise as love lifts the physical aspect of their intimate encounter into the magical *Yeziratic* World of Archetypes where where every slightest gesture and word takes on a poignant and symbolic meaning. This psychological level of communication is why a psychic connection is often made between lovers, who can perceive what is happening to each other, even though an ocean may divide them. The World of *Yezirah* has a different kind of time and space this is where the psyche has its being and the reason why love can be a paradise or purgatory.

In Kabbalah each of the *Sefirot* has two aspects: a positive and a negative, and a good and an evil side. The pillars can also reverse their charges, and the male can become passive and the female active. This reverse aspect was recognised by Jung. For example, an over-reactive right pillar or animus, can drive a woman to unconsciously take on an aggressive attitude towards life and especially toward men if she is convinced that they wish to dominate her. On the other hand her assertive animus may operate in another way by seeking out a man of a more primitive level, who will express and match her undeveloped Adam. An illustration of this was the normally prim Danish career girl who once a year went south to the topless beaches of Spain, in order to have two weeks of unadulterated sensuality with the local fisherman, before returning to her sedate banking job. Her Viking impulse had been satiated. Conversely, there was the young man who fell in love with but was rejected by his dream girl, who was frightened by his obsession for her. He pined for her over many years until they met again in their home town. By then she had lost her youth and golden hair. She was plump, cynical and exhausted by mundanity. Suddenly, he wondered what he ever saw in her. She no longer fitted his princess image. The full horror came when he realised that he had missed several opportunities to marry because his anima projection had blocked his view of what a real woman was. Modern advertising exploits the power of this projection in its constant presentation of beautiful women and potent men who symbolise the form and energy of the outer pillars. This projection can come from any of the functional *Sefirot* so that this or that quality can be emphasised in a particular archetype. Thus, for example, *Gevurah* can be evoked by a Battle of Britain fighter pilot with his stoic courage, while *Nezah* can turn a certain fashion model into the rage of the season. Here it should be noted that each pillar has its subdivision of masculine and feminine so that *Binah*, for example, can be the great grandmother or the Saturnine philosopher, while *Hokhmah* can produce the archetype of the great prophet or prophetess of Wisdom.

It is interesting to note that Jungians observe four levels of animus and anima which correspond to the four Kabbalistic levels. The first is the he-man hero or natural woman who have a strong sensual appeal; the second, the romantic poet or sensitive girl who evoke a psychological, rather than a physical reaction. The third is the man with the master mind and the profound woman who symbolises a spiritual Wisdom and Understanding. The highest order is exemplified by the illuminated animus and anima figures who are not just images, but actually live what they think, feel and do. All these levels and many more aspects of the animus and anima polarity form a highly complicated and yet essentially simple complementary system that operates between men and women, as they work within themselves and with each other in the pursuit of balance in their respective Trees. This comes, according to Kabbalah, when the Adam and Eve of each partner are face to face in a mutual as well as internal union. Jung would call this the integration of the masculine and feminine; in Kabbalah it is seen as 'the marriage of the King and Queen'.

The major Jungian archetypes, when placed upon the Tree, correspond almost exactly, although the terms may be different. For example, Jung's Great King would be placed in *Hesed*. His archetype of the Hero is certainly *Gevurah*, the beautiful maid or youth is without doubt *Nezahian*, while the Trickster clearly fits with *Hod*. These archetypes occur in many guises, but the Great King is always merciful and generous and the warrior courageous and discriminating, which are the qualities of *Hesed* and *Gevurah*, or the reverse if the dark side of the *Sefirot* are being invoked. The same is true of all the other archetypes. For example, the Trickster can appear as the Joker or clever Crook, the delightful Wag or the sinister Spy, using every aspect and skill of *Hod* to juggle, scheme and outwit the good or bad opponent. These archetypes crop up not only in dreams but in politics, business and family situations. They can also occur in myths, such as are found in the cinema. The old Western movie for example, usually contains a cool *Gevuric* hero and a *Hesedic* and rich rancher with a beautiful *Nezahian* daughter and a bent *Hodian* lawyer or gang leader. That is why the Western has such a folk story appeal. Seen in terms of the Tree, all great drama is the acting out of the tension between the various archetypes as good and evil aspects are brought into confrontation. For example, every play follows the pattern of first establishing a stable situation which is suddenly disrupted by an intruding element. The plot then unfolds a developing sequence in which the conflict between normality and disharmony is brought to a climax. Equilibrium is restored, be it by Hamlet finally taking action or the arrival of the U.S. cavalry to the rescue. These archetypal situations find echoes both in society at large and within the individual psyche, as they are moved from an old and fixed position into a new dynamic phase by an crises that are often reciprocated by evil archetypal symbols, such as the *Gevuric* terrorist, *Nezahian* seductress, *Binahic* dictator or *Hokhmah* type mad genius.

The realm of the archetypes is the World of *Yezirah*. Here collective and personal experience manifest in countless forms, expressing the interrelation of the ten *Sefirot* of the psychological Tree. As such, they may be combinations or the pure essence of an archetype that can be projected onto an external situation or be part of a private fantasy. The ever-changing watery nature of *Yezirah* does not allow any fixity to occur, as this fluidity is vital in order to meet the constantly shifting World of thoughts, feelings and actions. Indeed, flexibility is the basis of good mental health as the mind continually adjusts its balance in order to prevent any psychological stagnation. This leads us to the special archetypes of the central pillar that keep the pivotal balance at each level. The first to be examined is the persona, the mask that covers and protects the ego.

41. Persona

As the archetypes of the animus and anima seek out each other in sexual and psychological relationship, so the archetype of the ego, in the form of the persona tries to match the demands of society and make a place for the individual. The persona, as said, means 'mask' and Jung saw this as a particular kind of archetype, for it often took on an external projection, which was based upon an acquired personality, like an actor. Kabbalistically the persona is the appearance that *Yesod* puts on in order to protect the ego and relate to the outer world. An example of this is a party where people label each other so that they can assess their place in the social order. The business man, artist and doctor will present themselves as such, as will the farmer, factory worker and scholar as well as the Lord, general or callgirl. Each will dress or use some device or mode of speech to indicate what they are, despite the fact that they may all be wearing jeans and jerseys. This is the ego's way of preserving and projecting a *Yesodic* identity.

A persona is necessary because only a few individuals actually know who and what they are. The vast majority of people project an image of what they believe is them. Observe any gathering and you will constantly hear "What do you do?" The answer is usually given in terms of profession or status, such as bottle washer, housewife or Prime Minister. Even the unemployed or drop-out will say they are an ex-machine minder or poet. This image, although it might be a projection, enables people to respond to each other according to the local custom, whether at the White House or a meet of Hell's Angels. However, the importance of the persona and the archetype it adopts should not be underestimated. People will go to enormous lengths in selecting the kind of clothes they wear and how they move and speak in order to communicate what role they think and feel they wish to project. As Oscar Wilde said, "Anyone who does not judge by appearances is a fool". He was an expert on the persona as many of his plays are comedies of manners where the characters are expected to fill this or that social role. However, it is interesting to note that his novel *The Picture of Dorian Gray*, which is about a handsome youth whose appearance never ages while his hidden portrait takes on the ugliness of his odious life, is a remarkable study of an archetypal persona masking what is going on in the unconscious.

In its right place, the persona performs an important task. It enables the individual to take up a role while remaining secure within him or herself. One can be a good engineer, postman, peasant or queen without having to expose whatever may be going on at a deeper level. Moreover, the persona allows the individual to have different personalities in various circumstances, such as being a serious colleague at work, but a light-hearted companion in the cafe, although this can be confusing when one does not quite know which mask to wear when with two friends from very different spheres of life at the same time. There are individuals, however, who always present the same face. They are usually either limited in their repertoire of masks, because they have not developed a wide and flexible *Yesodic* ego, or they are so inwardly secure that they have no need for a facade. The former are often immature and the latter exactly the reverse, in that they can cope with and accommodate most situations without losing the sense of themselves. These individuals are operating from *Tiferet*.

In the relationship between men and women the persona can be crucial, for it will reveal the balance of the animus-anima factor of the outer pillars. Let us take an extreme example to illustrate the point. Most male homosexuals have a strong anima emphasis in their psyche which gives them their tendency towards the feminine side of the Tree which is often expressed in the persona. The same is true of women with a powerful animus, so that the force of the right-hand pillar is predominant. This pillar trend, however, is sometimes compensated by the persona in that the homosexual can project an excessively masculine image and the Lesbian an extraordinarily feminine personality. This over-compensation of course could be *Yesod* putting on an acceptable persona to cover a male soul in a female body or vice versa. In heterosexual relationships, the persona is important because men and women project their animus-anima through the *Yesodic* image. The girl who always dresses like Alice in Wonderland is projecting her anima, trying to attract a man with the same problem or someone who can take care of her like a father. The man who only wears black leather and never washes or cuts his hair is using this persona to appeal to some girl with an equally wild animus. The same goes for men and women who like to be seen in the smartest restaurants or hang out in a back street cafe. The persona they present of sophistication or toughness is designed to attract their own type, and anyone who does not meet their image is outside the clan. Here we see the persona as a major factor in the creation of social orders, and these are the *Yesodic* foundation of a society.

In some cases, the persona can reveal some deep lesion in the psyche of the person. For example, there is a particular phenomenon, known as the 'puella' or the 'eternal girl' syndrome. In this situation some event in early life, such as not forming a real relationship with the father, produces the distorted phenomena of the 'Darling Doll' persona, which takes on the image of a pretty little thing, in order to get the response the woman would have had as a child. In another case it can be the very reverse where the persona adopts the role of an 'Armoured Amazon', so that no one can hurt such a well-protected ego. In the former, the feminine pillar predominates and in the latter the masculine. The 'Dutiful Daughter' persona is yet another defence, but of greater complexity. Here the relationship to parents is an elaborate balance of love and hate, of need and resentment, held in by a mask of apparent filial goodness that can hide a frightening backlog of unreleased id-*Nefesh* energy. This situation can go on even after the parents are dead because the super-ego-ideal may still hold *Yesod* in its control until the individual matures into the Self of *Tiferet*. The 'Misfit' is the type of persona that seeks a masochistic comfort in disaster, as it constantly draws misfortune upon itself. Here the subconscious mortido impulse rises up as a powerful death-wish that uses the persona to destroy others as well as itself. Extreme cases can become psychopathic, as *Yesod* is cut off from the influence of *Tiferet* and the capacity to perceive reality. An example of this is the lunatic who says, "The end of the world is nigh because of its corruption". He is projecting and predicting his sense of destruction upon others so that he does not have to face it. This trend is seen in many revolutionaries who want the world to be in their own image. Conversely, the persona of apparent success can also cover an imbalance. The high official who uses his position to oppress people may be compensating for a lack of ego-esteem, and the brilliant and witty personality often masks a profound depression about his private life. Here, we see the Tree reacting so as to retain some workable equilibrium.

In some cases the persona meets an external need of a community, like the paternalistic president who ruled a primitive republic for decades. The individual who embodies the fashion of the moment is usually the personification of that society's ideal. Some ambitious people actually cultivate the persona that the fans want to see in their idol, but living up to such a mass projection has destroyed many talented individuals, who have counter-projected the image in order to get to the top. When the image begins to pall and their popularity fades, they often turn into burnt out cases. They do not have enough maturity to survive without adulation. This has happened to kings, generals, poets, and many celebrities who are no longer in the public eye.

The phenomenon described above is called 'inflation'. Here the ego is so caught up in its own image that the persona becomes the predominant focus of the psyche. This means that nearly all the psyche's activity is directed into the mask which expands outwardly and away from the path of honesty between *Yesod* and *Tiferet* to form a bloated personality that at some point must burst. For instance, Napoleon said at the height of his career, "I am the revolution". From that moment on the French-based movement to bring republican freedom to a feudal Europe started to become just another empire with Napoleon as Emperor. After his dramatic fall, he was confined to the little island of St. Helena where he became incredibly petty. The *Tiferet-Yesod* connection had all but gone, leaving the shell of a once great man. On another level is the example of the woman who saw herself as a psychotherapist who solved everyone's problems, but could not face her own. Moreover, her inflated persona could not conduct an ordinary social conversation without considering the motives behind every remark, which estranged many good friends. Such dominance by the persona can stem from an overactive *Gevurah*, which can produce a Spanish Inquisitor, or a faulty *Hesed* that can turn the persona into a 'Jack of all trades' who does everything for everyone else but nothing for himself. Just as many so-called religious people suffer from inflated personae as do business tycoons and pop stars. Possession by an archetype working through the persona is not always a spectacular matter. Many people are run by the mask they have adopted and remain imprisoned by it all their lives. Consider the professional soldier who always obeys and finds himself executing people he knows are good.

Jung observed that there were many individuals who realised that the persona was only a mask. These were usually people in middle life who had found that the role they had filled so well in the world was not what they wanted. The *Yesodic* personality, was after all, just an image by which one communicated thoughts, feelings and actions to others. This realisation created a sense of emptiness in many who knew there must be more to life than being acknowledged as a top professional, master craftsmen or just an interesting personality. Seen Kabbalistically all their *Sefirot*, triads and paths were at their optimum level. They could manage life well and even increase their scope, but greater proficiency or higher social status was not the answer. Worldly reputation no longer had meaning, for they knew it to be a fragile bubble. Nothing seemed to move or excite such people any more because time had shown that, despite the changes in the world, there were always the same essential human problems that no external solution could solve. The real question was why did they feel so empty. Was there a purpose to life and Existence, or not?

The persona is useful in dealing with everyday life, but it could actively prevent inner growth by preoccupying the mind with mundane issues. Jung noted that the people who actually asked the question "Who am I?" were those individuals who wished to grow beyond the ego and become conscious of the Self. Kabbalistically this question precipitates a rise up the path of Honesty from *Yesod* to *Tiferet*. However, such a process also stirs the dark side of the psyche, and it will seek to thwart any threat to its power, and to perpetuate the mask of the persona. Bringing the light of consciousness into the unconscious inevitably evokes the archetype of the shadow.

42. Shadow

In the Kabbalistic system each of the twenty-two paths between the *Sefirot* that compose the triads has a Hebrew letter assigned to it. The one between *Malkhut* and *Yesod*, or the body and ego, has the letter *Resh*, whose root means 'head'. This could also be interpreted as the face of the physical countenance of the ego image. On the liminal line between *Hod* and *Nezah* is the letter *Nun*, whose root meaning is to 'flower and decay' — that is, to resolve and dissolve whatever crosses between 'reverberation' and 'repetition' (the Hebrew root meanings of *Hod* and *Nezah*) and that which passes to and fro between the conscious and unconscious. The path of the particular interest to us is occupied by the letter *Tsade*, which is usually translated as 'righteous' or 'honesty', but it can also mean 'He who lies in wait'. This reveals the shadow side of the connection between the ego and the Self and the conscious and the unconscious. As such, the path is subject to both illumination and darkness, as the liminal level fluctuates between the outer processes of *Yesod* and the inner Watcher of *Tiferet*. This preconscious zone can open out or close down, bring forth realisations or repress them, make matters clear or cloud them with distortion. It is here that the light of honesty cuts a path through the milling thoughts, feelings and actions of the lower psyche to unite the ego and the Self, or to become benighted as the sinister side of the psyche eclipses our interior Sun and Moon.

Freud saw the shadow as the id intruding into ego consciousness, either to disrupt its order in irrational behaviour, or as a highly creative factor in which the instinctive energy of the *Nefesh* was harnessed to give a libidal drive to an individual, in contrast to the mortido impulse behind destructive and criminal acts. Jung agreed with much of this and the notion that the shadow contained what had been repressed by consciousness. The story of *Dr. Jekyll and Mr. Hyde* symbolised this dichotomy, in that the good doctor's dark side was embodied in the crude and violent character of Hyde — a character that he could not control once it had gained its autonomy. All of us have a Mr Hyde who is composed of everything we find unacceptable, according to the criteria we live by. Thus the do-gooder will repress meanness; the pacifist, aggression; and the law-abiding citizen represses any impulse to break the code. However, these suppressed elements reappear in unconscious behaviour. The do-gooders often neglect their families, the pacifists are frequently offensive in their cause, and the law-abiding person usually seeks ways of getting around rules, such as hiring accountants to help them avoid paying tax. Perhaps the most obvious case of this was the guru who slept with his female followers, in order, he said, to initiate them into his teaching. The ones he chose for initiation were always, his devotees noted, the most sexually desirable of his followers.

The positive aspect of the shadow is that it is mainly composed of our irrational impulses which gives us an instinctive flair for spontaneous action so that we can respond to situations instantly. This adds a vitality to our lives, which might be rather dull without it, but it means that there there is an unpredictable dimension to the psyche that gets us both into and out of scrapes, like the scholar-explorer who feigned madness so convincingly when captured by some tribesmen that they released him because he might bring them bad luck. An extremely sinister example of the shadow in a highly civilised man was Dr. Mengele who ran a clinic in a Nazi concentration camp. This educated and sophisticated man performed many perverse experiments on the helpless inmates. He removed bones from legs to see what would happen and deprived people of certain chemicals over a long period so as to observe the effect. Here, the *Hyde* had totally displaced his *Jekyll*. The path up to *Tiferet* and the soul triad of conscience was cut off or blocked by the 'He who lies in wait' aspect, symbolising evil.

The most common expression of the shadow is the instinctive attitude of people towards members of their own sex. Two men, who have very similar traits, may have a strong negative reaction to each other, finding the other's faults quite repugnant as they project their own dark side. Both Freud and Jung noted that such responses had a strong sexual flavour, as did the phenomenon of the unbalanced animus and anima in which the Tree exerts so potent an attraction for the opposite sex that it is seduced by its own power. This produces the 'Femme Fatale' or the 'Don Juan' psychology that takes over the person, who then seeks to conquer every candidate who comes within range. The situations of the brilliant man destroyed by a sensuous and fickle woman and the aristocratic virgin brought down by an enchanting villain are the basis of many myths, ranging from the ancient story of Merlin's fall brought about by a beautiful girl to the movie *Alfie*, which was about a man who just used women. Such a shadow has what Kabbalah calls a Luciferic element to it as it exploits the power to fascinate. This causes the path of integrity between *Yesod* and *Tiferet* to be cut off as the shadow takes possession of the ego and turns the persona into the archetype of the seducer. It is interesting to note that Lucifer, which means 'Bearer of Light', represents its very opposite since his fall.

From a conventional viewpoint what is considered by most people as evil is what the super-ego-ideal perceives as bad. This may be, in some societies, anything that offends local custom. For example, not dressing for dinner was just not done, while not paying your tailor was quite acceptable, according to the code of certain nineteenth-century regimental officers. The Spanish Inquisition saw all heretics as evildoers who must be destroyed in order to preserve the Faith. The use of torture was quite in order, as the shadow mortido impulse combined with the super-ego-ideal to extract 'evidence' from their victims. It is interesting to note that the Chief Inquisitor, Torquamanda, who could not abide Jewish or Moorish converts, was of mixed race himself and was therefore unacceptable in a Spanish society that was of *limpa sangua* (pure blood). His id-*Nefesh* took its revenge through the persona of Grand Inquisitor, who saw impurity everywhere and dealt with it most cruelly, even though his Order was called the Holy Office. This perversity is characteristic of the devil who can be seen as archetype of the shadow.

The devil, for many people, is the personification of all that they abhor. This may or may not be evil from an objective viewpoint. The morality of the ego is usually quite subjective because it is under the unconscious influence of the super-ego-ideal. Most people react according to their upbringing and social pressure. Consider again a war in which so many so-called normal individuals, once in uniform, do the most ghastly things to other people in a different uniform. Good and true citizens blast each other as the shadow side of the individual and the community is unleashed. This kind of madness reached its height in the First World War where organised psychosis was encouraged, and millions died futile deaths for a few metres of muddy ground. Any protest by those who could see what was really going on was thwarted, and indeed many were punished for exposing the reality. We can also see that the women who gave a white feather of cowardice to every man not in uniform were not actually being good patriots, but were expressing their desire to destroy whatever they thought was a threat to their own security and safety. This was because the enemy, whoever they were, took on the projection of all the bad thoughts, feelings and actions that had been suppressed during the nineteenth century with its Victorian ethic. The frustrated id-*Nefesh* of Europe burst out in 1914 in a frenzy of war fever, as propaganda encouraging the collective mortido was focused in a titanic effort to defeat a foe, who had turned overnight from being a cultured neighbour into a barbaric enemy that sought to destroy all that was good. In clinical terms this was mass paranoia.

Freud was quite pessimistic about the shadow side of humanity, but Jung felt that, if it could be acknowledged, something could be done to transform its function into a useful lesson. According to him, each person had a particular devil who was in charge of all their negative aspects. Such an interior creature might turn up in dreams or even be projected upon others as it served as the internal opponent who sought to test the good in an individual. Here is where the Kabbalistic notion of the good and evil impulse, so beloved of the rabbis, relates to the archetype of Satan, whose name means the 'tester'. Having once been the highest of all creatures, Lucifer now patrols the central column of the Tree as it passes up through the *Yesod* of ego to the Self at *Tiferet* and beyond. As Satan, Lucifer's task is to prevent anything deviant rising higher than the *Tiferet* of *Yezirah*, where the three lower worlds of body, psyche and spirit meet, and entering the 'Way of the Spirit'. This is the path, whose Hebrew letter is *Het*, which means 'Awe', which stretches up from *Tiferet* through the *Daat*, or the place of Knowledge to *Keter* where the three upper worlds meet. Thus the devil's role is to waylay, like the Amalakites in Exodus, the Israelites on their journey to the Promised Land. In developmental terms, if these shadow elements that 'lie in wait' are brought out into the light of consciousness, they can be neutralised and integrated into the psyche in the same way that the Israelites were forged into a unified nation out of a slave-minded and disparate collection of tribes. The whole of the Bible is a collective parable of this process.

In Kabbalah there are various techniques for discovering the shadow. One method is through trustworthy companions or a tutor who acts as *Tiferet* or the Self for the student. Another method is to examine dreams which reveal, by relating them to the Tree, what is going on in the dreamer. However, this procedure can only be useful to those who know and see the diagram as a living reality. As in analysis there are many subtleties to be observed before one's personal devil can be identified. Some Kabbalists have even seen this dark being standing in their way in visions when the shadow is playing a particularly significant role at a certain point in the process of development. Here is where the Kabbalist, like the analysand, has to observe with scrupulous honesty and reflect upon their conduct and the comments of their tutors, and to consider what is being drawn to their attention by external events. For instance, sometimes the shadow is revealed by a small incident, like a Freudian slip, while on other occasions it can take on the form of a major crisis like the choice between personal happiness and important work that can only be done alone. Many people on the 'Way of the Spirit' have had to face this one. Here is where the shadow in one can argue extremely persuasively in order to curtail progress. The devil is not always unattractive, especially when it uses people that we respect and love to seduce us.

The *Hod-Nezah-Tiferet* triad of Awakening illuminates the upper section of the path of Honesty as consciousness rises up from *Yesod* into *Tiferet*. This is accomplished by acute and sustained psychological observation, which grants direct access into the unconscious. As this occurs, so the individual's life becomes increasingly less influenced by the habits of the ego and the prejudices of the super-ego-ideal, because *Tiferet* sits upon the seat of Solomon at the pivot of the psyche. Here is the place of the Self.

43. Self

The place of *Tiferet* is called the Seat of Solomon because it sits at the centre of the psychological Tree. From here it has access to every *Sefirah* except *Malkhut*. It is also the focus of most of the paths and triads, occupying a point midway between the upper and lower faces of the Tree. Moreover, it holds a position where the *Keter* of the body, the *Tiferet* of the psyche and the *Malkhut* of the Spirit meet, which gives it access to three different worlds and realities. As such, the Seat of Solomon is the place of the Self, sometimes called the 'Wise One' or 'Watcher in the Tower'. Jung named it Philemon.

The notion of the Self is an ancient one. It is found in all esoteric traditions, although it has many forms. Among some primitive people it is perceived as the ghostly companion, who advises and sometimes intervenes in a person's life. Among the ancient Greeks, it was seen as one's 'daimon' who oversaw Fate, and the Romans acknowledged it as the hidden 'genius' that all people possessed. The Hindus, who had a highly sophisticated metaphysical system, saw the Self as having two aspects, one human and one Divine. This idea is also found among the Red Indians who call the Self, the Great Man. Here, we must differentiate between the Self and the SELF, the latter being a reflection, in Kabbalistic terms, of Adam Kadmon.

Jung differed from Freud in that he saw the Self as a quite separate entity from the ego. The Self was not under the control of any conscious process, nor could it be contained by ego. This is clearly seen when the position of the ego and the Self are set on the Tree. The ego at *Yesod* may be the Foundation of the psyche, but it only has command over the triads that focus in upon it, and these are confined to the lower face. In contrast the Self is acquainted with practically everything going on in the psyche and is the clearing-house for all the *Sefirot* and archetypes, except the body. The Self perceives relatively objectively what is going on, whereas the ego is only aware of what is going on in the lower face of the psyche. The archetype of the Self, as Jung saw it, was that it symbolised unity. This is borne out by its position on the Tree, where it acts as the focus of the psychological organism at the point of equilibrium between the two outer pillars and the upper and lower faces. As such, it operates as the harmoniser and the organiser of the psyche. Thus the *Sefirah* of *Tiferet*, which means Beauty (the fusion of many things into an exquisite combination), is probably what Jung had in mind when he defined the Self.

Taking it further, Jung saw the Self as the archetype of archetypes, and indeed this squares with the esoteric notion that a human being is the image of God. Such a concept is quite familiar to the Kabbalist, who sees him or herself as the microcosm of the Divine. However, as said, there must be a clear difference made between God and Adam Kadmon, who is a macrocosmic reflection of SELF, and the microcosmic Self of the individual, who is the smallest complete unit of consciousness. There are several other levels of Selfhood, and these occupy various points on the central axis of Jacob's Ladder in an ascending sequence of rungs of awareness. The Self at the *Tiferet* is the *first* stage of wholeness. As such it is concerned with the totality of the psyche, residing, as it does, at the top of the physical Tree and occupying the base of the Tree of the Spirit, as well as holding the central position in the psyche.

As a psychologist, Jung was mainly concerned with with world of *Yezirah*, which is the realm of formation. Thus he saw the Self operate, for example, through dreams. At this level it can take on many forms. In some cases, the Self appears as an old man or woman giving sound advice, and in others as a youth riding on a powerful animal that is the id-*Nefesh* of the body. In yet another instance the Self will adopt the image of a famous and respected person, or the countenance of a Kabbalistic tutor or analyst. In women's dreams it will often appear as a great queen or mother superior, while in a man it might occur as a sage or father figure. However, in spite of their variance, all these images will have the same qualities. Kabbalah defines these as Beauty, Goodness and Truth — that is, the finest expression of the body, psyche and spirit. Of course, this is an idealised image of the fully realised Self, but nevertheless, it reveals what is within each person and what they might become.

Jung recognised that for most people the Self was hidden in the unconscious. Initially it has little direct influence because the psyche is not sufficiently advanced to be aware that the Self is a crucial factor in their lives. It is only occasionally, when what Jungians call something 'odd' happens, that it is apparent that something deeper than the normal ego reaction is guiding one. This might come in a dream of warning, like the man who dreamt he saw himself in his own car being driven by someone else. Here was a symbolic piece of advice that his life was no longer under his control. Or it might be quite a direct communication such as the dreams said to have been had by some telling them not to sail on the doomed liner *Titanic*. This is possible because the Self has access to higher levels of time and space and knows the pattern of Fate. The Self working from the unconscious also has the power to manipulate like the id and super-ego-ideal, but for quite a different reason. It does not seek to satisfy an immediate bodily appetite or make the person conform to a collective view, but brings the individual to a realisation of their true situation. This might be something quite personal, like beginning or ending a relationship, or be related to a wider horizon, such as showing the individual what, in Kabbalistic language, they were 'Called forth, created, formed and made for'. Jung saw this as acquiring Selfhood, of knowing who one is and where one fits into the Grand Design of Existence. This meant to him not so much perfection, which was the completed process, but Self-knowledge. Here is the start of Self-realisation which is at the root of every spiritual discipline. Such a view must inevitably lead to what has been called the 'transpersonal'. In Kabbalah and other esoteric orders it is known as the *Beriatic* or Cosmic dimension.

The collective aspect of the Self is concerned with this level. As such it relates to the upper part of the psyche and therefore to the lower face of the World of *Beriah*. Here the Universal level of Creation manifests in the various cosmic archetypes. One example, taken from the Bible, are the spirits of the Nations, represented by certain archangels. Great Michael, for instance, watched over Israel and defended its honour against the Princes of Babylon and Rome. The spirit of a particular people was recognised in ancient times and often symbolised by a distinct character. The English adopted Saint George as their collective archetype, and much later the Americans, Uncle Sam, who was based upon a certain Samuel Wilson, who worked for the U.S. government during the 1812 War. This lanky, tall, grey-haired, wheeler-dealer figure with his high hat caught the patriotic imagination of the people, and he became the United States' equivalent to John Bull, the English yeoman. France's parallel is the revolutionary figure of Marie Anne carrying the tricolour, while Japan has the image of the Rising Sun and India has Oshoka's

Wheel. These are all images of Selfhood in nations. Britannia may no longer rule the waves, but she is still there in the mind of the British, especially if she is provoked to action, as in the Falklands War when a remote remnant of the Empire was invaded.

Returning to the level of the personal, the Self is mainly concerned with the process of psychological maturity. It plays its part behind the scenes, in the unconscious, making the individual increasingly aware of who he or she is. This is quite different from the super-ego-ideal of the side pillars with their conventional response to reality. The Self is not only at the centre of the Tree, but at the pivot of the triad of the Soul that hovers between the lower face, which is involved with the body, and the upper face, which is related to the transpersonal realm of the Spirit. The soul is said to be the place where one's conduct is reviewed. Not, it must be repeated, according to the criteria of the super-ego-ideal triads of emotions and concepts, but in relation to the synthesis that occurs within the triad, which is composed of the Self and the wings of Mercy and Judgment, which generates the phenomenon of Self-consciousness. Self-consciousness is that part of us which has the capacity to step back and look objectively as what we are thinking, feeling and doing. It can, as the processes of maturity makes us more sensitive to subtle factors, perceive with deep insight into our own psyches. It assesses a situation over the long term and advises on the moment, if we care to listen to it. This art has to be acquired, as one's whole education and upbringing tends to train us to note only what the worldly-wise or foolish ego suggests, according to its habitual patterns. One teacher remarked, "It is like regarding what the doorkeeper says. He only sees the obvious and does not know what is really going on". This becomes very apparent when the household of the psyche is very disturbed, for the ego cannot cope with anything outside its scope although it may try. The Self, like the master of the house, often has a way of dealing with crises that the ego does not understand. For example, a sudden 'spring clean' to clear out the mess of several decades of old habits can cause much confusion to the ego. A nervous breakdown is not always a bad thing. Sometimes some Self-administered psychological surgery can precipitate much suffering as the *Gevurah* aspect of the soul lances a mental boil in order to clear out some pus in the conscience, but it may be necessary before a fatal poisoning can occur. An example of this was William the Conqueror on his death bed. He went through an agony of remorse about how cruel he had been. This brought him the possibility of redemption before the post-mortem process of purgatory was initiated. This is the reason behind the esoteric saying that 'one must die before death' — that is, face our Self in conscience.

The Self, according to Jung and many spiritual traditions, is there to make what is unconscious conscious. This process shows in people who seek to develop themselves as profound changes of attitudes, and in the realisation that everything, including difficult times, are useful for inner growth. Crises become friends to people in touch with their Selves, and dark times are reversed into periods of illumination, as a deeper comprehension of their cause releases us from old patterns that have dominated life, perhaps since infancy. Thus, long-forgotten and unseen influences in the psyche are revealed by insight and converted into a continuous study, not only of one's own experience, but of all humanity, so that we recognise that all individuals are both unique and universal in their journey towards Self-realisation as the atoms of Adam Kadmon. However, before we have any idea what this might mean, we must examine the complex interactions that go on within the psyche so as to glimpse what the Self has to administer.

44. Interactions

We have now built up a developmental and structural picture of the psyche and seen how it relates to the scheme of the *Yeziratic* Tree. We have become aware of how all the general elements fit into a working organism that gradually matures from infancy into an adult whose inherent tendencies interact with the environment. These interactions were defined, both by Freud and Jung, according to the science of their time. The terms used in defining and analysing the structures and dynamics of the physical world were applied to the psyche. This is the esoteric 'as above, so below' technique used in reverse in order to perceive the same laws at work within a different reality.

Jung saw the psyche as a relatively contained system, which converted external inputs, like sensory impressions and food, into psychic energy. Such intakes, he thought, continually disturbed the equilibrium of the psyche, so that it was always in movement. Seen Kabbalistically, the stimulus coming up from the body is transformed from a coarse into a finer order, which can then enter the psyche through the lower face of the *Yeziratic* organism. An example of this is a good meal and conversation. Both generate nourishment, as the psyche, like the body, extracts what is needed to sustain it. Jung went on to observe that the psyche could never obtain a perfect balance because of all this activity. However, it did seek a working stability — as each side of the psychological Tree came into prominence, it was countered by the *Sefirot* and triads of the other pillar. He also speculated that, if the psyche was deprived of external stimuli, it must eventually become becalmed like a stagnant pool. This occurs in total madness when a completely isolated psyche is turned into a mental cesspool because there is nothing fresh flowing into it.

The normal psyche, it appeared, is in a state of continuous change, with internal and external pressures shifting between the poles of quiescence and crisis. The latter were necessary for the psyche to remain interested and alert, and not sink into indolent inefficiency. This is why people seek out excitement and even danger. However it was noted that the average person did not go to such extremes, but kept their Tree gently swaying and alive. Jung used the term 'libido' to define this process, but he expanded its range to mean not only the id-*Nefesh* needs, but also to include the drives that all people have to achieve what is important to them, be it the pursuit of worldly satisfaction or something of a higher order. Thus the energy of the psyche could circulate in the lower face of the Tree as thoughts, feelings and actions to be used in maintaining the side triads, or help in transforming experience into the personal and collective unconscious. This energy was the fuel of the dreaming process and the driving force of inner growth. Jung also saw a reciprocal action between body and psyche, in that they could stimulate or stultify as well as feed and prompt each other. This exchange is the process that passes through the *Yesod-Daat* combination of the ego which acts as a two-way transformer. Psychosomatic events are based upon this direct reciprocation as well as upon the principle of resonance transmitted by the side pillars. An example of this is the man who literally gets scared stiff before a parachute jump.

Another innovation introduced by Jung about the general operations of the psyche was the idea of psychic values. According to this concept, a person distributes what psychic energy he or she has in various ways, depending upon what the individual considers most important. Thus a woman interested in sport will devote much time and energy to that occupation, while a man who writes poetry will allocate an enormous amount of his libido into that area. This means that the loading of the psychological Tree will be different for each individual. Out of this a hierarchy of interests will emerge as the person selects their priorities. In one person security may predominate over everything, while in another freedom might be their chief preoccupation. These values, Jung observed, were not absolute, but relative, so that while an artist might love painting, his family would nevertheless takes precedence because he considers them more important. It is also noted that those who invest their energy in many things cannot focus enough attention upon any single subject in depth and so fail to become a master of their field. Leonardo da Vinci was an exception, but even he had his limitations for he left many unfinished projects. Here we see how the emphasis of values can effect the balance of a Tree. Take, for instance, the poor Scots boy who went to America, made a fortune, and then returned home to live like a laird. He spent all of his energy and substance to compensate for a lack of ego-esteem. However, within himself he still thought, felt and acted as the poor boy because he set such a high value on frugality.

Jung saw psychic values as the basis of the various complexes. Thus associations of interest clustered together in important constellations. Less-focused topics only had a tenuous relationship because the charge they were infused with was not strong enough to assert any force, or because they were checked by an equally strong anticathexed concept or emotion, such as the desire for, but fear of, pregnancy. The clusters of high value elements were, for example, easily observed in the person who loved riding or doing business, pursuing pleasure or study, and they were equally apparent in the things some people avoided, like work or responsibility. Not so clear were those complexes that were of high value but not manifest, which nevertheless influenced the person from their unconscious in 'odd' attitudes, neurosis and psychosis. These might be a hidden fantasy or an obsession that could only be observed in dreams because they were so heavily disguised by a 'reaction formation', such as excessive common sense or reasonableness. Here is the unconscious counterbalance to an unconscious drive in the psyche, as energy seeks to find a working solution within the fabric of the Tree. Another example of this is the person who is exceptionally fastidious. Such people often have chaotic psyches that are suppressed by the ego because the person cannot admit to their true state of mind. The energy used to hold back what is seen as grave interior threat builds up a highly organised external world in order to preserve the image of complete control. This often leads to what is known as 'neurasthenia' or chronic fatigue which only allows the person to function at a lower standard of performance. However, this condition does not solve the basic problem. Many people live in such states of compensated imbalance for much of their lives.

As will be seen, a great many things can occur within the apparent simplicity of the Tree, as layer upon layer of associations and constellations activate this or that complex or concept. These emphases will both enhance and oppose others, causing some to take up enormous quantities of energy while others will be depleted. In the case of extremes, like any malfunction of the body, the psyche's system can sicken into various forms of pathology.

Observation, deduction and intuition led Jung to a concept that he called 'complex indicators'. This might be a person's outspokenness or reticence on certain subjects. Such things caused him to believe that the 'laws of equivalence' were at work. For instance, when a boy reaches adolescence, he switches his focus from games to sex. Thus, all the id-*Nefesh* passion he put into football will go into the strategy of outwitting rivals and getting the girl. This redirecting of the libido and mortido impulses is a sign of equivalence, as one set of values loses its power to another set, as it absorbs and uses in counting that quantum of energy now available. Such events happen all the time as the psyche shifts in the process of growth and transformation. This discovery was extremely significant because it explained how the psyche adjusted to different situations by borrowing from Peter to pay Paul.

Jung also saw equivalence at work in the relationship between the conscious and unconscious, as psychological energy was bound into *Yeziratic* form and then passed into the unconscious to lie dormant or only surreptitiously active, except for the occasional flicker across the *Yesodic* screen of the ego, or an outburst in a cathetic release such as anger or love. It was also noted that, when the persona took more than its quota of energy, the ego was often debilitated. For instance, there are professional sergeants major who are quite docile at home when they are out of uniform. This was equally true of the young woman with a dominant anima, or left pillar, in her psyche, who cultivated an excessive femininity to attract a strong male who would supply a protective substitute for a feeble right pillar.

A second and complementary principle is 'entropy' which determines the way the energy pattern flows. In this the greater tends to drain its energy into the lesser, even as hot water loses its heat into cold water in the search for equilibrium. Within the systems of the psyche many such exchanges occur as various elements discharge their tension into ease, as when an intense feeling is put into a poem or letter. This process of entropy is vital, or the Tree would indeed atrophy. For instance, opposing values breed conflicts that need solutions which move the person on. Weakness in one complex can generate a strength in another, like the fear of failure that drives a man to work harder, likewise an archetype, prominent for a period, has to give way under the law of entropy to the one that takes its place or is its opposite. An example is the beaten bully who becomes totally submissive in defeat as the emphasis is reversed and power flows into the hands of the now-victorious ex-victim. In the young or under-developed, these exchanges are simple and sometimes dramatic, because the energy is not defused like it is in the well-developed psyche of a mature Tree. An adult mind is more complicated by checks and balances, but these give it stability. Such structures, built up by experience, can hold or soften a surge of pleasure or pain, even as fine sand absorbs the blast of an explosion. The resolution between opposing flows, like wishing to have the privileges of adulthood but not its responsibilities, is one of the processes of maturation as the psychological Tree fills out and differentiates into a more subtle vehicle for the individual to use.

Entropy directs the incoming energy to where it is needed, while equivalence maintains its potency as energy is used up or is locked into new forms within the psyche. Here we see the interaction of active and passive sides of Tree as *Sefirot*, paths and triads operate in pairs up and down and from side to side. An example of these complex operations is that *Gevurah* can complement anything in the Tree that is directly related to it. *Tiferet* can act as a partner, as can *Binah* or *Hod* or *Hesed*, which means that each principle can have many combinations. This process is vital when one is working through a problem from several angles and levels. The triads are also subject to the law of entropy as are the upper and lower faces, the Self and the ego and the ego and body. So too are the conscious and unconscious and the dimensions of Soul and Spirit. All these and many other possible combinations reveal the wide variety of movement within the psychological Tree. However, all of this involves another major process that Jung speaks of, and this is synthesis.

45. Synthesis

Jung, like many other psychologists, observed a polar principle at work throughout the psyche. This manifested in reciprocations, such the animus and anima, and in oppositions, like the resistance of ego to the mortido impulse. Pairs also operated within larger and more complex systems. For example, the psychological functions of thinking, feeling, sense and intuition worked in various paired combinations of introversion and extroversion around the *Yesod*, while the active consciousness of the ego is polarised with the passive unconscious, which becomes the active partner during sleep. The side pillars are the most easily identified pair as they take up the masculine force and the feminine form in individuals. Here it is interesting to note that the role of the pillars is sometimes reversed in a quarrel between a man and woman, when a tiff escalates into a confrontation between the man's anima and the woman's animus. This kind of polarisation occurs within the psyche when different impulses, desires and ideals contradict each other, and they form a lock between two aspects of the Tree that cannot find a resolution. Such a situation is often rooted in a log jam in the psychological flow, or in a loss of control. These can range from an afflicted *Gevurah-Hesed* that is obsessed about injustice, as is found in many protesters, to a faulty *Hod* and *Nezah* that seeks a completely hedonistic expression to all of its impulses.

Fortunately, there are processes that eventually overcome these problems in most people as they mature psychologically. Jung called this 'progression'. The term was used to describe how the psyche was continually in a state of change, although it might have reached its optimum stage of development, so that even a saint still had to process what life presented and to adapt to continually changing conditions. This meant, for example, that there was an endless process of adjustment which would call forth different functions. For instance, at one point the function of action might predominate, pushing its counterpart of intuition into the background. At other times when action could not cope, then intuition would come out of its unconscious role to compensate for what the sense triad could

211

not do. An example of this is the mountaineer in a panic. All of his tools are quite useless in that state of mind until suddenly his intuition, calling upon all the experience stored in the unconscious, reminds him of a spiritual discipline that will calm him down. This is the most important technique he needs to get out of his difficulty.

The above kind of crisis, when a person finds him or herself without any procedure to deal with a new situation, occurs when all familiar patterns are redundant, leaving the individual puzzled and sometimes in a quite unstable position. Here is where the process of synthesis starts to obviously operate. Such events occur at the onset of puberty when there is a draining of energy from a juvenile set of ideas or emotions into an adolescent system of interests. Out of this comes all the drama of conflict with parental authority and the making and breaking of relationships with peers of both sexes. Hopefully, a new person in body shape and mental outlook emerges to cope with the situation. This traumatic period is more than just an equivalence exchange. It is a fundamental reorientation in the use of time and energy that dissolves a whole way of life as the maturing psyche takes on a new kind of balance. Some have gone through this crisis but not synthesised their experience which means that they often continue to regard their sexual partners as parental substitutes, or just people one plays with for amusement or excitement. Such individuals often suffer much as a result, in that they cannot relate as adults. Fortunately the principle of progression moves us on, whether we like it or not, and life usually offers a solution in some fatal meeting with just the right person, although that rightness may not be apparent until later, because they may be the hammer that breaks the shell.

In complement to progression is 'regression'. Here again Jung uses the term in a special way. Progression for him was the addition of energy to a psychological element, so that it is nourished and maintained, while regression takes energy out of a given system or function, so devitalising it. Thus an adolescent no longer reads comics or is interested in childish games as he or she becomes preoccupied with more interesting matters. All the subtle skills and grace of childhood disappear as the individual copes with a dramatically altering *Yesodic* image. Unfamiliar thoughts, feelings and actions, which are often initially expressed in crude and gauche modes, are experienced as regression takes one back to learning to handle one's body and mind anew. Jung observed that many old problems disappeared during such transitional periods. This seemed to be due to the loss of power in opposing elements as a new order took up the energy. For example, belligerent tomboy girls have been known to turn into the most loving sweethearts. Moreover, he noted, this not only applied to natural changes in the process of maturation, but also in psychological situations which can not be resolved by opposing interests. For instance, a woman who hated her job, but was worried by the idea of being financially insecure, might become ill and so get herself on paid sick leave. This is an unconscious solution that could give her time to look around for a new job. Or take the man in a bad marriage. He may start fooling around with other women in order to be thrown out of the home, which would perhaps solve the problem. In both cases a regressive response pushes the person into a crisis in which they are forced to break a situation they could not deal with consciously. A phase of regression is not at all uncommon just before a breakthrough into a new stage of development. However, it is often a heavy price to pay for development.

Seen Kabbalistically, progression and regression are the oscillation of the Tree in general, or of a part in particular. Structures and energy patterns are built up to perform a certain task, and, once this task is done, the configuration begins to dissolve. The interim phase is when the Tree is in momentary equilibrium. This is perceived as a certain psychological quiescence, in which the person seems calm or even indifferent for a brief time, or as a state of apparent imbalance, when a panic or profound sense of insecurity sets in. This continues until the *Sefirot* and triads start to work again, and the person is once more involved in the action. For example, the man with the excessive *Gevurah* is often severely censured by others. This may reach a point when he is no longer sure what discrimination or judgment is. However, out of this reaction may come a greater tolerance generated by the swing from a momentary pause at the Self on the central column towards the compassion of *Hesed*. This leads us on to the notion that the resolution of opposites is more than mere exhaustion in a war of attrition, or just the shift of emphasis to another system. It is the intervention of what is called by some spiritual traditions the 'third force' or Grace.

In all esoteric systems, there is, as said, always the principle of the Trinity. In the Vedic teaching, they are called *Rajas*, *Tamas* and *Sattva*. These correspond to the active, passive and conditioning principles of the Gurdjieff system, which in turn relate to the *Yang*, *Yin* and unseen reconciling *Tao* of Chinese mysticism. In Kabbalah the three are sometimes called the *Zahzahot* or Hidden Splendours that generate the three columns of the Tree of Life. The interaction of these three factors was the subject of much metaphysical study, for their various combinations can be multiplied and sub-divided into greater and greater complexity as they work their way down through all four worlds. For our purpose, it is sufficient to recognise that any new event only occurs when the three principles come together. When just two are involved, nothing new happens since they merely oppose or accommodate each other, but when the third element is introduced, then the focus shifts and something quite original occurs. The most obvious example is in intimate relationships. Two people can meet but not necessarily relate. However, if there is a third force, such as a common interest, then a quite new situation can arise. It is not enough just to bring a man and woman together. There has to be this third force to make them fall in love. It may be sex, temperament or karma. It can be anything that unites the male and female (or the active and passive) in them, even though they may reverse or periodically exchange the positive and negative roles. These are seen in Kabbalah as functions, the third or central factor being consciousness which can act as a catalyst even at a hidden level.

The same principle occurs within the psyche. At one period, a reciprocal relationship between a pair of elements may be necessary to hold the stability of, say, the ego, but there will come a time when this situation holds back an important adjustment, such as a change in attitudes that could save a job or marriage. Then the third force, whatever it may be, prompts the person to act or think in another way. For instance a man could suddenly become remarkably interested in his job if he is threatened by the sack and the discovery of a mistress has made many wives revalue neglected husbands. This third factor is often unnoticed because it is either an unconscious element or so remote that it remains obscure but nevertheless potent. An example of this was the startling dream that made a woman migrate. So, too, was the pressure of unemployment which stimulated a man to leave the stagnation of his home town. Sometimes the intervention is direct as in the case of the woman who could not make up her mind. One day she suddenly decided to marry when she realised that she was only happy with the suitor she had constantly rejected. The Self had shown her this in a moment of realisation, which had galvanised the ego and loosened the opposing lock of the side columns that had been jammed in a conflict.

Progression, regression and then synthesis is a continuous process within the psyche. It goes on day after day, at every level. At any given time, something is dissolving and something is resolving. If this did not occur we would learn nothing and would not grow. Madness is a state in which too many functions and reciprocations have become knotted in the Tree. In this situation there is no movement, except to repeat a series of short circuits that sometimes blow out any possibility of change. When this happens the psyche becomes a collection of split off elements that cannot respond to the unifying principle embodied in *Tiferet*. In the healthy psyche, the checks and balances are flexible but firm, so as to be able to accommodate the various psychological mechanisms and aid the process of inner development. The fallow periods we all experience from time to time are the psyche's way of making us pause while we synthesise the past and prepare for the future. Jung advised people to take time off for this very purpose and so allow whatever needed to alter its centre of gravity to be given the space to do so. In Kabbalah, the daily cycle of remembering who one is, where one is, and WHO else is present is designed to facilitate such changes as one walks the Way of the Lord. This path, however, is not easy, because one is beset not only by the squeaks and grindings of inner processes such as described, but by the gods and demons that inhabit the *Yeziratic* world of the psyche. This is a realm few psychologists will admit exists outside the imaginatio, but all esoteric traditions acknowledge the possibility of intrusion and possession and take it into account. Here is where Freud drew his limit in his rejection of the occult.

46. Possession

The upper worlds of Existence are seen as different kinds of reality in their own right. Many mystics have described their topography and dynamics in great detail. The esoteric traditions of Tibet and Mexico, as well as those of Europe, the Middle East and India, share similar views of these higher realms, which indicates that they are an objective phenomenon. Jung found similar accounts of these non-physical Worlds, both in the mythology of widely varied cultures and in the dreams and visions of many people. In Kabbalah, the reality of these Worlds is accepted. However, what is of particular interest to us are the many observations of their inhabitants, who were called *Malakim* and *Sheddim*, or angels and devils.

If we consider that the psyche is a *Yeziratic* organism, we must differentiate between what is subjective and what is objective. The objective is what resides in the collective unconscious and is common to all humanity. The subjective elements are all those things that have passed through an individual ego to be stored in the personal unconscious. As such, these memories have a very subjective flavour, according to the psychological type of the person, their stage of development and the way they accept or reject the experiences they have had. The collective element is quite different, in that it is too deeply buried to be greatly influenced by the ego level. An instance of this is the universal belief in nature spirits, although they may be called by a thousand different names all over the world. The fact that the so-called educated do not believe in them does not make them disappear. This division of the psyche into objective and subjective areas is crucial, as it explains many things that some psychologists find disturbing because they cannot go beyond their mechanistic view of the psyche.

Jung saw the objective aspect of the psyche as the realm of the archetypes. Some of these were cosmic in scale and others more psychological. This was the difference between the collective and personal levels. He also perceived that, besides the symbolic elements, there were many minor archetypes that were entities in their own right. Some of these were related to the split-off elements of a person's psyche and some were not.

In the normal psyche, one that is relatively balanced, the arche-types play a remote role in the individual's life. The pattern of a love affair turning into a courtship, and then moving on towards marriage is a natural progression of archetypes at work. Each partner is stimulated to make a reciprocal response to the other as anima and animus pass through the various stages of physical, then psycho-logical reaction and fusion, before both enter into the universal archetype of a marital union. In most cases the archetypes work through the personal unconscious, and each party feels they are caught up in something bigger than both of them, which, indeed, they are. Choice, however, is never lost, and many prospective brides and grooms have backed out of the seemingly inevitable process before it was completed. The reasons may be real or fantasy, but the individual has the power to accept or to decline to go on, which someone who is *possessed* by an archetype has not. Such people are ruled by a principle, be it a preoccupation with money or their mother, a total identification with their job, or the idea that they are Attila the Hun. Here, there is no question of choice. They 'are' that preoccupation — often so much so that they lose the vulnerability of the rest of humanity and become like ciphers of their ruling passion or idea, like Napoleon, who became a caricature of himself as Emperor of the French. The same thing can occur to a tax inspector who is so identified with his task that he puts the Spanish Inquisition to shame. This kind of possession has been touched upon, but here we are going to look at it in a slightly different way in order to see that it is not always just a malfunction of the psyche, but something intrusive and alien.

Jung saw many of the old gods of mythology as projections of archetypes in the psyche. Kabbalah, however, goes further and states that the upper Worlds not only contain symbolised principles at work, but have actual objective entities who live their lives as we do, but in those other realities. These were referred to in many texts as good and evil spirits. The idea that such creatures exist was quite common in the West until the industrial revolution. In recent years there has been renewed interest in such things, perhaps as a reaction against technology. Kabbalah saw these inhabitants of the upper Worlds as creatures going about their business rather like people and animals do in the physical World. However, besides the goblins and fairies, as some see them, there are human entities who are without bodies. This may be because they have just died, or because they cannot leave the lower level of *Yezirah*. The reason for this might be that they cannot accept the fact they are dead or that they prefer to stay there between the Worlds in the hope that they might be able to find a new body without going through the post-mortem and prenatal processes. A few, tradition says, wander about looking for someone living to attach themselves to. These were known as *dibukim* who sought to take possession of weak or unbalanced psyches so that they could retain some contact with life on Earth. Psychiatrists have called the phenomenon of two or more identities within one body 'multiple personality'. While this may be the case in certain individuals with fragmented psyches, it is not always so. Sometimes what takes over the psyche is not just its shadow or even a recognisable archetype, like the seductress or miser, but a distinct character with decidedly different qualities from the patient. An example of this was the man who disappeared from his home for many months and turned up many miles away in a new town with a new name, having started a completely new way of life. Then suddenly he 'woke up', took possession of himself again and returned to where he had come from. This was no ordinary psychotic episode for he appeared to be quite normal in both personalities.

From a scientific viewpoint, the concept of a discarnate entity entering the psyche and taking over is medieval. Here we have a modern subjective reaction when confronted with what is not contained within the current paradigm. When the Age of Reason destroyed the ancient picture of a multi-level, interacting Universe, the upper Worlds were lost from view. Fortunately those like Jung, who were not closed to such dimensions, saw beyond the physical and opened up the Western mind to the Universal dimension again. Many who have continued his work have begun to recognise that what the ancients said was not untrue. Indeed, Jung saw many of these phenomena, which are spoken about in Alchemy and Kabbalah, manifest in the consulting room and psychiatric hospital, so that the notion of entities and possession are no longer regarded as just imagination. Indeed, one quite eminent physician confessed in private that he was acutely aware of, in his own case, quite benign entities aiding him in his work. Not all entities are sinister. Returning to the theme of gods and demons, Kabbalah speaks of each individual having an angel on one shoulder and a devil on the other, urging the person to follow their good or evil impulse. The idea that the Tree has its shadow side is quite compatible with the notion that any one of the *Sefirot*, triads or paths can malfunction and produce a negative or demonic effect. This is observed in the cruel warrior or afflicted *Gevurah*, or the unscrupulous trickster of *Hod* who cannot but cheat, and the oppressive lawyer of *Binah* is seen in the hanging judge. Less spectacular devils come in the form of certain attitudes that always condemn or negate both oneself and others, and as ideas or emotional experiences that block out any insights. Likewise distorted complexes can disrupt harmonious constellations of concepts, so that there is an internal battle between the angels and devils within the psyche. The problem of devils or intruders which plague the psyche is not just confined to the disturbed or mad; it has particular meaning to those who wish to develop further inwardly and who begin to go beyond the place of the Self at *Tiferet*, for there is a counter-movement to hold to hold them back. This was called by one sage as the 'rising up of Evil'.

We have already spoken of the shadow, the devil and the Luciferic principle, but what is now encountered is peculiar to the person who has reached and established a contact with the Self at *Tiferet*. Here the sense of achievement thus acquired attracts the Tempter who sometimes offers many benefits at quite reasonable seeming terms. Such a moment often comes when it is least expected. Satan will set up an inner or outer situation in which all of the shadow side of the psyche is encouraged to undermine and yet exploit all the gains of years of work. This might be the belief that illumination makes one special or that the ability to see what others do not makes one superior. Many people on the Path have been possessed by their own sense of Self-importance, and not a few have fallen because they were seduced by their own charisma. Here it must be remembered that, according to Kabbalah, the Self has three distinct components. If the *Keter* of the body or the *Tiferet* of the psyche and the *Malkhut* of the Spirit are separated (and this can happen by design or neglect), this split can allow the archetype of any of those levels to take possession of the person. This is why the intelligent insane often have such remarkable faces, like Biblical characters. They are in *Tiferet* but there is no connection between Earth and Heaven. Their delusions of grandeur are centered in the archetypal realm of *Yezirah* which is full of all that can be imagined by a Self-possessed mind. Being neither under the spiritual law of *Beriah* or the restraint of *Assyatic* reality, they live, half disembodied, in bemused bliss or agony betwixt the Worlds. Satan, the Tempter, opposes the Self so as to prevent any unbalanced or unworthy person from proceeding further for beyond that point is what all traditions call the 'Way'. In Kabbalah this stretches up from the Self to the place where the three upper worlds meet. As said this path has been given the Hebrew letter *Het*, which means 'Awe'. Here is where the process Jung called 'individuation' takes on a new dimension as it unifies the three aspects of the Self and enters the Spiritual Kingdom of Beriah. Let us look at individuation more closely.

47. Individuation

According to Jung, a person starts life in a condition of undifferentiated wholeness. As the acorn has the oak tree within it, in potential, so the individual has all the elements that will go to make up their fully mature being, including traces of its ancient origins. Jung acknowledged the effects of environment and the influence of parents upon a child in as much as their psychological state and relationship were transmitted to the child along with cultural and genetic tendencies. He even went so far as to say that children's dreams were not always their own because they were within the psychic orbit of the parents, and they sometimes acted as the mirror to the adults. This left its mark upon the child's psyche before it developed a separate identity. Seen Kabbalistically, Jung perceived the embryo of the *Yeziratic* organism emerging at birth, which then began to grow and develop according to the various forces at work upon it. Jung's interest in Astrology no doubt made him take into account the fatal tendencies of the psyche which were usually not apparent for many years.

To differentiate means to develop and refine, so that what is in potential reaches its maximum manifestation and function. An example of this is the process of gestation. Here the fertilised seed splits, multiplies and specialises, so that by the time the body has reached full maturity each cell is in its place performing a specific task in relation to the whole. It is exactly the same with the psyche. The difference is that the process of development from a primitive to a sophisticated state is in a more subtle reality.

Jung recognised five distinct phases of unfoldment. Childhood, youth, young adulthood, middle age, and old age. That is, the Mercurial-*Hod*, the Venusian-*Nezah*, the Martial-*Gevurah*, the Jovial-*Hesed* and the Saturnine-*Binah*. The Lunar-*Yesod* epoch, when the ego is emerging, is included within the childhood period, because Jung felt that the parents acted for the ego until the child develops a cohesive memory. Until that stage the child operates within the parental field, its instinctive impulses being contained and directed by them. When the patterning of the parent and the ability to

221

perceive and react to the environment begin to be established, so the first differentiation between the child and the outside world occurs. Out of this arises a primitive 'I' which becomes the nucleus of the ego. Thus the *Yesod* of the psyche, together with its adjacent triads, starts to operate as thoughts, feelings and actions are activated in the lower face of the Tree. Later the four functions of 'sense', 'thinking', 'feeling' and 'intuition' begin to separate out, although initially in a very primitive form. This is the first phase of differentiation.

The various stages of development, such as going to school, forming relationships outside the family, and getting to know the world at large, fill out the psyche with experience. These, we have seen, also undergo a differentiation process into various complexes and conceptual clusters that congregate around the archetypes to create an elaborate lattice which hangs upon the pillars, *Sefirot* and triads of the Tree. At puberty, Jung observed, a totally new factor appears. He called it the 'psychic birth' — which closely corresponds to the esoteric notion that the three organisms of body, psyche and spirit adjust and integrate in a new way at certain points, such a puberty. The sudden influx of energy in adolescence is not just the release of more hormonal energy, but is an increase of the psyche's influence upon the physical. The links between the body and mind are more efficiently fused as the *Binah* and *Hokhmah* of the body lock fully into the *Hod* and *Nezah* of the psyche as the person deepens their state of incarnation. This developmental process works down as well as up as the *Yesod* of the psyche and the *Daat* of the body, on being more fully integrated, become active as the child moves out of the sexually latent stage to become pubescent and still more fully involved with life as an independent entity.

The next stage of individuation is when the adolescent starts to withdraw from the parental environment, rejecting family customs and values in order to establish a personal identity. This is a shift from the structural side of the Tree to the dynamic — that is, from *Hod* to *Nezah*. The more powerful the parental restraint, the greater the resistance, as the young person seeks to find individuality. Those who are not strong enough to actually break out of the home environment will rebel inwardly, often nurturing a deep resentment that they are not being allowed to grow up, that is, be able to move from *Nezah* to *Tiferet*. This stunting of the individuation process is often at the root of many psychosomatic and psychological disorders. The sour spinster, who stays at home and nurses the aged parent she hates while appearing not to mind, is a classic case of someone locked into the left pillar of Rigour, as it is sometimes called. However, those who go too far away from what has been parental protection often swing excessively over to the other pillar of passion and love in reaction. The ex-convent schoolgirl will have a forbidden love affair while ex-rabbinical students have been known to become Muslims and wear the dress of Palestinian Arabs. All these, and many other similar ploys, are attempts to free the individual from the power of the super-ego-ideal. This initially unconscious process of trying to reach the Self on the central column takes much more than just leaving home, or breaking tribal codes. Many youthful renegades have found themselves on some far, foreign shore, fighting the parents within their own psyche because they are still dominated by the functions of the side columns. Many suffer defeat and revert to being what their society would consider to be an ideal member. For most people this might be correct for they have not yet moved from *Yesod* to *Tiferet*. An example of this are the two school fellows who remained cronies even though one had become rich and was the mayor of the town and the other a milkman, just like his father. Both were still under the influence of their super-ego-ideals in spite of their social differences.

It will be recalled that, in Kabbalah, there are several levels of humanity. The first is the *Malkhutian* or elemental person, who only values what is material. Such people are so identified with their possessions that only wealth distinguishes them. The second is the vegetable or *Yesodic* level. These people see physical survival and comfort as their chief priority. They do not search for individuality, but seek safety in a conformist society. Identity comes with being a staunch trade union member or a time-serving company executive with a secure pension. Neither type strives for promotion because they do not wish to take the risks that animal level individuals run in order to gain the prize of being top. The animal people, however, who relate to the triad of *Hod-Nezah-Tiferet* are trying to be different, if only to be ahead of the crowd. This gives them that certain individuality that independently-minded people have. However, for some this is not enough as they see through the illusion of a worldly image or the idol of self-esteem. The people who came to Jung for treatment were often of this class. They sensed that there was more to come. This is the work of the Awakening Triad that takes them up to *Tiferet* and gives them an insight into the Self.

Many people arrive at this point in middle life which, according to tradition, is the right age to begin the study of Kabbalah. This is because one has reached full maturity and has solved most of the problems and crises that ordinary people have. There are those who seek to arrive at such a point in early life, but often this is an attempt to escape reality and Fate's lessons, and so avoid the responsibilities of their karma. Such people frequently retreat into some kind of introspective seclusion where they pray or think out what they should be doing. This does not always have the desired effect because, more often than not, they revert to reverie or fantasy, which is a form of infantile regression. Individuation requires one to face and master both the outer and inner worlds and, indeed, the old Kabbalists would not train individuals who could not support themselves both outwardly and inwardly. This was the reasoning behind the principle of not studying the Kabbalah until mature. The same applies to advanced analysis, which is not so much concerned with healing as with development.

Individuation, as Jung saw it, was the gradual differentiation of the various parts of the psyche, their co-ordination and then integration so as to bring them all into harmony with the whole. Seen Kabbalistically, the body level of *Malkhut* is first brought up to physical maturity as the various triads of thinking, feeling and action are developed in relation to the ego and outer world. Then the four psychological functions are brought into being, completing the lower face of the Tree as the conscious part of the psyche, while the unconscious absorbs and differentiates both personal and collective experience. Next, the *Yesodic* ego is transformed from being a dominant steward into a useful and obedient servant as the master at *Tiferet* emerges in dreams, and through thoughts, feelings and actions to guide the individual when they are able to recognise the voice of the Self. Here it must be said that this process is no smooth passage. The journey is full of storms beset with calms, rocks, whirlpools and monsters as well as pirates who seek to plunder the ship of the psyche, enslave the crew and kill the captain. The book, *Pilgrim's Progress* plots the same course on land, as does the story of Cinderella and many other myths about individuation.

The aims of individuation is to find an increasingly better way of expressing the Self through the many skills and arts learned from experience on the journey. This requires great vigilance and a deep integrity, because it is possible to be shipwrecked at any time. For example, some, on discovering that they are indeed individuals, believe they can do what they want because they are above the laws that govern most of humanity. Many a highly individuated person has succumbed to this temptation, and marooned themselves in madness or disgrace. Such an experience can range from a moment they would rather forget, if it is a minor misdemeanor, to physical or psychological imprisonment where all credibility is gone. The remarkable magician Aliester Crowley said, "Do what thou wilt" and paid for it, as did Oscar Wilde, who flouted his society's sexual code. Both of these talented and highly individuated people fell at the height of their powers and died in miserable poverty. Individuation means living one's fate at a higher and deeper level so that we may find our destiny and to see how we fit into the Grand Design. Let us look at this more closely so as to perceive this as a pattern behind individuation.

48. Pattern

Fate is a pattern of development. It is set at birth and is based upon karma, which is in turn formed by the other incarnations that the individual has passed through. This chain of embodiments follows a distinct line, called 'destiny', which is concerned with the purpose of that particular human entity and its place in Existence. Thus, the individual and their environment have a specific relation to one another. No one is born at a random time or place. Free will, however, allows personal modification and so an individual may progress or regress from life to life, or even remain for a period in stagnation, until the cosmic flow moves them on.

Each fate, according to esoteric tradition, is designed to give the maximum opportunity for growth as it passes through the various physical and psychological stages of development. This gives many possible combinations of situations because no two people are at the same stage of evolution. Some, for instance, will find themselves well placed and others apparently disadvantaged. The cripple with deep insight, the beach boy with no brains, the strikingly beautiful poor girl with great intelligence and the privileged aristocrat with none are no accidents. Everyone is exactly where they should be in order to meet just the right circumstances and people to help them correct imbalances and move on in their journey of destiny.

As said, each one of us is shown the general outline of our lives just before birth. This memory is usually lost to consciousness shortly after we are born, but some people retain a trace of it that may be recalled when they encounter a person or place they are sure they have seen before, although they know not where. Dreams sometimes grant access to this inner programme, and sometimes we are shown what is ahead in premonitionary glimpses. This pattern, buried within our unconscious, is not unlike an interior birth chart, for it describes the general configuration and path for a particular life. Some psychologists would argue that this is a rigid, preordained pattern but the Kabbalist sees it as somewhere in between the poles of fixity and total freedom. Take, for example, the clever farm boy. He may see life as an imprisoning drudgery into which he was fated to be born, live and die, or he may regard it as a challenge to be met and overcome. Many labourers have remained where they were and have died in the house where they were born, having learnt little or nothing, whereas others on the same farm have risen to the situation and become their own masters in more ways than one. Some have even left their croft to make their way in the wider world, to become publishers or presidents of nations. Here we see a pattern that is not fixed but flexible enough to accommodate development. It is not the form that is inflexible but the principles. What is ordained is not that this or that particular is to be acted out, but that certain situations are needed to stimulate the right response so that the farm boy may learn about tenacity and practicality, which he might not have acquired in the family of an Oxford don. The timid girl who has avoided life by living on a legacy will eventually have to learn how to fend for herself when it is gone, but she could shorten and ease the lesson if she went out and met the problem while she is still ahead financially. What might be said is that fate is designed to bring the person into a consciousness of the very thing they may have avoided in their last life. This may be, for example, the very opposite to hard circumstances, like those born into situations of wealth, power and glamour. They may have to learn about the problems of temptation, corruption, responsibility, and the consequences of using and misusing such things. Good fortune and bad fortune are not always what they seem. The pattern has many convolutions and reverse dimensions, as well as broad and dominant lines.

Jung recognised many of the principles spoken of above and no doubt took them into account in his work with analysands. His ideas on synchronicity (meaningful coincidences and their origins) come very close to the esoteric understanding of omens. The notion that a significant incident may be a hint about the future is an ancient one. The principle is that, because the Self has access to the World of *Yezirah*, the psyche can become conscious of an approaching event by recognising the signs of the unfolding pattern. These may be in the form of selective projection, which draws the attention to something that symbolises what is to happen, such as the falling down of a favorite tree signifying the end of an epoch. Or one may dream about a certain town to which one must go in order to meet a particular person. Such precognitions are not uncommon, nor is the phenomenon called *deja vu* in which people experience something as having happened before. Psychologists write these incidents off as brain malfunctions, which some may be, but nevertheless quite a number are not so easily explained. Many incidents have the quality of just being familiar, either because it is already in the unconscious from the prenatal period or because of some coincidental event, like the man in the midst of a breakdown who discovered that his house had a massive structural fault. Such synchronicities, and Jung put great store by them, are the work of Providence or the World of Creation, which is responsible for the organisation and unfoldment of the Universe. A parallel can be seen in the 'critical path' analysis technique used by builders who have to plan just when to bring in each component so that everything comes together at the right time and place. Nature uses the same process each year, as does the embryo during the gestation sequence. The dynamic comes from *Beriah*, the format from *Yezirah* and the manifestation occurs in *Assyah*.

Now, while precognitive dreams and omens can be seen as emanating from Providence or the Self, which sees the situation objectively, it does not mean that the hint has to be taken, for we always have the option of choice, which means that our fate can be altered. However, this event is quite rare, because it is only possible to change the fatal flow by a conscious effort, and most of us work from habit and repeat the old and ordained pattern until we learn our lesson. Take, for example, the woman who decided not to marry because it was too difficult and messy. She will still have to face her animus in some situation or be confronted by her dreams in which the masculine will demand attention. Fate does not mean that one will marry a particular person, but that we repeat our lesson, with that type of individual as the psyche projects its needs upon the outer world and attracts the people required. It may not be our soul mate as most of us are not ready for that yet. Those inclined to the right pillar, like the workaholic, will inevitably find themselves excessively busy in city or country while those on the left column, such as the fearful man, will always be afraid, no matter how well protected they may make themselves. Free will operates when one is liberated from the domination of functional pillars and triads and acts from the Self of *Tiferet* on the central column. Here in a moment of insight, something can be done, as consciousness illuminates and offers a solution. This alone can alter our fate. The masters have said, "Live in the present" and not in the past or future over which we have no power.

In the normal sequence of development, all the phases described unfold in a general way, so that the body and psyche pass through a form that is appropriate to each period, until physical maturity and a general kind of mental stability have been established, which most people take for adulthood. However, as observed, many individuals are not psychologically mature. Some remain essentially babies, their lives dominated by infantile desires, while others still play juvenile games or retain the values of adolescence. The fate of each level is usually well monitored by various counterbalances to these discrepancies, giving all the possibility of forwarding their development. This again is the work of the *Beriatic* World of Creation that operates the larger pattern so that everyone can find their place in the Universe. The Holy One is exceedingly merciful.

Most people do not notice the extraordinary thought that has gone into their fate because of repression, projection and a dozen other defence mechanisms that prevent them seeing what is actually happening. One esoteric tradition calls this 'sleep' or *Katnut*, the lesser state. Because of their problems, many consider themselves victims of circumstance and they are right, but not in the way they see it. Their fate is the direct result of their own effort or lack of it. Others, more open to reality, look for what might be the cause of their difficulties and learn by trial and effort to alter their pattern. Those who seek to grow will mature quickly each lifetime and become adults who see every event as a teacher. They accept life as it is, and exploit every moment to gain the most from their situation. There are some, however, who look even deeper and inquire as to what the purpose of Existence is. They are shown, if they only heed the hints, the pattern underlying their own and others' lives so that they begin to see the dim shape of a cosmic pattern in which everyone is involved. Sometimes the veil is drawn and they catch sight of a chain of lives as ancient memories return of other times and places. This can lead them to a point where they recognise a distinct direction that indicates what their destiny might be. Here we stand on the edge of a quite different dimension.

49. Direction

There are three general stages of development. The first is the bio-psychological, the second of education and occupation and the third is of the Soul and Spirit. Nearly all individuals go through the first two stages without too much difficulty and find their place in society, be it priest, ruler, merchant or labourer, for most people can fit into the four basic castes of mankind. There are, of course, the misfits. At one end are the criminals who act as the demonic element of humanity, and on the other are the 'outsiders' who do not fit into the conventional pattern for some reason. In the earliest of times, such people went to the local wise person for advice. If the problem was just psychological, it was often resolved there. If, however, the issue was more serious then they were sent onto a shaman or magician who understood something about what lay beyond ordinary problems. Later priests and rabbis performed the same function. This indicates the difference between healers and those concerned with development. In our own time, we have specialist healers who deal with the psyche. These can range from the mechanistic behaviorists to the way-out alternative practitioners. Both extremes hold limited views that can, it must be said, sometimes solve problems that need their kind of solution, such as surgery for the man with a brain tumour or spiritualism for the woman who was healed by a conversation with her dead mother.

Freud and Jung occupy the middle ground in the spectrum with Freud orientated to the bio-psyche and Jung to the psyche-spirit. As such they dealt with the people who were attracted by their particular way of working. This is the law of like being drawn to like. It is also part of a fatal pattern. Thus a person with problems related to parents or sex would seek the Freudians, whereas the individuals in search of themselves would find the Jungian approach more appropriate. This finding of the right help is crucial, and it may take many years and several false starts to arrive at the door of just the person one needs. There is an esoteric maxim which says that 'when the student is ready the teacher appears'. This is related, not so much to the healing process, as to the third stage of development in which one seeks to go further than just becoming so-called normal. However, before this stage can occur, a balance in the psyche has to be established because it is quite dangerous to proceed with deeper growth if there is a major discrepancy in the mind which could be magnified and produce a madness more serious than any ordinary psychological disability. The average neurotic or psychotic usually only makes life difficult for themselves and their immediate circle, but the highly developed mad person can do a great deal of damage. A classic example was Shabbertai Zvi in the sixteenth century. He claimed to be the expected Messiah, and because he clearly had enormous charisma and great knowledge of Kabbalah, he convinced not only ordinary Jews but many rabbis that he was indeed the Annointed One. When his growing messianic movement became a political threat, he was given the choice to convert to Islam or die by the Sultan of Turkey. He became an instant Muslim and the Sultan's honourable doorkeeper. Thousands of Jews, many of whom had sold all their possessions in readiness to return to the Promised Land, went into deep shock. This event shook world Jewry to such a degree that Kabbalah was forbidden to anyone under forty, for such knowledge could, it was believed, drive one insane.

For most people any enquiry into the deeper levels of the mind is disturbing, because it is the unconscious area of the irrational and spiritual. Both of these could be a threat to the rationale of the ego. People seeking help for strictly psychological problems are usually dealt with by the techniques of observation and analysis until they reach a point when they perceive the difficulty. They can then resolve it by untying the knot and moving on to the next phase of balancing their psychological Tree. This can go on for years, or it can just be a period of a limited number of sessions in which they and a psychotherapist examine a particular problem. Such may be right for those seeking healing, but it is not for people who are in the pursuit of development. Many individuals have spent decades in analysis and gotten nowhere, except deeper into their problems, because the sessions lack the spiritual dimension. Unless the analyst or therapist themselves has such a connection or direction the psychological process can only go round in a *Yeziratic* circle. The healer also has to be a priest or rabbi, in that he or she must be aware of the higher worlds and familiar with their reality. This, alas, is quite rare because of the split in the West between science and religion brought about by the Age of Reason. Fortunately, there is a process of correction going on in that there is a renewed interest in the esoteric, even among psychologists. This is why this book is being written.

The Indian term *Guru* means 'spiritual teacher'. In Kabbalah such an individual is called a *Maggid*. However, before people come under the instruction of such a person, they are supervised by a *Moreh*, which means 'to oversee'. In analysis, the analyst performs much the same function, up to a point, in that they sit in the position of the *Tiferet* on the analysand's Tree, and act as the Watcher over the analysand at *Yesod*. The Freudians, however, do not form a personal relationship with the analysand, so that there is a relatively objective connection between the two. This allows any *Yesodic* ego projection on the part of the analysand to emerge and be seen upon the blank screen of the analyst's professional persona. This technique is very useful in revealing unconscious elements, such as desire for approval, manipulation and resentment, that may have marred the person's life. Having perceived these, the analysand can redress old imbalances, removing blockages and dissolving fixations that have distorted their Tree. The skill and impartiality of the analyst in this process is tested to its limit, for the analyst has to avoid their own counter projection. For example, if the analysand sees the analyst as a parental figure, the analyst must not react like one, or the relationship will lose its objectivity and they will both be repeating an old pattern. This requires the therapist to know his or her own psyche very well, which is why most analysts have been through the analytical process themselves. Here it must be said that we are still dealing with the healing operation of balancing the Tree.

The Jungian approach is somewhat different from the Freudian. In this, the analyst enters into a personal relationship with the analysand as a friend with analytic background. That is, a *Tiferet* to *Tiferet* connection is established. This creates a mutual flow in which whatever emerges is examined frankly and without any *Yesodic* double-dealing. Here is the path of honesty between *Yesod* and *Tiferet* in action. The openness and acceptance that is generated allows many things to surface, so that 'transference', that is, any projection coming from the analysand, is dealt with tactfully but firmly by the analyst, who acts as the *Moreh* or overseer. An instance of this is when the analysand sees his own aggression in the analyst, so that whatever the analyst says or does is perceived as a threat to his *Yesodic* ego. If the analyst accepted the role of aggressor, then the analysand would inevitably take up the pole of victim and their mutual Tree would be under strain. However, if the analyst reflects the situation from *Tiferet*, the analysand might realise what he was doing as he was drawn up the path of Honesty out of an old ego pattern into the Self. All these methods and many other devices and counter-devices were used by Kabbalists down the centuries in both counselling and teaching. One twelfth-century rabbi asked, "How can you expect me to be perfect when I am full of contradictions?" This is a very precise definition of the problems of differentiation and integration. The chief difference, however, between the psychologist and the Kabbalist is the *direction*. In this sense it means to be instructed by a teacher, which is quite a distinct process and different from psychological therapy.

In Kabbalah, the *Moreh* acts as tutor to a student for many years. During this time the theory of psychology and cosmology is taught and many techniques of self-observation are practised. This is common to all esoteric traditions. Kabbalistic psychology may not use modern terms and there are differences of nomenclature even within the Tradition, but the basic structure and dynamics of the psyche are the same. The id is the *Nefesh* or *Nafs*, as the Sufis call it, and the description of *Yesod* and the surrounding triads are, as we have seen, an extremely accurate account of the ego and its functions. It is simply a question of translating terms into the modern idiom. During early training a Kabbalist has to become familiar with all the aspects of the lower psyche. Exercises in action, thought and feeling, give experience of these triads and how they work through the ego at *Yesod*. Later, the student learns to tell the difference between *Yesod* and *Tiferet*, and note the qualities of all the *Sefirot*, as well as recognise the character of each triad and pillar. Tutors will instruct the student in group-work and in private consultation. Comments are made about their own Tree's balance and the effect of patterning. Dreams will be examined, as will omens or incidents of synchronicity. Such events are considered in the light of both the student's overall development and their relevance to the present. Progress reports and advanced studies and exercises are carried out as in-depth tutorials and seminars that increase the students comprehension of their individual paths and the Tradition, that is, the collective dimension which includes the study of mythology, history, metaphysics and philosophy as well as more penetrating practices. This can only happen in a Kabbalistic school that is under the direction of a Master.

Masters or *Maggidim* are extremely rare. Freud and Jung were teachers to their generation of psychologists. They saw much more than the average and even brilliant researchers of their time. They opened the door into the unconscious for science, even as a Kabbalistic Master, like the eighteenth century *Maggid*, Baal Shem Tov, introduced the spiritual dimension to those without rabbinic learning. Such *Maggdim* are originals. This is the creative quality of the World of *Beriah* which changes the psychological forms of *Yezirah*, that in turn affect the workaday world of *Assyah*. Sir Isaac Newton was of this order, as was Rabbi Azriel of the thirteenth-century school at Gerona, whose reformulation of Kabbalah into the philosophical mode led to its wide acceptance among both Jewish and Christian mystics who trod the Path of development. Such masters are part of a long chain of evolved human beings who, over time, have slowly been filling in the rungs between the first fully realised man, Enoch, and the most innocent newly-born person who has never been incarnated before. Somewhere in the middle of this Jacob's Ladder of humanity are those who wish to rise above the dominance of the id-*Nefesh*, the *Yesodic* ego and the super-ego-ideal to become true individuals. Jungians would call this process the 'Inner Journey', Kabbalists, the 'Ascent of the Ladder'. There is no difference. In most esoteric traditions it is simple called the 'Work'. In Hebrew the word *Avodah* means both 'work' and 'worship'. Jung came across it in alchemy as the 'Great Work'.

50. Work

In Kabbalah, the relationship between tutor and student has much in common with the modern psychological approach. However, the objectives differ in that the aim is directly concerned with the spiritual and Divine dimensions. As a working method it has been evolved over several thousand years. This means that many of the pitfalls, which the solitary seeker falls into, can be avoided because of the backlog of much experience. For example, an individual can be in a psychological cul-de-sac without knowing it. He may carry out exercises, such as watching the mechanism of *Yesod* and its triads, which were correct when he first started beyond their point. This could make him become excessively egocentric, if he were unaware of it. A tutor observing this will indicate that a change is needed to order to move him on in accordance with a progression related to the Tree. A person on their own cannot perceive their situation objectively; help is needed not only to advise, but sometimes to apply a certain stimulus or check. This means quite a high degree of trust is initially needed between tutor and student. Such a situation has it hazards, but the Tradition has its ways of balancing discrepancies by always referring to the objective principles of the *Sefirotic* Tree.

In the Jungian method, the Self is the *Maggid* as it guides both the analyst and the analysand through the process of analysis. Dreams, current personal events and the situation unfolding during each analytical session will lead the couple into many areas that need to be brought into consciousness. In the case of the Kabbalist there is, in addition to the Tree, a vast body of tradition to which one may refer. Ultimately, however, the inner contact that the tutor and the student have with their own and their common *Tiferet* is the one that is important. This is the same Self in all of us which gives access to both the conscious and unconscious. This place where the three lower worlds meet is the first stage of the Spiritual Path. Let us look at the theoretical situation in order to see the parallels between Kabbalistic and psychological methods.

Malkhut, as we have seen, is the contact point with the physical and external world. Here the student learns to observe events in the light of the larger picture. Social as well as psychological phenomena are observed and analysed in order to see the interaction of the macrocosm and microcosm. This keeps the tendency in psychological work from becoming too limited to the personal. *Malkhut* also relates to the way a student participates in ordinary life. Can they see the lesson being presented by Providence, and how are they responding to it? These are the questions that the tutor asks, or gets the students to address themselves. An understanding of what is going on both externally and internally is crucial because some events are vital keys in the process of development. A series of mishaps, an offer of a new job or relationship are seen as indications of inner conflict or change. Synchronistic events of both the personal and collective level are viewed with great interest for they may reveal something about the Grand Design and where the school or individual fit in. An instance of this was the move of Freud from Vienna to London and the shift of psychoanalytical operation into the English-speaking world. This opened the door to a new epoch of psychology, which prepared the ground for a revival of interest in the Kabbalah some decades later because the ground for self-examination and interior exploration had been laid by Freud.

Observation of *Yesod* is carried on from day to day. The Jungian expression 'to be a stranger to oneself' exactly describes the Kabbalistic notion of observing the ego mind from *Tiferet*, which entails constant awareness of the various processes of the lower face of the Tree. The Buddhists call it 'mindfulness'. However, in this exercise, the triads are worked upon to bring about a balance if one is weak or too strong. In this way the student not only gets to know how the ordinary mind works, but can correct any discrepancies. For example, perhaps one of the four psychological functions needs developing so that the ego is not biased in one direction or another. What *Yesod* projects is of great importance and so students note in great detail what image the ego presents. Flashes of *Tiferet* consciousness will reveal much about the persona and whether or not some unconscious impulse is overly influencing what is being felt, thought or done. Continuous vigilance on the student's part, in conjunction with the tutor, will teach him or her how to observe impartially and follow through the flow of life, as the psyche responds both inwardly and outwardly to the situation. This objectivity is vital if one is to perceive who and where one is.

The examination of the *Hod-Nezah* level of the psyche is the next

stage. Here the student learns the theory and does the practice —
that is, the study of the principles of Kabbalah and their application.
The theory is learned by observing the Tree in every kind of field.
For example, a given situation is analysed according to the various
Sefirot, triads, paths and pillars, so that the pattern and balance of
it and where it is going are seen. This kind of contemplation is
combined with the practice of meditation and conscious action in
order to bring the *Hod* and *Nezah* and the three ego triads together.
Thus a person can, for example, conduct a love affair and see it as
a way of development as the partners explore each other and
themselves. This can, however, cause problems, as any two people
in analysis, and in love, will know. But then it also gives a growing
element to the situation, which if correctly handled, can enrich the
relationship.

The path between *Yesod* and *Tiferet* is the one of Integrity. If this
is lacking between tutor and student, then nothing worth while can
happen. Any interaction must be honest because the tutor, like the
analyst, acts at least for a time, as the *Tiferet* of the student. When
the student becomes a peer to his mentor, then the Selves of both
can combine to produce a unique situation in which things can
be revealed, that were hidden in the unconscious of both. Many
remarkable events can occur in such a situation. The discussion of
a dream can open out a deep vista into the transpersonal, where an
insight is gained into the cosmic dimension. A seemingly casual
comment can turn a conversation into one of profound personal
revelation. The path of *Honesty* gives access not only to *Tiferet* but
to the whole psyche. It also, as noted, can release the Shadow and
Luciferic principle and this requires all the skill and integrity of the
Kabbalist to identify and deal with. The dark side of the psyche is
a mean enemy, as is the external intruder from the Astral World of
Yezirah. This opening up into the domain of the unseen or unconscious is one of the reasons Kabbalah was considered dangerous,
but then so is falling in love, having a baby or, indeed, living.

The level of *Hesed* and *Gevurah* operates at a much deeper
stratum. Here is where the emotional life of the person is lived,
usually totally unconsciously. In the case of people under Kabbalistic
discipline, the power and influence of this level is crucial for it is
from there that the super-ego-ideal operates, as it draws upon the
complexes and concepts stored in the side triads above and below
Judgment and Mercy. These areas have to be brought out into
consciousness by close observation of all that is thought, felt and

done. After much work there is the recognition of what one learned as a child, which is purely conventional, and what is real, as regards, for example, morality. When this occurs an inner code of ethics begins to be established, not according to accepted custom, but according to eternal laws. To fulfil the Commandments at this psychological level may mean contravening local regulations, such as apartheid or a military code, if it goes against what is essentially right. Thus a true conscience starts to be developed which does not reward or punish according to the parental model, but acts in line with the heart of the psyche or the *Hesed-Tiferet-Gevurah* triad of the Soul.

The reality of *Hokhmah* and *Binah*, at the level of the collective unconscious, can only become apparent after years of study and practice, or in a flash of vision. Here is an area in which, at first, only an inkling of comprehension is to be expected, although many people think they grasp the meaning of these *Sefirot* once they have labelled them. To possess Wisdom and Understanding takes a lifetime, if not many, and for most of us it is the collective effort of Mankind that gives us some insight into this cosmic and spiritual level. Myths and legends, be they of the Bible or some of remote pagan people, point to the spiritual dimension in which the personal is transcended. Encounters with this level through various traditional exercises of meditation and visualisation gives the Kabbalist a sense of a vast pattern that is unfolding over the ages. Such a comprehension is acquired by accumulation and much pondering, which is a slow and thorough process that goes on deep in the psyche. Wisdom is something that may be given in a revelation, but this is not always understood. There has to be a combination of *Binah* and *Hokhmah* in the Kabbalist so that their *Daat* or the non-*Sefirah* of Knowledge can bring a moment of realisation to *Tiferet*. Such a moment may occur on the top of a mountain, in bed, during supper or while with one's tutor. It is not something that can be commanded, but is granted by Grace, and this is something beyond the range of psychology. Newton's insight into universal law on seeing an apple falling was of this order. The dark glass of *Daat* was suddenly clear and illuminated.

The work done by a tutor and student or analyst and analysand should take them over most of human experience. Their path will wend to and fro, sometimes advancing straight with great rapidity and, at others, almost inert. At moments the Work might seem pointless, and many people drop out of the process at such stages using this or that reason to depart. The reason for this, and it can occur anywhere along the Way, is often to hide some block or baulk some difficulty that might move them on from the familiar and safe and into that awesome area of change where they feel their psyches will be transformed and they will lose themselves. This, of course cannot happen. The Self does not alter. It may grow, shift its balance or emphasis, but it will never cease to be anything but itSelf, for it is an expression of the eternal SELF. This process of development is graphically described by many traditions in the simile of the butterfly, as it moves through the stages of caterpillar and chrysalis towards its exquisite fulfilment. Such phases are passed through at each level, as the right pillar is activated, then the left is consolidated, before eventually emerging as the Crown of *Keter* at the top of the column where the three upper worlds of psyche, Spirit and Divinity meet. People deeply involved in the Work trust the process, and although they may be old campaigners with a background of immense experience, they are still inevitably amazed at whatever happens because it always contains the miraculous. To catch a taste of the Work (for no book can convey its reality) let us look at one individual life so as to catch an insight into Fate, the ways of Providence and the path of Self-realisation.

---

[1] For an outline of Kabbalistic exercises, see the author's *The Work of the Kabbalist*, Gateway Books, Bath, 1984, and Samuel Weiser, York Beach, Maine, 1985; *School of Kabbalah*, Gateway, 1985, and Weiser, 1986; and *The Way of Kabbalah*, to be published by Gateway Books and Samuel Weiser in 1987.

51. One Life

In this chapter we will look at one life, with notations, in order to see some of the processes we have examined at work. Sarah Alvarez was born in England in the 1930s of Spanish parents, who had migrated because they foresaw the Spanish civil War. Sarah was a love-child (fate) and her birth had been easy (*Malkhut*), in contrast to her elder sister, who had given her mother a difficult confinement. Her infancy (*Yesod*) was spent in London where her father was an artisan in leather, a family tradition brought from Cordoba, an ancient centre of this profession. Her earliest memories (lower face and ego) were of the small flat in North London and its surrounding streets. Everyone was poor at that time, but her father, a good craftsman, could provide for the family. Her mother was a kind woman (*Hesedic*), given to occasional moods, but her father was stern (*Gevuric*) and maintained many of the customs of Spain (collective unconscious), including lighting candles on Friday evening, although no one knew why they did so (super-ego-ideal). Sarah and her sister were taken to Mass quite regularly, and this left a deep impression on Sarah, as did her sister who kept Sarah firmly in her place (personal unconscious). The mother triad to show no favouritism towards Sarah, but it was nevertheless felt by the elder child, who continually forced Sarah to retire into a reflective and defensive posture (sense-intuitive introvert), even though deep down she felt quite secure in her mother's love (*Hesed-Yesod*). The father also preferred Sarah, but out of fairness and duty to his first-born he had a marked difference in behavior to the elder sister (*Gevurah-Binah*), which Sarah resented (id-*Nefesh*). (Note the reversed emphasis of male and female pillars in parents.)

Here we have all the signs of a karmic situation within a cross-cultural setting. Sarah has been born at a certain time to a particular family because events in a previous incarnation have drawn her there to learn certain lessons. Thus she has a specific racial and collective type of body and psyche which interacts with an individual kind of psychology and fate set at the moment of birth. Let us suppose her Sun is in Scorpio, her Moon is Virgoan, and she has a

Libran Ascendant. That is, the Self is fixed, watery and probing in quality, while the ego is mutable, earthy and concerned with detail. The Ascendant would give rise to a cardinal, airy and attractive physique. This particular combination would place the Sun in the House of possession, generating a desire to acquire a wealth of sexual, emotional and spiritual experience. The Moon in the twelfth House of privacy would make the ego tend to be reserved and analytical. As a character, Sarah would appear to be a good-looking, intelligent, forceful but introverted girl with a need to penetrate and explore what lay behind life.

When the Second World War came, Sarah's family moved out into the country, while her father joined the British army and was sent overseas. Childhood was outwardly uneventful. Except for the occasional air raid, the war was just the background to her *Yesodic* consciousness. However, this semi-rural life did not quite exclude a strong sense of national unity that prevailed in wartime Britain, as she was dimly aware of distant historic events (collective unconscious) affecting all their lives. Sarah knew her mother was worried about her father (left emotional triad), but each letter from somewhere in North Africa indicated that he was all right up to that moment (right emotional triad). Perhaps the most important memory of that time was not the great Battle of El Alamein, but the competition as to whom would be the May Queen at school. Being both pretty and intelligent, Sarah, to her mother's delight, was short-listed as a candidate to be Queen. Her sister feigned family pride, but she was jealous (id-*Nefesh*) and revealed it in a spiteful remark (mortido) when Sarah lost the crown to the school's most popular girl (anima). Her sister's behaviour upset Sarah deeply and left a scar (personal unconscious) that made her realise that families were not always loyal and loving, as she had been brought up to believe (super-ego-ideal). The other significant memory of that time was the wearing of a traditional Spanish costume, which her mother had made for the Victory Day fancy dress party. This stirred something deep within her (collective unconscious). It was as if she had worn such a dress many times before (prenatal memory). It also triggered something yet deeper in her soul that made the party more than a pleasant childhood episode. She sensed that she was a stranger who was staying with her family only until she was ready to go out and find something or someone in the future (precognition of her fatal pattern).

By the time Sarah was sixteen, she was a leggy, talented and conscientious student (*Hod*) at the local art school. With the war over, life became a routine with her mother endlessly cooking and cleaning, while her father and now her sister went to work in London each day (vegetable level). The only drama was the love life of her sister, who chose wild boys (*Nezah*). Her father saw all but said nothing. Something terrible had happened to him during the war (split between *Yesod* and *Tiferet*) and he was content just to sit and reminisce about the old country (*Yesod*). Her mother (*Tiferet*) said that 'his' Spain had vanished with the Civil War. Sarah was fascinated by her father's stories (ancient memories). At eighteen she fell in love with a boy who was the exact opposite to her dark beauty and reserved manner with his fair hair and extrovert ways (animus). This experience awakened (*Hod-Tiferet-Nezah*) all of her Scorpionic sexuality, until he wanted to sleep with her. Her Catholic up-bringing (collective unconscious) plus her Virgo ego prevented her (libido) from succumbing, even though her body (*Yesod-Malkhut*) desired to be taken. The boy dropped her when he could not get what he wanted, and she grieved for a whole year, although for what she was not sure (feeling triad). This experience had aroused a deep longing for a soul mate. Sarah hoped that this fulfilment would come at art school in London, but she did not find it there. Her work went well, but deep down (*Tiferet*) she sensed that this student epoch was a training for some task she had been given (destiny). Her admirers were many, but none came up to the standards of her Virgo Moon which expected the perfect (animus projection). Besides, when it came to sex, her super-ego-ideal held the field. This created problems (*Nezah* versus *Gevurah*), and she became quite neurotic when she was reproached for leading men on by the way she had dressed and moved (nun-courtesan persona). She saw this (*Tiferet*) but could not accept it (*Yesod*). At twenty-two she left home in an act of rebellion. Her parents said this was against Spanish custom, but she still went ahead, saying that she was English (collective), to share a London flat with three other girls. She got herself a job in a graphics studio where she met a designer who seemed to have all the qualities she sought in a man (her *Yesodic* image of her animus). She fell deeply in love (*Hesed*)and decided to lose her virginity (*Nezah*). After the initial shock (to her super-ego-ideal) the affair became an idyll (*Hod-Yesod-Nezah*). On holiday to Spain they visited Cordoba. It moved her profoundly as she had the strange sensation of having been there before (soul), especially in the Juderia which seemed incredibly familiar. When asking her father about family history, she touched something deep within him (*Tiferet*) as he told her that they were descended from converted Jews. She was particularly moved (*Gevurah-Tiferet-Hesed*) when she heard that there always had to be a Sarah in the family. This made her realise why the candles were lit on Friday evening (Jewish Sabbeth), although the reason had long been forgotten (collective). Her research came to an abrupt end when she thought she had become pregnant, and her wonderful affair dissolved overnight (*Yesod-Malkhut*) because her lover could not face reality. When it proved to be a false alarm, he wanted to return, but now she did not want him back. Fantasy had no future. She had to grow up.

Her twenty-ninth year (Saturn cycle return) was one of a total desolation and despair (super-ego-ideal crisis). Suicide was considered, but her Catholic and now Jewish collective unconscious forbade it. All her *Yesodic* dreams had withered. She now knew she was not a genius, nor, it seemed, could she make a real relationship. At her most desperate moment she had a memorable dream (*Tiferet-Yesod*). It was of a wise old woman (Self) who offered her a book containing all the secrets of Life. She awoke the next day and perceived that something had lifted her depression (synthesis). That afternoon she decided to become a freelance designer. This notion had often been in her mind, but her mother's voice (super-ego)always said that it is not good for a woman to be too independent. This advice she now disregarded. She moved into a flat on her own and set up as a professional woman (Awakening triad).

Within two years she established herself as a book-jacket designer. Her dealings with publishers taught her much about herself as well as her craft, and she made a place for herself in the world. At thirty-five she reached her peak, for her style was in fashion (fate). She lived well and occasionally took lovers (id-*Nefesh*). Through a series of coincidences (Providence), she met a woman who seemed to possess some kind of deep knowledge (Kabbalah). The lady was an analyst by profession, and although they met socially, they had many important conversations about psychology and matters of the Spirit, which Sarah now found interested her more than anything else (Seeker state). About the same (fatal) time she met an editor at a party whom she seemed to recognise. They had much in common (Astrological reciprocation). Soon it became obvious that they had something to work out together (karma) that could not but end in marriage. There were problems over religious issues but that did not deflect them. They married and lived for a year in great happiness (balanced marital Tree).

During this time Sarah's wise-woman friend (acting *Tiferet*) introduced her to a study group which she tutored. There she saw a
diagram of the Tree. It was the same design she had seen on the
book of her memorable dream. The group, moreover, was full of
seekers like herself. This was her real family (soul group). She told
her husband, but he did not seem to understand. He was invited to
the group. He came once but declined to return as he was hostile
to the tutor (ego versus *Tiferet*).

This distressed Sarah, for the work of Self-development was now
vitally important (*Tiferet*). Her husband liked things as they were
(*Yesod*). They made love (*Yesod-Malkhut*) but the sense of (soul)
union was no longer there. He did not wish to meet Self to Self
even though they had a *Tiferet* contact. They began to drift apart.
The choice was between him and the *Work*. She did not know what
to do. However, the unconscious intervened. Her husband had a
memorable dream in which he and Sarah went to a new country
and started a fresh life. When he told her, she saw it as an omen
about their relationship, but he interpreted it as a sign about a job
offer in Canada. He would accept the post and Sarah, as his wife,
must come with him. She was divided, for she loved the man within
(soul mate), but going to Canada meant leaving her London life and,
most of all, her family of seekers. What to do (*Yesod* versus *Tiferet*)?
She decided to be a good wife (super-ego-ideal prevails).

On the day they had their papers cleared for Canada Sarah found
herself (awakening triad) sitting in a Kabbalah meeting, listening to
a discussion about the symbol of the Promised Land. The group
were Israelites who, having left the bondage of Egypt, were bound
for the country of the Spirit. It was then that Sarah saw the real
significance of her husband's dream. They had understood it literally.
Suddenly all was clear (*Daat*). Which did she want — slavery or
freedom (Path of Honesty crisis)? That night she told her husband
of her decision (soul triad). He became very angry, and after an
intensely troubled few weeks he left for Canada. Sarah grieved for
their marriage, but knew she had to be true to her Self in following
something greater than social convention. It had been her hardest
test (initiation) of integrity. Time confirmed her decision because
her life began to flourish in a quite new way. She now waits to see
what else Fate will bring. Perhaps when the most vital lessons have
been learned, Providence will show her what her destiny is.

The above story, composed of several people's experience, shows how the Fate sets tests for the individual to meet and carry out. It might not always be easy but the opportunity for development is there especially at crucial moments in a life. These points are when a major decision has to be taken and this is the prerogative of the Soul, which is the agent of free will.

52. Soul

The soul proper is a major component of the psyche. In Tree terms, it is the triad *Gevurah-Tiferet-Hesed*. As such it is midway between the upper and lower faces of the psyche, and adjacent to the active and passive conceptual and emotional triads. It is a purely psychological or *Yeziratic* triad, quite independent of the physical and spiritual Trees. This gives it the unique capacity of free will. It is here that the person makes their decisions, processes experience and develops Self-consciousness. It has several names in Kabbalah and so here we will use the English word 'soul'. Some people equate the soul with the Self, but this is not so. The Self is concerned with the totality of being. The soul relates principally to the psyche and to that particular person as the emotional *Sefirot* of Judgment and Mercy balance and check each other in conjunction with *Tiferet*. The soul is a vehicle of consciousness rather than function because it is anchored and pivoted upon the Self. From its central position it acts as the monitor and synthesiser of both conscious and unconscious activity within the Tree.

As we have seen, the psyche is composed of many systems. These are in constant motion as each strives to perform its work. In the process of individuation these processes are dispersed into complicated and subtle configurations that cluster round various *Sefirot* to form a working hierarchy. Sometimes, however, they oppose each other to such a degree, like passion versus common sense, that major conflict can generate anything from mild nervousness to a psychotic state in which there is a split in the psyche. It is the task of what Jung called the 'transcendent function' to resolve these confrontations within the psyche and bring harmony, or at least a tolerant co-operation. This transcendent function is the work of the soul triad which has the power to manoeuvre and adjust the imbalance. An example of this is the conflict a woman may have about two admirers. She is drawn to one because he is vital and gives her sensual pleasure and security, and she is attracted by the other because he is intellectual and spiritual and gives her peace. She is in a quandary for it is a time of, perhaps, fatal choice.

Within her psyche there is confusion for none of the side triads can make a decision, as each clamours for its own satisfaction, and her inferior animus based upon the id-*Nefesh* opposes her superior animus, which draws upon the Spirit. In this situation she could be torn apart, especially if her sado-masochistic shadow takes a hand and destroys both relationships. At such a point the soul, under the auspices of the Self, can react to the crisis if the person wants a real solution. If this is so then *Gevurah* will see the limits and *Hesed* appreciate the gains made by each relationship. The Self at *Tiferet* will then consider the balance of such a situation and its effect upon the souls of the woman and the two men in the long term. The conclusion arrived at may be that neither are suitable mates, and so the soul, in its role of Self-consciousness and conscience, would advise her to drop both suitors. This largely unconscious process would then surface as thoughts or feelings and eventually action. If she compromises and chooses one of them anyway, because of an ego need, then the soul will let her know that something is not quite right, perhaps through a dream or some externally manifested omen, like quarralling with one man. If the signs are ignored, then the process she has initiated will proceed until the issue can surface again. If she continues to suppress the soul's advice, then the process will go on until the reality of the situation eventually asserts itself years later in the breakdown of a marriage. If, however, she acknowledges what the soul indicates then a synthesis may occur in which she sees that neither will do. This will allow other possibilities which she can work with to emerge, such a knowing without question who is the right person to marry when she meets them. This is the hallmark of the level at which the soul operates.

The process of synthesis, in which elements are related through a higher order of consciousness, occurs in various ways. For example, some issues will occupy the soul for years until they are resolved, while other matters may be dealt with in a flash of insight as a moment of Self-consciousness sees into the essence of a problem. The synthesising process is vital to the balance of the mind and goes on all the time, and it is monitored by the soul which helps the psyche to adjust to what the automatic processes cannot handle. This means a continual dynamic shifting of structure in the Tree. Such a flexibility is only possible because of the soul. No animal or angel has this particular capacity to synthesise and therefore develop. For example, if the soul is isolated, as in psychosis, then the psyche ceases to develop until a working balance has been established and the soul triad can operate again. Once this has happened, the lesson learned can be incorporated by insight, discrimination and acceptance. These are the qualities of *Tiferet*, *Gevurah* and *Hesed* that compose the soul. The soul is where the person assesses him or herself. It is the place where all the experience gained through the body, psyche and spirit is made individual. Thus, while a man and woman may have a love affair like ten million others going on at the same time, it will be the soul of each that makes it unique. The pillow talk and cliche's may be archetypal, but it will be the soul that transforms the relationship into something special. People who make love without the soul connection experience bodily passion or some psychological attraction but there will be no real intimacy. A man may come from a similar background and share the same interests in art or sport as a woman, and they might even be physically well matched, and have egos that correspond perfectly at the social level, but if there is not the soul connection, no deep and unique relationship can occur. When two people have this element in common there is a fatal meeting that is much more than just animus and anima mating. The profound sense of mutual recognition in such a situation is because either they have a common karma to work out or because they are soul mates who have at last found each other. It is rare, but it does occur. Most people do not operate at this level because they relate through the body, the ego or the collective dimensions, and they do not recognise their true helpmate when they meet. This is why real marriages are so unusual.

The state of the soul is crucial to the health of the psyche. This is dependent, initially, upon its condition at birth. Being the essence of that individual, the soul brings into incarnation all that has happened to the person before. As the emotional level of consciousness, it will tend to be either more *Gevuric* or more *Hesedic* in its loading, according to what karma has been incurred. Thus the person starts off with, perhaps, an inclination to be optimistic or even the reverse. Here is where the astrological chart is most useful. For example, the *Gevuric* planet Mars might be in Aries, where it is very powerful, giving the soul an impetuous demeanour, or it may be in Pisces, which will dull its sharp sense of discrimination. Jupiter, the planet of *Hesed*, on the other hand, might be well placed, and support the Mars from Taurus, giving it a fixed and steadying power. Conversely, Jupiter could be in a difficult aspect in Gemini, feeding a counter-productive excess of defused emotional power into an already indecisive *Gevurah*. There are many possible combinations of these two planets, and a good astrologer can gather much about the state of the soul at birth by considering their relationship to the Self of the Sun.

Generally speaking, most souls are in a relatively balanced state because the laws that govern incarnation will choose a situation in which the person will be given just the right planetary combination to meet whatever lessons have to be learned. In some cases, however, the configuration of Mars, Jupiter and the Sun will reveal a particular gift or problem that has to be used or dealt with. An example of this is the person with Mars and Jupiter conjunct in the House of Partnership. This could indicate issues of conscience in marriage or any long-term or legal partnership. From a psychological view, such a person might find that their super-ego-ideal came into conflict with what they really felt about formal arrangements, like the soldier who despised his commanding officer, but nevertheless obeyed his orders out of discipline. For the Kabbalist such a situation would be seen as decidedly karmic and an opportunity to untie some deep and ancient knot that had brought the two men together again so that they need not repeat it life after life. As the ego can be stunted by such a fixation so the soul can be distorted by excessive emphasis towards *Gevurah*, which makes it too strict, or too much *Hesed* that allows it to be lax. A soul can also be quiet contrary about what is right, because free will can be used for good or bad. An example of evil is the master criminal who has deep insight into the psyche and uses this knowledge to manipulate others for his own purposes. Morality begins at this level because choice opens up the kind of options that are closed to the side and lower triads of psychological function. A person working off ego will not even notice any moral issue because they will react according to local custom, like accepting slavery or apartheid.

The soul is the place where the individual comes to know him or herself. It is where the person's essence is held. This may be expressed in a particular form or symbol in a dream. Thus a man might see his soul as hunter or a woman perceive herself as priestess. It has been known for people to portray their soul's state in the form of a derelict town or a delicate temple. Some people unconsciously encapsulate the state of the soul in a personal motto, such as 'I am a rock' or 'waiting' or even 'I am a born loser'. These phrases often arise quite spontaneously as the soul hints in revealing phrases about how to handle the lessons of this incarnation. As part of the individuation process, the soul plays a most important role. It is the principal agent of Self-observation in that it holds an independent position between the side triads and the upper and lower faces of the Tree. As such, it can participate in most of the processes, although it can also be denigrated by the inferior elements of the psyche. This is described symbolically in the story of Cinderella who, as the soul, is dispossessed of her true place in her own house by her stepmother or shadow side of the ego. Made to live and work in the cellar, the symbolic lower level of body and psyche, Cinderella is helped by the fairy godmother of the Self so that she can meet the prince of the Spirit. This process is blocked, however, by her stepmother in favour of the two ugly stepsisters, who represent distorted side triads which dress up in their personas, but who cannot match the Beauty of Cinderella nor even recognise her after the transformation scene when the mice and pumpkin, or animal and vegetable levels, are changed by the Self into horses and coach in order to get the soul of Cinderella to the Ball. Here the prince has eyes for no one else, despite the attempt of the ego to keep Cinderella from her destined union. Let us now look at the palace of the Spirit that exists deep within the psyche where the Sacred Marriage of the inner King and Queen will occur.

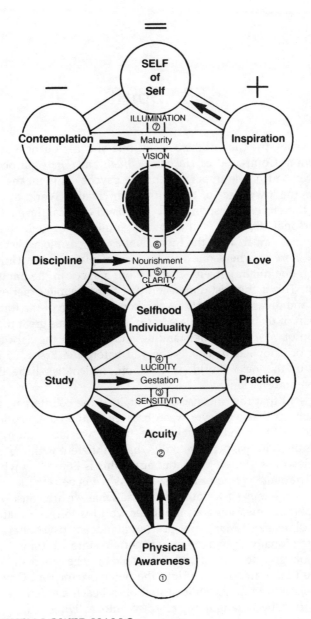

12. SEVEN LOWER HALLS

This describes a Kabbalistic view of psychological development. The sequence follows an ascending flow of consciousness from being aware of the body and the lower face of the psyche up through the Halls of the Soul and Spirit to the seventh level at the Crown where the Self and the SELF commune in the Divine.

53. Spirit

Like the soul, the triad of the Spirit is one of consciousness and not of function. Composed of *Hokhmah*, *Binah* and *Tiferet*, it occupies the lower part of the upper face of the psyche. This means that it overlays the lower face of the spiritual or creative World of *Beriah*, and it therefore corresponds, at the psychological level, to the transpersonal. By this is meant that, unlike the soul, it is not concerned so much with the individual as the cosmic aspect of the psyche. Here is where one has a sense of place in the Universe, although one might perceive that it is but a speck in the immensity of Spirit. This is the vast dimension that some people experience in visions and dreams, meditations and contemplation of the transpersonal part of their being. Situated at the centre of this great triangle, made up of Wisdom, Understanding and Truth, is the dark mirror of *Daat* or Knowledge. This is the veil before the *Yesod*, or Foundation, of the next World of Creation, which lies beneath the collective unconscious.

Jung said that the unconscious contained the counterpart to the conscious, so that whatever was observed in the outer world was mirrored in the mind. For example, when we look towards the heavens at night, we perceive only what is inherent within us. With radio telescopes we see more, but again this is limited by what we know. The same is true of the psyche. As we penetrate the cosmos of the unconscious so we only recognise what we are conscious of. To deepen our awareness of the inner world is to reach that same cosmic dimension. Many mystics (and, indeed, psychotics), who have intentionally or inadvertently penetrated into this transpersonal dimension, give descriptions of what could only be called an interior universe that granted insight into the outer macrocosm. One man, a physicist by training, while seated on a beach suddenly saw all that he had been taught transformed into a living reality as he perceived the cosmic dance all about him. This spiritual experience became the basis of a book that related ancient metaphysics to modern science. Indeed, there are many accounts of similar experiences down the ages. Some call it 'cosmic consciousness' while others a 'peak experience' while others termed it 'a view of the Heavenly halls'.

For most people this cosmic level is as removed as the Milky Way because their gaze is fixed upon earthly events. The daily round of life is more than enough to occupy them, and they are not aware of the subtle but great changes going on in the Universe and the collective unconscious. A prophet is someone who is sensitive to this reality, and perceives the trends of the time. Such people can sometimes discern coming events with fine accuracy. This is possible if one has access to the patterns and forms being created in the upper part of the World of *Yezirah*. People who have developed the *Binah-Tiferet-Hokhmah* triad within themselves can perceive the state of a society and prognosticate its future in the same way doctors predict the patterns of growth and disease. Seen Kabbalistically, prophecy is an insight into the workings of Providence. Thus, a person who operates from the Spiritual triad of the psyche can sometimes see the way events will unfold. For example, there was in the sixteenth century a seer called Brahan who foresaw railways. Such foresight was not uncommon among Red Indian medicine men and other primitive shamans. These people could pick up on forms that were yet to manifest in the physical world. This gift requires either many years, if not several lifetimes, of development, or an Act of Grace that sometimes grants such visions. The Bible called them lesser prophets. In modern parlance they are called *psychics* who, it must be said, are not always reliable when it comes to interpretation because they work off the side and not the central pillar and are therefore often biased by a dominant function.

The triad of the Spirit is concerned with a *Yeziratic* and psychological appreciation of Universal Principles. This is seen in archetypal formulations such as mandalas. For example, the sixty-four Hexagrams of the *I Ching* are a set of metaphysical images of the interaction of the basic processes that govern the Universe, while the Astrological system is a Middle Eastern view of the outer and inner cosmos. Yet another formulation is the Hebrew *Alef-Bet* in which the script of the drama of Creation is written. The vision of Ezekiel of the Chariots, Throne and fiery Man is a *Yeziratic* picture of the universe, as are the Books of Enoch and Revelations. These come from the psychological triad of Understanding-Beauty-Wisdom for there is no form beyond in the World of the Spirit. At the center of this triad is the non-*Sefirah* of *Daat*, the black hole of Cosmic Knowledge. Here is where one enters into cosmic consciousness.

This is the level where Buddha saw the chain of all his lives in a moment, as the upper face of *Yezirah* came together with the lower face of *Beriah* and allowed the light of the Divine World of *Azilut* to flood through the dark gate of *Daat* to illuminate him. He was a greater prophet.

If we look at a mature Tree of the psyche in the light of what we have learned, we will see that it is composed of many different parts that have slowly been building up and refining their capability over the years. If this was all that was involved in development, we would be nothing more than a collection of psychological mechanisms ordered by a central controlling system. But this is not so, for there is also a process of integration and unification going on which enlarges our capability. Thus, a person who contains the mineral, vegetable and animal kingdoms in their body and the various human parallels in their mind can encompass these levels and relate them to the Universe. It is this that makes a human beings part of a larger process and gives them access to the collective experience. Thus, a person can know what others have done, thought and felt in any time and place if they have reached the cosmic degree of awareness that the *Binah-Tiferet-Hokhmah* represents. This psychological triad of the Spirit is an individual's contact with the Grand Design. It enables the person to *see* where they fit into the flow and manifestation of time and space. By this is meant what point they have reached in their development and where they can operate most effectively as a useful unit in the unfolding of Evolution.

Take the person who has an imbalance of side pillars. Such an individual could not be relied upon to be objective about the relationship between men and women. However, an individual, who has actually attained a blend of the masculine and feminine within themselves and can relate to both with equanimity, is extremely useful because their counsel will be understanding and wise. That is to say, they have married their Adam and Eve. Such people perform a great service to the Universe in more ways than one. They are the psychological androgynes that Jung speaks of. Neither bisexual nor sexless, they have the capacity to appreciate both pillars because they have brought the King and Queen of *Hokhmah* and *Binah* together. When an individual reaches this point of interior development, their centre of gravity shifts from the individual to the transpersonal. This means that they are capable of perceiving from an objective level, even though they may be this or that sex. That is possible because the integration of the Spiritual triad focuses the personal consciousness, and its unconscious counterpart, into an alignment with the Collective at the place where the lower three worlds meet in the Self, giving it the Universal view. The addition of the Spiritual dimension to the place of the Self, moreover, brings both the physical and psychological into direct contact with the Cosmic so that the individual may come to know who they are and what their destiny is.

This cosmic aspect of life is meaningless to most people, although they may perceive it in their culture and religion, which are external projections of that level. The devout Jew, Christian and Muslim may have different versions of the Spiritual dimension, but if they saw behind the *Yeziratic* 'form', they would perceive the same essential reality as the Hindus, Confucians and other traditions. The cosmic archetypes of mankind, as Jung observed, may vary in style but there is no real difference between them. Good and Evil, Order and Chaos are universally recognised. Life and death, growth and decay are seen in the stellar realm as well as at the level of plant and animal. Human beings, however, can operate in any of the Worlds so that it is possible for them to perceive, experience and work where they choose, if they have the will to develop all the aspects of their Divine, Spiritual, psychological and natural possibilities.

From a cosmic viewpoint the human race has only been on the Earth for a relatively short time. Those who came at the beginning and have spent many lives learning about life in materiality have now matured and lead the younger members of mankind, who have been descending generation by generation into incarnation over the last few millennia. Some of these elder individuals are well known to us as prophets, sages, and saints, but many are quite unrecognised as those who make history. For example, some are those who introduced important ideas or inventions. No one knows the name of the man who brought printing blocks into Europe from China, but this act changed the course of Western history as printed books gave millions access to knowledge. That traveller from China was an instrument of destiny. Whether he was conscious of what would be the result or not we will never know. But some individuals do see their task, like the man who compiled a dictionary of a long-dead language, which is now the vernacular spoken in Israel.

Originality is the hallmark of Creation. People who work from the *Beriatic* level alter our view of Existence by introducing something new, like a Greek who said the world was round or the Americans who proved that it was possible to fly. These discoveries shift mankind's perception of reality. This triad grants access to the *Beriatic* celestial atmosphere where inspiration originates. Freud and Jung drew upon this level when they opened the Western mind to the inner cosmos of the unconscious. Their work has affected science, art and commerce, warfare and advertising, police work and education. They brought about a breakthrough just as orthodox religion began to fade and lose its hold upon many people looking for an entrance into the Way of the Spirit. It is interesting to note that both Jung and Freud were born at just the right times and places so that they could meet and then part in order to pollinate and stimulate clinical psychology and so move it out of its mechanistic phase. This is the work of Providence as it operates through the Spiritual triad of the individual and collective unconscious to open up what is hidden behind the non-*Sefirah* of *Daat* that overlays the *Yesod* of *Beriah*. When a person is chosen to carry out some cosmic task they are not conceived and born under the ordinary laws of karma or Fate but of Destiny, which will train and then direct that individual to meet the time when their whole being is in tune, not only within but without, so that the microcosm and macrocosm act as one.

The triad of Wisdom, Understanding and Beauty is the sixth level of seven 'Halls' within the Kabbalistic organisation of the psyche. A person enters this Hall when they reach the third stage of the Self. This means that they are masters of their body and lower psyche, can control the side triads and are conscious at the Soul level. This allows them to contain the Worlds of *Assyah* and *Yezirah* and to move at will into *Beriah* so that they can walk, talk, think and feel, and yet be in contact with the World of the Spirit. Such an achievement indicates that the psychological process of maturation is almost complete. The last and highest Hall of the psyche is the triad formed by the *Binah-Hokhmah* and *Keter* of *Yezirah* just below the place where the three upper Worlds meet. Here at the Crown of the psyche of the individual comes into direct contact with the Divine World of Adam Kadmon.

54. Divinity

The Divine dimension of the psyche is contained in the Wisdom and Understanding and Crown Triad of *Yezirah*. Here the apex of the psychological organism touches the place where the three upper Worlds meet. As such it has access to the highest limit of the psyche, the central zone of the Spirit and the lowest level of the realm of Emanation. This gives this place a special quality, as it is where the Light of Divinity touches the psyche, giving it an insight into the World of the *Sefirot*. In terms of human experience, it shifts consciousness out of physicality, through the ever-changing forms of the psyche, into the deep spaces of the Spirit and into Eternity. Such a moment is granted to everyone, at some point in their life. Some see it as a moment of profound illumination, others as a glimpse of what holds Existence together, yet others perceive it as an instant of Self-realisation.

The image of pure consciousness symbolised by Light comes directly out of the World of *Azilut*, through the *Keter* of *Yezirah* or the Crown of Formation to pass straight down the central axis of the psyche and and into the Self, where it is perceived by the Spirit, soul and body. Indeed, anyone who has experienced this Divine connection will realise that it is, in fact, always reflected there in the 'Luminous Mirror' of the psychological *Tiferet*. It is only when we rise up out of the dominance of the body and pass through the limitations of the personal and collective unconscious that we see the source of our illumination streaming down from the triad *Binah-Keter-Hokhmah* at the top of the psychological Tree. A symbol for this level is the ever-open eye which is used to indicate the Higher SELF.

Seen Kabbalistically, this higher SELF, where the three upper worlds meet, is the Watcher over the Self where the three lower worlds focus. Between them is the *Yeziratic Daat* that not only veils the *Azilutic* Light coming down from the Crown, but conceals the *Beriatic Yesod* or Foundation of Creation. Here too is the *Ruah Ha Kodesh* or the Holy Spirit whose messenger, the archangel Gabriel, acts as annunciator when the SELF wishes to address the Self.

Paradoxically *Daat* or Knowledge is the dark curtain that hangs between a person and their 'Lord'. Traditionally this is the Divine Name given to the *Malkhut* of *Azilut*, through which the SELF is expressed in conjunction with the *Tiferet* of the Spirit and the *Keter* of the psyche. Together these compose a cosmic and Divine communication point with the Crown of the psyche. As such, they have the deepest effect upon the unconscious in that they are the groundbed of the psyche's inner reality. Without these two upper levels touching the psyche, life is crude, petty and purposeless. People who deny these higher dimensions find themselves in a terrible dilemma. Nothing makes sense. Everything is an accident, death is the end, and their existence is pointless. An example of this was the brilliant physician who believed the psyche was a product of the brain. He feared madness and death because he saw God as a human projection. For him there was nothing beyond ego consciousness or the grave. Such a position is remote from the Light of *Azilut* and in what some call the 'Outer Darkness'.

At the upper end of the scale, for those who rise to this highest triad of the psyche and bring about the union of *Hokhmah* and *Binah*, or the *Sefirot* of Revelation and Reason, there is the direct contact with the World of *Azilut* as they reach *Keter* of *Yezirah*. This final process unifies the psyche and brings the Spirit and Divinity into a conscious relationship. Such an exalted state is called being 'Anointed' as Grace descends and permeates the individual. The meaning of becoming 'Anointed' is that whoever reaches this stage of integration attains the condition of full earthly SELF-realisation. It is said that there always has to be one human being walking the Earth who is conscious at this level while being in the flesh. According to one tradition everyone will go through this experience at some time in their journey of evolution although only a few will be publically recognised, like the Buddha and Jesus of Nazareth. Many mystics have left hints of attaining this sublime state. Plotinus said, "This Light is from the Supreme and is the Supreme". The Sufis call the person who holds this position the 'Katub' or 'Axis of the Age', and this is for good reason, for they are, at that moment, the pinnacle of incarnate humanity and its contact with the Divine through the Crown of their psyche.

To obtain this Divine level of consciousness, it is said, takes either many lifetimes, an intense burst of physical, psychological and spiritual effort, or an Act of Grace. However, not all who seek this goal are genuine in their motive. Not a few, including at least one

Roman Emperor, believed that they were Divine. These people, in Jungian terms, are often possessed by the archetype of the Deity, which is expressed in a megalomania in which a Luciferic-held Self worships its own image. On the other hand, it is quite possible for the good and true to receive an illumination which comes from direct contact with Divinity which give such people a strange quality of being suffused with Light. Both Moses and Mahomet possessed such a radiance because of their encounters with God, and both had to cover their faces with veils — that is, close down the *Daat* and don a *Yesodic* persona so that people could relate to them. A trace of this Divine quality is seen in certain children, nuns and monks, rabbis and Sufis who have an *Azilutic* connection. This radiant presence is also observed about happy pregnant women, people truly in love and highly evolved individuals as the Light of Divinity descends from the psyche's Crown to penetrate and give the body a distinct luminous quality. Those who meditate sometimes acquire this sheen, as do deep contemplatives and people who always try to act from the highest in themselves. This indicates just how potent an instant of Divine awareness can be. Such an event is not as rare as it might seem. Most people have had a least one encounter with the Divine. Many dismiss it as a trick of the light or the mind being in an odd state, but some see it for what was, is and shall be as one of the most memorable moments of their life when they saw that all is One.

From a strictly psychological point of view, there is no way of defining such an experience. It is said that mysticism is a form of madness, but this cannot be the case because the mystic sees nothing but beauty, order and purpose whereas the psychotic usually perceives just the reverse. The insane may glimpse the upper Worlds, but their perception is not the same as the mystic, who is disciplined, focused and in control of the psychological Tree so that the shaft of Divine Light and Cosmic Winds do not blast their way through and disrupt the lower face of the psyche. This is the reason why the Children of Israel were forbidden to go up the Holy Mountain. They were not yet developed enough to receive the Holy Radiance that rested upon the summit of Sinai, which represents the Crown of the psyche. Here the Fire or Light of *Azilut* and the Cloud, which is a mixture of the air and water of *Beriah* and *Yezirah*, meet at the upper place of the Divine, Spirit and psyche. The Lord said to Moses in Exodus XIX:21, "Go down, warn the people not to force their way through unto YHVH so as to look, for many of them will perish".

However, it goes on in the next verse "But let the priests come near to the Lord, although they must sanctify themselves, lest the Lord break forth upon them". In this free translation two distinct levels are set out. There are the priests who are as yet undeveloped, symbolised by the Israelites, and the priests, who possess some knowledge and experience. Even so, these initiates still had to prepare themselves and be sanctified for an encounter with the Divine. This means a long and arduous training under competent direction. Here is where psychology reaches its limit and the progression turns into a spiritual discipline, which has quite a different order of criteria. The spiritual path is a deep commitment to the Work of Unification, as it is called in Kabbalah. It must be done, not for oneself but the SELF.

In Jungian terms, the archetype of the SELF is the Divine Principle of Unity. As such, it seeks to bring everything to a wholeness as it moves Adam Kadmon from innocence to experience. Sent down to be the lowest level of Existence, we slowly make our way back up through all the Worlds, life after life, in a journey of individuation that differentiates and integrates the particular part we have come from in Adam Kadmon. When everyone has fulfilled their destiny, Tradition says, the education of Adam Kadmon will be complete. In that ultimate realisation of SELF-contemplation, gazer and reflection will become one as God beholds God in the image of the Divine. Then, we are told, all the *Sefirot* will fuse into a dot of total consciousness known by the Holy Name I AM THAT I AM. Until that time let the Work of Unification go on.

Amen: So be it

Index